GW00937914

'The Adoration of the Magi', as used in St. David's, Sime Road, was drawn from the original sketch still in the possession of the artist, Stanley Warren. The figures were drawn from life using other P.O.W.s as models.

PRIEST IN PRISON

Four years of life in Japanese-occupied Singapore
1941–1945

The author in 1940, aged 25.

PRIEST
IN
PRISON

Four years of life in Japanese-occupied Singapore
1941–1945

John Hayter

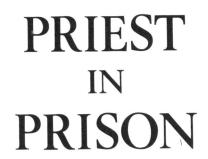

GRAHAM BRASH
SINGAPORE

First published in Great Britain in 1989 by
Churchman Publishing Ltd

Second revised and enlarged edition published in 1991 by
Graham Brash (Pte) Ltd
227 Rangoon Rd
Singapore 0821

ISBN 9971-49-268-7

Printed in Singapore by Chong Moh Offset Printing Pte Ltd

For
JOHN LEONARD WILSON
Bishop
and
REGINALD KEITH SORBY ADAMS
Priest
two very good companions

'It is only when we dig up those faded records, which, once written, are stored away unread, that we remember with a shock the truth of those days, when weary in body we gave expression to the anxiety of our minds. We find in those close-pencilled pages the impressions of forgotten days which are happily erased from our memories.'

J. M. Scott, *Life of Gino Watkins*

Contents

Readers write in ...

The author was deeply moved by the many letters he received from readers of the first edition of his book. Below we give extracts from a few of them.

"One night I read your book until three in the morning! When I came to the Double Tenth, tears streamed down my face ... Yes, we did learn something from the dangers, trials and difficulties of the war ... I think the younger generation of Singaporeans should read your book so that they can know the sufferings and hazards of the Japanese War and Occupation." *Elizabeth Choy*

"Your story helped me to appreciate, as I had never done before, the magnitude of the suffering and courage and above all the faith which kept people going." *A citizen of Malaysia*

"How wonderful that you have been able to tell your story. I have been fascinated, moved, uplifted and filled with admiration. It deserves to be a great success." *Niece of an Internee who has died*

"Within forty-eight hours of receiving my copy of 'Priest in Prison' I had read it from cover to cover. It is a wonderful story of Christian faith and courage and endurance." *Bill Purcell, Archdeacon of Guildford*

"There is a lot of interest in Australia, in (the Japanese Occupation) because it was OUR war. Not only did the Japanese capture 22,000 Australians, but they threatened and attacked Australia. As a member of the post-war generation, I feel it is important that it should all be written down as you have done. How else will we know?" *An Australian author born in 1944*

"The chief impression I gathered from 'Priest in Prison' was that the author at the outset was a kind, observant, well-disposed young man - and interested spectator of people and events. At the conclusion he was a wise, mature, compassionate priest who could write the sermon on 'Charity' delivered in Sime Road in Holy Week, 1945." *Head of an English Teachers' Training College*

List of Illustrations

Preface

by
The Right Reverend Mervyn Stockwood
formerly Bishop of Southwark

Had this book been written by an observer rather than by a participant it would have been suitably entitled *Courage amid Adversity*, as it tells the story of men and women who experienced in themselves the effects of a war in which the Japanese were guilty of appalling atrocities and subhuman behaviour.

It also tells of remarkable bravery and unselfishness on the part of some who never lost hope, nor failed to encourage and serve those who suffered alongside them.

I first knew John Hayter when he was training for ordination at Cambridge, and subsequently when he started his ministry, shortly before the war, in the lovely town of Romsey in Hampshire.

Leonard Wilson came into my life shortly after the war, when, as the hero of Singapore, he won the admiration of the young people of my parish in East Bristol. So impressed were they that they contributed to the training of one of his priests.

I remember being told by a history lecturer, when I was a student at the University, that there had rarely been a time since the crucifixion of Jesus when the Christian Church had not been persecuted. No doubt his listeners entered his remarks into their note books for examination purposes, but thought that such barbarism could not occur again. How wrong we were.

It was in the early thirties. A year later Hitler was in power and, when I was in Munich on holiday with undergraduate friends, synagogues and churches were being burnt and Jews and Christians imprisoned. The situation was bad, if not worse, in Soviet Russia, where hundreds, probably thousands, were put into concentration camps and murdered.

11

PRIEST IN PRISON

Then came war in the Far East, where the Japanese quickly proved by their inhumanity how well they had learnt their lessons with regard to persecution. Alone of all Japanese occupied territories, Singapore, owing to the early intervention of an Anglican Japanese officer, avoided the worst of religious persecution. There was, however, a devastating system of persecution of anybody who might be regarded as an opponent of their vicious regime. And the story is little different today in other parts of the world, particularly in Chile and South Africa.

It is for this reason that I hope John Hayter's book will be widely read. Not only is it a thrilling account of heroism and horror, but it serves as a warning. It confirms the words of Jesus in that it demonstrates the costliness of Christian belief. We may be free from religious persecution in Europe for the time being, but there is nothing to suggest that it is more than a temporary lull. When persecution reoccurs, and it may not be in such a dramatic form as with Bishop Wilson and others with him in Changi, how shall we react? A possible answer may be found in this valuable guide and text book, *Priest in Prison.*

✠ Mervyn Stockwood

Author's Preface

In an introduction such as this the names of most of those to be thanked are there in the book itself. If it had not been for them, the events of internment in Changi Gaol and Sime Road Camp during the Japanese occupation of Singapore would have been unendurable. It was their humour, their kindness and consideration, often their courage and many times their patience and forgiveness which made it all possible. Remembering them helps to lift the whole experience above the level of nightmare. Of all those mentioned in the book, chief place goes to Bishop Leonard Wilson and the Revd. Sorby Adams, as is, I hope, made very clear.

Preparing the book so long after the events described could not have been done without much help from Philip Reed and his secretarial staff at the Imperial War Museum, and, too, a great deal of typing by Sylvia Sheppard. Nor would it have been attempted without the insistence and encouragement of Margaret Duggan, a journalist of repute, and of Andrew and Elizabeth Barr, both formerly of the B.B.C., he now of Television South, and too of Yahya Cohen, F.R.C.S., recently Professor of Surgery at the Singapore College of Medicine. He was himself a Singapore internee.

To Freddy Bloom, besides a most valued friendship, I am grateful for permission to quote from her book *Dear Philip*; as also to Dorothy Moreton, interned in Sumatra, for many quotations from *An Irishman in Malaya*, her biography of John L. Woods; and to Tan Sri Datoh Mubin (Mervyn) Sheppard, for the use of his book *Tamin Budisman — Memoirs of an Unorthodox Civil Servant*; and to Mary Thomas, for her *In the Shadow of the Rising Sun*, an account of life in the Women's Camp at Changi and Sime Road. It has also been a great help to use the map of Singapore Island from *Changi Photographer: George Aspinall's Record of Captivity* by Tim Bowden.

Iris Parfitt, R. W. E. (Harry) Harper and Stanley Warren have generously allowed their drawings to be used, as have the families of Bert Neyland, W. R. M. Haxworth and Richard Walker.

To Bishop Mervyn Stockwood I am deeply grateful for his encouragement and for his Preface. Besides being there at my first beginnings of life as a priest, he heard of many of these events soon after they happened and has remained a much valued friend ever since.

Finally, I know that if it had not been for the support and encouragement of my wife, Rosemary, this book would never have appeared.

May, 1989

AUTHOR'S PREFACE TO THE SECOND EDITION

It is a strange thing for an author to write what he thinks is one kind of book — in my case a straightforward account of events and the people who shared them — to discover from some of those who have read the book that in fact it is quite different. I had not realised that *Priest in Prison* revealed how much we grew up!

The writing of the book has brought me unforeseen benefits. There have been friendships renewed, many of them totally submerged since 1945. There have been new contacts made. Two particularly valued, Mr. Hans Schweizer of the International Red Cross and Sir Edward 'Weary' Dunlop, Australia's best known and most highly respected P.O.W. Surgeon, have contributed to 'Afterthoughts' with its new material.

Once again in the preparation of this edition, as in the first, I owe much to the encouragement, skill and expertise, and most of all the friendship of the 'One Man Team' of Denham House.

My friend Colonel Peter Chitty of Boldre Developments has been an invaluable helper in the book's postal and local sales.

The first year of the life of *Priest in Prison* was saddened by the grave illness and eventual death of Churchman's Publisher, Peter Smith, who, faced with many problems and difficulties, continued working to within a few days of his death.

It is to Mrs. Choo Campbell of Graham Brash, publishers in Singapore, that this second edition is due. It was she who began a telephone conversation from her office with the immortal words — 'I want to save your book!'

March, 1991

14

Introduction

WRITING OF THE DIARIES — AND OF THIS BOOK

Most prisoners of the Japanese who kept a diary during their captivity from 1942 to 1945 knew the risks they ran. If they were caught they were liable to very severe punishment. All the more credit, then, to men like Dr. Robert Hardie. While he was a P.O.W. on the Burma—Siam railway he kept a diary secretly and illustrated it most beautifully. In 1983 it was published by the Imperial War Museum in a finely produced edition.

Equally remarkable was George Aspinall, an Australian P.O.W., who took a camera with him to Thailand. He only destroyed it after several times coming near to discovery. He finally decided that the risks were too great. Some of his photographs of Changi Barracks in Singapore and the 'Selarang Incident' there, and, too, of his journey north to Thailand, with the appalling conditions he and all who were with him endured when they got there, are quite extraordinary. They are all published in his *Changi Photographer.*

Stan Arneil is another of many Australian P.O.W.s who, in his *One Man's War*, has preserved a day-to-day record. It begins with the fall of Singapore, moves to Changi, north to Thailand, back to Changi again and then home to Australia, all in total secrecy — and fearful risk.

Ronald Searle, too, with the magnificent collection of 'War Drawings' in his book *To the Kwai — and Back*, has also included an interesting written account of his experiences.

I can claim no such cunning of concealment in producing and preserving this record. The Japanese imposed no ban on the keeping of diaries by civilian internees, either before internment, while still living in Singapore under the Japanese, or after going to Changi Gaol and, later, Sime Road Camp.

Even so, while I was still free in Singapore with Bishop Leonard Wilson before we were sent to Changi Gaol in March,

1943, I had to write this record with some caution. I could make no reference, for example, to the activities of the Bishop and the Revd. R. K. S. Adams, with both of whom I was also involved, as illicit middle-men in contacts between the P.O.W.s in their camps and internees in Changi Gaol.

Nor could I write about the highly dangerous activities of Norman Coulson on behalf of internees while he was still allowed to be free in Singapore and which, later, were to cost him his life. They are, however, mentioned here in another context. These and other incidents and opinions had either to be veiled in code or left out of the original diaries altogether.

In fact the first two sections of this book did fall into the hands of the Japanese Military Police. At the time of our internment in Changi in March, 1943, they were put for safe keeping into the Bishop's study at the Cathedral, with no attempt to hide them. When the Bishop became involved in the 'Double Tenth' enquiry on October 10th, 1943, and was arrested by the Kempei-tai, the Japanese Military Police, many of his papers were removed from the Cathedral. At the end of the investigation of his case all of them were scrupulously returned to him. Amongst them were my diaries, on the cover of which had been written in pencilled Japanese script 'Religious Writings'. It was a relief that I had not included controversial comments or sensitive material.

A FIVE PART STORY

The book is made up of five sections. First, a brief autobiographical note leads up to my arrival in Singapore to work at the Cathedral' in March, 1941. This is followed by a short account of the rest of that year and the start of the Japanese attack on Malaya. The story of the war period as I saw it, from December 8th, 1941 to February 15th, 1942, I wrote down soon after the fall of Singapore. I had not been able to write a day-to-day account during the campaign. There was too much else to do. The details, however, were still very clear in my mind. This completes the first section of the book.

I made no record at the time of the four months from February 18th, 1942, when Sorby Adams and I returned with the Bishop to his house, though I have since written briefly of this period.

It was not until June, 1942, that I began to keep a diary. Somewhat shortened here it tells the story of much of the life of the three of us for the rest of our thirteen months of freedom. It has much to say of Singapore under the Japanese and particularly of Church life at St. Andrews Cathedral and at St. Hildas, Katong, a district church in south-east Singapore, of which the Bishop made me Priest-in-Charge.

The third section of the book begins with our internment in the Goal at Changi in March, 1943. It includes full details of life there, including the 'Double Tenth', the devastating enquiry by the Kempei-tai, starting on October 10th, 1943.

In May, 1944, we were moved from the Gaol at Changi, changing places with P.O.W.s at Sime Road Camp. From then until the end of internment in September, 1945, I kept a diary again. It appears here as section four.

There follows a brief description of two fascinating months of freedom in Singapore in September and October, 1945, before the Bishop left by plane to join his family in Australia and I flew home to England.

The book closes with two short chapters — 'Where are they now?' and 'Forty years on', brief extracts are also included from several sermons preached in Changi and Sime Road.

THE ROAD TO SINGAPORE

For someone just setting out across the globe on his life's work, mine was not a good start. In the fading light of a bitterly cold day in early January, 1941, the SS Tosari, a 7000 ton Dutch cargo boat, sailed from Liverpool with six passengers in a snow storm on the first stage of an eight-week journey to Singapore. At a time when German submarines were particularly active in the North Atlantic, special precautions were needed. Sometime during the night the ship took her place as third in the most westerly line of a convoy sailing north up the Irish Sea.

At about midnight we were woken by the violent sound of the Tosari scraping throughout the whole of her length along a shingle bank. We fared better than her sister ship immediately astern of us on a course fractionally to the west of ours. She went onto the bank — and stayed there. The Tosari showed no apparent sign of damage, but back to dry dock in Liverpool we went, with the threat that there might be a delay of several weeks before our next sailing. Fortunately we were called back within a week and got away without incident. It was still snowing!

A strong rumour alleged that our whole convoy had been out of position, some miles off course to the west. The rumour also continued that an incoming convoy had met ours in total darkness on a collision course and that the two had passed through each other's lines without mishap. The mind boggles!

FIRST BEGINNINGS

The events which put me, a young Anglican priest of twenty-five, on the *Tosari* had begun eight years earlier. A Sunday evensong in October, 1932, had taken its ordinary course in the College Chapel at Lancing in Sussex. The sermon was by Dean Foxley-Norris of Westminster Abbey. I remember thinking, almost vaguely, as I processed out with the choir (and I give the form in which the thought came) 'It would be funny if I were to become a parson'.

I doubt if I should have remembered that at all had it not been for what followed three weeks later under very similar circumstances. The sermon, again at evensong, was preached by the Reverend Gordon Day, Candidates Secretary of the S.P.G. — the Society for the Propagation of the Gospel. I was completely bowled over, totally pole-axed. I knew I had to be ordained and specifically that I should work overseas. There were no inner voices or blinding vision. I just knew. As there was bound to be with such a discovery, there was a strong emotional reaction. It was very like falling in love for the first time. This stayed with me for several days. I knew that a bombshell like this had to be tested and thought about very carefully, and I knew too that, however sure I might be, other people also had to be equally convinced.

Chief amongst them were the elder statesmen of the S.P.G., who accepted this raw and not at all clever boy as a candidate under their care and direction. Their financial help and affectionate counsel then and later were invaluable, especially after the death in 1934 of my father, a much loved schoolmaster at King Edward VI School, Southampton.

Three years at St. Edmund Hall, Oxford, followed by eighteen months under Canon B. K. Cunningham at Westcott House, Cambridge, were not marked with any particular intellectual attainment from me, but with great enjoyment and much benefit.

For anyone newly ordained, both the parish and the priest under whom he serves are of great importance. A wondeful preparation, not only for what was soon to follow, but for a lifetime as a priest, were two and a half years at Romsey Abbey with Canon W. B. Corban as Vicar. Canon Cunningham knew him well, having trained him in earlier days at Farnham Hostel. He decided that W.B.C. and I would fit. We did.

Figure 1: The Vicar of Romsey, Canon W. B. Corban (centre), with the Revd. Adrian Somerset-Ward (right) and the author (left).

PRIEST IN PRISON

Why, after Romsey, was I on my way to Singapore? As soon as I became a candidate of S.P.G. they hoped I would allow them to take the lead in recommending what work I should do and where it should be. I was very ready to accept this. Both at Oxford and at Westcott House, as also particularly at Romsey, were those who, in consultation with S.P.G., were far better able to arrive at the right answers than I could be.

There was, however, one decision which only I could make. With huge numbers of people being called up from 1939 onwards after the outbreak of war, there was a great need for Service Chaplains. I was asked if I would defer going abroad. In spite of the pressing thought that by leaving England I would be turning my back on the war, nothing had happened to change what I always regarded as 'orders' to go overseas. By the middle of 1940, after talk of going to Moulmein in Burma, S.P.G. suggested my name to Singapore Cathedral, who needed an Assistant Chaplain. It was agreed I should go as soon as I could get a sea passage.

The voyage as it developed was without further incident, broken only by an overnight stop at Cape Town and a day at Durban, although it was constantly enlivened by the bitter animosity between two Dutch naval officers, who shared a cabin, and nothing else but their dislike of one another!

FIRST LOOK AT THE FAR EAST

My first sight of Malaya as we approached Penang with the dawn was unforgettable. The sea was carpeted with what seemed hundreds of small fishing boats with their postage stamp sails. To arrive in Singapore two days before Palm Sunday, with Holy Week and Easter to follow, could not have been better if it had been planned.

The impact of Singapore on a new arrival, especially on a young priest, was very great. This was particularly true for me coming into a Christian community wider and more fascinating than anything I had known in England. The Cathedral was a revelation.

It had not in 1941 achieved that level of total inter-racial worship and action which it has now reached nearly fifty years later, although there was then no suggestion of any kind of racial distinction. Its large congregations of Chinese, Indian,

European and Eurasian, a high standard of music and the entree which it gave to so many aspects of Singapore life I found totally absorbing.

To name only a few, there was the chance to see the high quality of work being done by our own missionaries and the nurses they were training at St. Andrews Mission Hospital, and at the Childrens' Orthopaedic Hospital, with lawns going down to the sea at Siglap. Within days I had been shown and saw a little of the work of the Government Leper Hospital. Our schools were of a high quality. The Chinese and Indian Churches, their clergy and people were unfailingly friendly and welcoming to this newcomer from the west.

A sharp and unpleasant attack of dengue fever two months after I arrived could not by any reckoning be put on the credit side. Convalescence in the cool and the beauty of the hill station at Fraser's Hill north of Kuala Lumpur and the chance of seeing something of Malaya certainly could.

Keen as I had always been on most kinds of sport, I did not need to be warned that, for health reasons, regular exercise was essential in the tropics. Besides, it was made plain that it was part of my job as a way of 'getting to know people'. What a bonus, to be able to play soccer, cricket and golf regularly without asking whether it was a proper way of spending the time of a young priest!

Never far from my mind were the war in Europe and the people affected by it whom I had left behind, but I was spared the frustration of a lot of my contemporaries in Singapore, who at that time felt that they were 'out of it'.

One thing Singapore lacked in the first half of 1941 was an Anglican Bishop. Basil Roberts had returned to England to become Secretary of S.P.G. In April, when I arrived, no appointment had been made, though there were those, including Archdeacon Graham White himself, who thought that it might be offered to him.

ARRIVAL OF LEONARD WILSON AS BISHOP OF SINGAPORE

However, the choice fell on Leonard Wilson, who, since 1938, had been Dean of Hong Kong. He was consecrated Bishop in the Cathedral there on July 22nd, 1941, St. Mary Magdalene's

Day, the anniversary of his wedding. His coming to Singapore at the age of fifty-four was a milestone in the life of the Church.

The very new Assistant Chaplain of the Cathedral and the Bishop and his family seemed to get along pretty well from the beginning. That this was so was partly because we were all newcomers. Perhaps even more it was due to the very special friendliness of the Bishop, of Mary Wilson and of their young children, Susan, Timothy and Martin. James was born in Australia in 1942.

Within no more than two months of his arrival, the Bishop began a very successful tour which, in eight weeks, took him to every part of his diocese. It has been said of him at this time 'Wherever he went those of all races who met their new Bishop were struck at once by his friendliness, his sympathy and his understanding. They were delighted by his humour and his gaiety. They found in him a preacher and a teacher who really helped them to understand.' Bishop Baker of Hong Kong said of Leonard Wilson's time there 'He brought a breath of fresh air into the life of the Church and the community'. That was certainly the experience of their new Bishop of the people of all races in Singapore and Malaya, Thailand, Java and Sumatra.

At the end of his tour he flew home to Singapore from even further afield, from Saigon, on the day before the outbreak of war on December 8th, 1941.

Section One

War comes to Malaya

AN ACCOUNT OF THE MALAYAN CAMPAIGN
and
THE ATTACK ON SINGAPORE
as seen by the author

December 8th, 1941 to February 15th, 1942

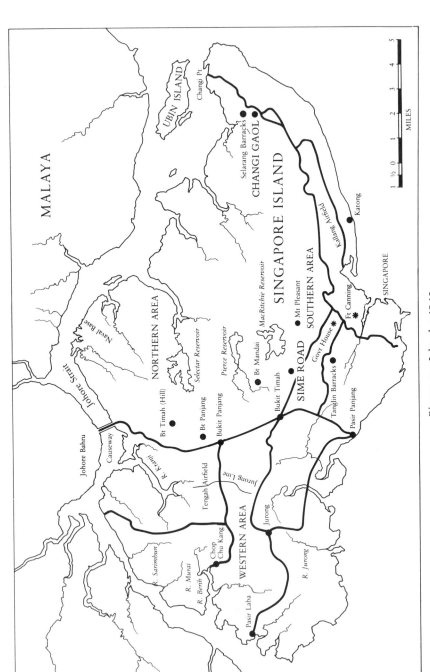

Singapore Island c.1942

War comes to Malaya

At the beginning of December, 1941, a whole day's drive took me from Singapore to Kuala Lumpur, where I was to have been in charge of the parish until the New Year. It was a Friday, the fifth of December. Everything was so normal. There was not any sense of a lull before the storm. War with Japan we thought of as a possiblility, but that last week-end of peaceful living bore none of the marks of strain and tension of Munich week in 1938 or of the period between the invasion of Poland by the Germans and our own entry into the war in the West in 1939. This was still true as late as the Sunday night, with the Japanese landing at Kota Bahru in north-east Malaya no more than a few hours away.

December 8—19th, 1941. In the early hours of Monday, December 8th, a telephone call came through to Norman Jarrett, British Resident of Selangor, with whom I was staying briefly. The Japanese had landed at Kota Bahru. Later we heard that Singapore had been bombed.

THE SCENE IN KUALA LUMPUR —
REFUGEES FROM THE NORTH

The next days are a succession of confused pictures. There was the tragedy of the sinking of the battleships *Prince of Wales* and *Repulse* off the east coast. Evacuees from the north started pouring through, amongst them a pathetic trainload from Penang, women and children packed into second and third class carriages. Amongst them were Honor Sawyer and the twins, Edward Sawyer's Colonel's wife and her two children, Mrs. Crowe with her two, all of them grey with dust and weariness after twelve hours in the train.

Five hours later they were all back in the same train — but how changed. There was not one of them who had not been taken off for a bath, a meal and a rest. The many cries of

'Thank you' as the train steamed out were greater reward than we either expected or deserved. There was far more reason for us to be thanking them for the first of the many examples of heroism — and that is by no means a word to be used lightly — of the women who came south, leaving their homes and their men.

Then followed days of ceaseless activity and endless confusion. Trains came and failed to come from the north and from the east coast. Cars loaded to the last inch rolled into the yard of the Station Hotel at all hours of the day, disgorging their occupants, who made straight for the lift and the reception desk, where they were met by the patient and perspiring head and shoulders of Pendlebury, with Day and myself either at his elbow or hovering in the background. It had become the official Refugee Reception Centre. Pendlebury (who died in Bangalore shortly after his evacuation from Malaya in 1945) was magnificent during the whole of that time and carried on single-handed right until the very last moment, when both Day and I had each in our turn made our way down to Singapore. It took some time to realise that, behind his appalling hesitancy, his boundless patience was worth any amount of slick efficiency.

Patience there had to be, not only with the people we were trying to help — though that was made easy enough by the wonderful patience which they showed — but also with chaotic orders, no sooner issued than they were countermanded. There were some who had definite instructions that they were to leave South Perak, only to be placed in the impossible position of being allowed, on the following day, to go back or not as they liked. Others were issued with train permits through to Singapore — permits which we were empowered and instructed to give — only to find themselves back in Kuala Lumpur on the following day, having been turned out of the train at Seremban. It is true that a very heavy strain was being put on the civil administration under almost impossible conditions, but the tragedy of it all was that it undermined public confidence. 'What are we to believe?' was a question on everybody's lips.

There were some who carried on quietly and confidently in the face of terrific pressure of work. Norman Jarrett was a

glorious example. He was left practically single-handed, even
to answering his own telephone and deciphering his own
telegrams. On the morning when the Government Offices
were bombed, a visitor to the Resident's office found him
still there, with hardly a soul left in the building.

During the whole of this time I was at the Parsonage, for
the first time in my life host in my own house. And there
were many opportunities of hospitality. It started with three
from the Malayan Broadcasting Corporation, who arrived in
Kuala Lumpur on the 8th fresh from a tour with a recording
van in Province Wellesley; the Bishop for a few hours on his
way through from Ipoh at the end of his two months tour of
the diocese. It was so good to see him. The Revd. Colin King
and his wife arrived from Bukit Mertajam on the 15th,
followed by Marjorie Broadhurst, Pat, Sarah and Richard,
who stayed for a riotous two days and then on to Singapore.

Finally, the Revd. G. S. Clarke arrived from Taiping, where
bombs fell at the back of the Parsonage as he drove away
from the front! In spite of the fact that there was a great deal
I could do and was being able to do in Kuala Lumpur, I was
very anxious to get back to Singapore. Clarke's arrival made
it possible. A hurried telephone conversation with the Bishop
at 9 p.m. on the 20th was followed by several hours of handing over to Clarke. By 9 a.m. the following morning I was on
the road and, with the last light of day, at Bishopsbourne to
one of the nicest and warmest welcomes imaginable.

DISILLUSIONED RETURN TO SINGAPORE

December 20th, 1941–January 19th, 1942. It was altogether
an odd return, in many ways a very great disappointment and
anticlimax. To leave the atmosphere of bustle and urgency of
Kuala Lumpur, with so many people travelling south who
needed immediate help; with men coming back from the line;
hospital trains waiting for hours, their darkened windows
phosphorescent blue in the shadowy gloom of the station;
troop trains carrying others north to take the place of those
pyjama-clad figures, who sat smoking and talking, or lay
deathly quiet, while doctors and orderlies passed to and fro —
to come from all that to a Singapore shrouded in a cloying

pall of false security was heartbreaking. For days I had been longing to get back, with the thought of so much to be done amongst people I knew and was beginning to know well, but for several days there was the bitterness of inactivity, until, after a gloriously happy Christmas at Bishopsbourne, the Bishop, with me in tow, plunged into the many complex problems of the reception and billeting of evacuees from the north.

HOMES FOR THE HOMELESS

For the greater part of January I found myself in a new world, tied to an office desk, first in the Public Works Department (P.W.D.) building and then in the Supreme Court, with an endless stream of people who had lost their houses, their belongings and, in a great many cases, their whole means of livelihood. The telephone was continually busy with incoming and outgoing calls. There was hardly a moment when we were not faced with some new and pressing personal problem which had to be solved at once — a home found for an elderly couple, or a woman with four children, all of them young, with nowhere to go!

Requests for information about shipping became so frequent that we had to introduce someone to deal with that alone. Fortunately, with the help of the already hard pressed A.R.P. Wardens, lists, very nearly complete, were compiled of houses, number of bedrooms, etc., and we had something to go on.

There were four things which made possible the partial success which we managed to achieve. First, the very real co-operation of the people of Singapore who, once they became aware of the necessity, did everything they possibly could to help. Even in cases of glaring misfits — of which, be it said, there were very few, though probably more than we knew — our blunder was pointed out with quite undeserved generosity and tact.

Another of the factors which made things at all possible was the founding of the 'Nelson Arms', formerly the Japanese Tojo Hotel, the child of Stanton ('Bird') Nelson. After a very short time, a hundred people could be housed there in comparative comfort and security. The 'Bird' was invaluable.

There was nothing and nobody he could not 'fix'. If we wanted beds, they were produced. Coolies to black-out the Nelson Arms or sugar and rice bags as bunding for the Supreme Court, the magician's wand had but to quiver and they were there. To walk into the office and to see the 'Bird' beaming and twinkling always meant that some particularly outrageous scrounge had been accomplished. One of the pleasantest interludes of each of those days was our picnic lunch shared on the verandah of the Cricket Club with Mrs. Kathleen Nelson, who had walked over the bridge from her Medical Aid Service (M.A.S.) office in Fullerton Building.

Help of a different sort, but just as useful, came from Sorby and Eunice Adams at St. Andrew's School. In the first days we were faced with the most difficult problem of knowing how to dispose temporarily of the large numbers of people whom Pendlebury in Kuala Lumpur and his opposite number in Seremban were sending us by the morning trains. It was impossible to billet them privately on the same day or to send them to one or other of the married quarters put at our disposal at Changi, Tanglin and Gilman Barracks. But St. Andrew's did nobly and Mrs. Adams was always equal to the occasion, even to providing meals for nearly a hundred and fifty people at no more than a few hours notice!

The thing which made the scheme at all possible was the week's work of the Bishop, creating and co-ordinating and producing order out of chaos. It was sad and a little alarming to see him go, but fortunately his confidence was justified. For a few days we were at sixes and sevens, but S. M. Middlebrook when he arrived was a very useful pilot. I think it can reasonably be said that we did the job at least adequately.

DESPERATE DEPARTURES

Before leaving this business of billeting and evacuation, there still remains one aspect of it which is worth mentioning, partly because it was, if anything, the most difficult and the most vital, and also because it kept me on the run on one occasion until six in the morning. Throughout the whole of this time we kept in close touch with the P. & O. shipping office. They were responsible for all bookings for passages in British ships. The difficulty with which they were faced was being told in the evening of one day that they could fill ships which were to sail within twenty-four hours with anything between five to eight hundred women and children. This meant the most frantic telephoning and furious driving all round the town in an attempt to locate people who had often given incomplete addresses or, worse still, failed to correct them when they had moved elsewhere.

It was on one of these all-night forays that I had an experience which was both disturbing and alarming. I cannot remember the hour at which it happened but I was driving alone along a deserted street in the middle of Singapore when I was stopped by two soldiers, both of them with rifles. They asked for a lift back to the Naval Base. I replied that I couldn't help. When one said to the other 'Shall we take the car?' I decided it was time to leave. As I drove away I looked in my rear-view mirror and saw one had his rifle to his shoulder. Far more angry than alarmed, I slammed on the brakes, got out and walked back. I told them who I was and what I was doing and that, if they took the car, an untold number of women and children would not get onto a boat to leave Singapore in the morning. I walked back to the car and drove away. Fortunately, the anger I was feeling was stronger than the fear of a bullet in my back!

The worst of these nocturnal 'scavengings' found me at 11 o'clock at the P. & O. office which, for the purpose of booking passages, had been moved to one of their big houses on Cluny Hill. For the next three hours I was in turn making a nuisance of myself at the Oranje, Raffles and Adelphi Hotels, finishing up with about an hour and a half of indiscriminate telephoning from the Rex, knocking up one boarding house after another, trying to get in touch with people who wanted to leave. Stupefied with sleep as they all were, proprietors would have been perfectly justified in sending me packing, but they were, without exception, charming, and the amount of charm which the average English man or woman can muster when summoned from bed at three in the morning is usually not very noticeable! The P. & O. staff were still hard at it when I got back at about 3.30 in the morning to some more telephoning until 6.

While I was there Dicky Pyper and his wife, Helen, came in,

she very worried as to whether she should leave or not. It was very hard for so many of them, having to make up their minds at such terribly short notice. And now she has left and Dicky is dead. Ten days before the capitulation he got a commission in the R.A.S.C. Within a week he was gone. Before the surrender the Changi Military Hospitals were evacuated, but he, with one or two others too ill to move, was left behind with a minimum nursing staff and there he died.

ORDEAL BY BOMBING

During the whole of this time the intensity of air raids was increasing. Fortunately they did not become really bad until we had broken the back of the billeting and I was able to move about freely, doing the job I had been given as Chaplain to the Civil Defence Services. During the first fortnight of January the Japanese were obviously testing our defences. Initially they concentrated on night raids. Their techniques differed from that of the Germans in the west and, with the searchlight crews here at the top of their bent, the Japanese achieved nothing by these methods. Night after night they came over in close formation and I never saw a time when the searchlights did not find and hold them. There was one night when they caught and fastened onto two groups flying on courses crossing and at right angles to one another and they were still on the mark when the planes had passed beyond the shores of the Island. Heaven knows how many German planes I have heard droning their way across the fields and towns of a darkened England, but only once did I see the probings of the searchlights bear fruit — on the first night raid on Southampton.

All of us knew that the time of our testing could not be very far off. Day raids might — almost certainly would — mean that our own fighters would have a chance to retaliate, although it was a very long time before badly needed Hurricanes began to arrive to relieve some of the valiant but hard-pressed Buffaloes. But daylight raiding would also mean damage on a far larger scale, and so it was to prove.

Tuesday, January 20th. The first heavy raid on the town itself came on January 20th, when a large number of bombs were dropped and we had our first taste of pattern bombing. Twenty-seven planes — from now until the end that was to be the usual number of the raiding force — made their run in over the target together, and at a signal from the leading plane — usually three sharp bursts of machine-gun fire — they started dropping their bombs and carried on until the racks were empty. Orchard Road, Scots Road, Cairnhill Road, Stevens Road, Government Hill, Cavenagh Road, Monks Hill and Newton Circus had it on that day.

DEATH AT CATHEDRAL HOUSE

By the greatest of good luck the majority of bombs fell on open ground, although the Archdeacon had a really unpleasant shaking with two in his garden. For him and for Mrs. Graham White there was the shock of the tragic death of Joseph, his secretary. He was standing out on the verandah when the bombs fell and was killed instantaneously. He cannot have known anything about it. It was all too sudden. The Archdeacon tried desperately hard to appear matter-of-fact — almost casual about it, but in spite of his barking and roughness in his dealings with Joseph, there was a great affection between them.

By this time we had moved the Billeting Office from the insecurity of the old P.W.D. building to the massive bulk of the new Supreme Court, which also housed the A.R.P. Control Room. This meant that when the siren sounded and all work stopped — though it was hardly ever necessary that it should stop — I was able to slip through to the Control Room and get first-hand information about the raid, where the bombs had fallen, the extent of the damage and the estimated number of casualties.

Wednesday, January 21st. On the day after the raid on the Orchard Road area I was with the Archdeacon at Cathedral House at about ten in the morning when the siren went for the second time. The first raid had caught me at Tan Tock Seng Hospital. Several groups of planes flew over the town and dropped their bombs. As I drove back into town it became obvious from the fires that the damage had been considerable. I went on, down Bras Basah Road to the Church

Bookshop, on the edge of the bombed area. All was well there. The Revd. L. St. G. Petter, resplendent in his uniform as Chaplain to the Malacca Volunteers, emerged as I arrived, quite unmoved, although he had been thrown out of his chair by the force of the explosion and shot halfway across the room.

Turning into North Bridge Road, I went up into Victoria Street, past several fairly small and isolated fires on which the Brigade were working, down Bras Basah Road and into North Bridge Road again. The M.A.S. had done their job well and all the casualties had been removed from that area. But there were about half a dozen bodies lying on the five-foot way — a food hawker beside his stove, a man who had been killed while walking upstairs — there was not time then to think fully of the horror of it all. Madrid, London, Coventry, Rotterdam, Chungking, Berlin, Hong Kong — and now Singapore.

We, an A.F.S. man off duty who had come along 'to see if he could give a hand', a soldier and I, covered the bodies as best we could — sacking, a gaily covered canvas cinema poster, corrugated iron torn from its place and a large piece of green baize ripped from the back of a shattered show case. On broken doors and shutters we lifted the bodies into a passing lorry and for the first time had a moment to stop and look around. The pathos of it. A large hole in the road, houses and shops blasted and battered, stock in trade scattered all over the place, the air thick with smoke, dust and the smell of blood and death. There were so many small and pathetic Pompeian things. In the little kitchen at the back of a shop, two charcoal burners, on one of them a pot of stew, on the other a boiling kettle. Half an hour before the kettle had been empty and the stewpot had been given its last pinch of salt.

There was nothing more to be done there and I drove back to the Supreme Court, prompted largely by the alarmist report that there was little of it left and that the Cricket Club was a smoking heap of rubble. In fact, both were still very much there, although the combined effects of eight bombs on or around the Padang — one of them bringing down the wrath of the shades of Drake when it made a gaping hole in one of the corners of the bowling green! — had served to

33

hurl the smoking remains of Dr. Hopkin's car through the billiard room window. It started a very small fire and lolled there for days, in a sort of drunken stupor, half in and half out of the window. The Supreme Court, except for a mass of twisted metalwork and plaster which had fallen from the porch ceiling onto the tarmac below, was untouched.

Jeans, the A.R.P. chief, was the first man I saw, hunting vainly for the driver of an M.A.S. ambulance standing idle outside the Supreme Court. Every available ambulance was needed in Beach Road, where there were still many casualties. While he jumped into the driving seat I got up behind. Beach Road, and especially the market, which had had more than one direct hit, was indescribable. The dead and the wounded were mixed up amongst a tangle of girders, corrugated iron and wooden boxes. Four of them we got out and drove off in the ambulance to Kandang Kerbau Hospital, where we were told there was no more room and we must go to the General Hospital. For sheer stoicism I saw little in the days which followed to equal the cheerfulness of a young Chinese of about twenty who had had his thigh smashed, but who laughed and talked the whole time.

CIVIL DEFENCE HEROES

It was on this drive that I saw the real solid worth of the M.A.S. for the first, and by no means the last, time. Before leaving Beach Road we had picked up a boy of about sixteen who had his water bottle and first aid equipment with him. From the time we left Beach Road until I left them at the junction of Coleman Street and Hill Street, he never for one moment stopped looking after those people; they were his people, his responsibility, his special charge. Sips from his water bottle, a field dressing put on gently and carefully, a blanket straightened and another rolled to go under an uncomfortable and sorely aching head. No one had told him in his long and often unintelligible M.A.S. lectures, that these were things of real importance. They were not things which could be taught. One would do them, another would not.

There is this much to be said for war and all its ghastly accompaniments. It does show up real worth as little else can. And there's the pity of it. It takes a major disaster to bring out the best in people. There were so many examples of quiet and uncomplaining sacrifice, and so many of the noblest deeds of Singapore will remain unsung, though not unhonoured in the minds of those of us who were there to see them. There will be no George Cross for one young Chinese M.A.S. volunteer. He had been on his way to duty at his Aid-Post and had taken cover behind a sandbag shelter in North Bridge Road when the planes were heard. When they were almost overhead he saw an old woman crossing the road with two small children. He ran out from the five-foot way and hurried the children back to the bunding, while a warden who was with him helped the old lady. The bombs fell. The children were saved, the warden and the old lady were killed. The young M.A.S. man had his arm shattered. I saw him several times in hospital and, although he was in great pain from a poisoned stump, I don't think he would have had it otherwise.

Another example of quiet heroism amongst thousands of others was Nellie, the young Chinese nurse, who stayed kneeling beside a wounded soldier in an open corridor at Kandang Kerbau Hospital, while shells were falling on and around the building, shielding his body with hers, covering his ears with her hands.

A WORLD STARTLED AWAKE

Just after writing this I came across a quotation from Dorothy Sayer's book *Begin Here*, which had a close bearing on what I tried to say about the response to service in times of peace and of war.

> 'The great obstacle, in times of peace and prosperity, to improvement in the social order is the inertia which society presents to any kind of change. The reformer spends nine-tenths of his energy in endeavouring to make his voice heard above the snoring of well-cushioned indolence, to smash his way into the closed circle of vested interests, to disturb complacency and generally to overcome the disposition of his hearers to let sleeping dogs lie. But war does this part of his task for him. The world is startled awake, complacency is destroyed. His

chief difficulty now will be to catch the distracted attention of agitated people and get it focussed on what he has to say'.

What is lacking in peacetime is any form of social consciousness. Although distraction and agitation startle the world into wakefulness, there is still the question of wakefulness to and for what. At least the world is now in some sense awake, shocked and frightened out of its former stupor, and there is, being prepared, the seed bed in which a new interest, a new desire for reform, may grow. The Church has been accused many times of lack of interest in reform and of a reactionary and even obstructive attitude towards it. It has a real opportunity to correct the balance. Here in Singapore now, early in 1942, the opportunities of service and the really vital urgency of its being given, become increasingly apparent almost daily.

RETURN TO BEACH ROAD

On that day, January 21, I left the ambulance and drove back to Beach Road in the car. A great many casualties were still there and a small crowd was gathered round the ruins of a shop-house which had had a direct hit. There was an Indian buried in the wreckage, who was not only alive, but practically fully conscious. His head and his arms were free and after about two hours of careful digging we managed to get him out unhurt, save for an extensive scalp wound on the side of his head. He was lying against a wall which had been completely demolished down to a height of about three feet from the ground. He lay in the angle of the wall and two large slabs of stone with a sheet of corrugated iron resting with one end on the top of the wall, supporting a mass of rubble. Slowly and carefully we moved the bricks and tiles and paraphernalia of the ship chandler's shop, all of us infuriated by reel after reel of white cotton which was everywhere. It tangled itself round bricks and beams, even the wretched man himself, and the more we pulled the worse it got! But it was the chandlery which saved him. When we had removed the bricks we found that he was lying on his side with his face to the wall, his knees raised slightly. At his back were a number of large coils of rope, while another, supported on either side, was resting lightly on his hip. After the tenseness and anxiety of those two hours, we finally got him out and saw him carried away in an ambulance.

The anxiety very nearly led to bloodshed at one stage, when a horde of Tamil coolies swarmed onto the ruins and, with the greatest enthusiasm, began pulling at the first thing on which they could get their hands. I had to knock one man's hand away when he started hauling at the precious sheet of corrugated iron. Dr. Hopkin arrived just as we were getting him out and, after we had seen him driven off in the ambulance, the two of us went off to another part of the building. Someone came running up to say that they had heard cries, muffled and very faint, coming from the middle of the wreckage. It seemed impossible that anyone could be in the centre of that and yet still be alive, but by the time I left we had uncovered his back and shoulders. Even that was not all. Hopkin told me the following day that they had heard still another cry and had finally, by the light of car headlights, got another man out at about 8.30.

GATHERING IN THE DEAD

The full tide of war burst on most of us in all its fury on that day of the Beach Road raid. The streets further inland, too, had as much to bear and the wardens in this division had more than their share of work during the days which followed. I tried to spend as much time as I could with them and was now more than ever glad to be free to come and go as I pleased. The most distasteful job with which they were faced was the recovery of bodies from the ruins, sometimes as long as four or five days after death, although they were to a large extent relieved of this job by gangs of Tamil coolies under the direction of Asiatic overseers. It was with one of these gangs that I spent a more than unsavoury morning, although afterwards it was even possible to see the comedy of it.

One of the difficulties for the last month was a great dwindling in the ranks of organised labour. More and more people were leaving the town, with the result that those who remained were able to demand high wages. Nothing can be said against that. They were, in many cases, being called upon to do unpleasant and sometimes dangerous work. But they needed very careful handling and a great mistake was made when no added supervision was given. Judging from my own experience of this particular morning, that supervision, if it had been there, would have been of the very greatest value. Some of the Asiatic overseers did their job and did it well, but there were others who were not so successful. The conditions under which they were required to keep a firm hand on their men called for qualities which could never be expected of them. The pity of it was that there were several hundred men in Singapore, planters and tin miners, many of them in the up-country detachments of the Local Defence Corps, who had little or nothing to do at a time when their experience would have been invaluable. The European Municipal Officers did their best, but the areas which they had to cover were too large to make adequate supervision of each gang possible.

THE CURATE AND THE COOLIES

It was about four days after the raid when I found myself in Muar Road, a narrow street just off Rochore Canal Road. A row of four small houses had been completely demolished and the road blocked with debris. Within a length of street no more than forty yards long, two gangs of Tamil coolies were working, each of them about thirty strong, one on the road and the other on the ruined houses. There were, in the first place, many too many of them, with the result that the amount of work each man did was negligible. They stood about in sulky groups talking their heads off, while the Eurasian overseer shouted, cajoled and swore, without making any impression on them. One o'clock came and one of the gangs knocked off, in spite of the fact — or perhaps because of it! — that there were four bodies in a heap, partially uncovered, in one of the houses on which they were working. In another hour the other gang would be off as well, but something had to be done. Without much hope of success, I told the overseer of the road gang to get his men onto the house. He stormed and 'yammered' at them, one of

them started a counter agitation and then to crown it all two
of them started a fight. We soon stopped that and, after re-
moving an ugly looking crowbar from one of the contestants,
sent him and the agitators packing.

By this time the noise was terrific. The overseer had lost
all control and was crying with rage, screaming at me, his
men, and the world in general, in a loud, high-pitched falsetto.
The gist of his remarks to me was that he was a good Catholic
which, reiterated time after time, seemed very little to the
point and contributed little of value to the discussion, which
was now general! Something, I thought, has got to be done!
Feeling the whole weight of Empire pressing down on me, I
mounted aloft on a pile of rubble and commanded silence.
Almost as difficult as claiming attention at a Christmas party
for five hundred child evacuees at Romsey in 1939, but in
this case, as then, I was successful. I called for, and got, eight
volunteers. I might or I might not have got them without
glittering promises of 50 cents a time, but I had arrived at
the stage when I was taking no chances, and anyway there was
a *terminus ad quem* and 2.30 was not so very far away. But
we removed enough debris for the bodies to be got out and
at long last the disposal lorry arrived and we turned our backs
on Muar Street after an extremely unpleasant morning. To a
certain extent the situation had been relieved by elements of
comedy. The boy who 'stood on the burning deck when all
but he had fled' had nothing on me in my lonely isolation!

Raids on a large scale were a common occurrence after
this, though mercifully, until the shelling began, Beach Road
had nothing further to contend with. But Geylang and Tiong
Bahru, as raids on Kallang Aerodrome and the Harbour
Board increased, had more than their share. Memories of
these days are rather kaleidoscopic. There was the heavy raid
along Geylang Road with many casualties on the five-foot
way. Death, ghastly in its violence. Young and old — no one
was safe. I helped Tim Denison Smith and Jack Wilson clear
things up as best we could, with the aid of a squad of police.
Four wardens did magnificent work carrying bodies from the
ruins of an atap house — an old woman, another who might
have been her daughter, and three young children.

Another morning, after an equally deadly raid, I went to

Yock Eng School, the Revd. Jack Bennitt's Aid Post. I clumsily bandaged one or two superficial wounds, I watched with admiration and envied the bustling efficiency of Mrs. Orton, with time to notice how absurdly comic she looked with her head almost enveloped in a bakelite helmet several sizes too large. I hoped against hope, but in vain, that Olga Neubronner's attempts to slap life into a wounded baby might have their reward. I then made my way down to Grove Road, which had also had it pretty badly.

THOUGHTS ABOUT LIFE – AND DEATH

Why was it that so often I found myself having to deal with the dead during these raids? Our job should really have been with the maimed and the frightened, but there were many who had far more unpleasant jobs than mine to do, amongst them A.R.P. wardens, who did not meet death just here and there, but every day. It was worth spending some time with them and perhaps to help them in more ways than by just carrying the bodies. Thank God – and I did then – that He did not allow me to suffer too deeply the pain and the sorrow and the agony of it all. Emotionally I was dead, not for the living and for those who had to try and mitigate for themselves and for others the dread of each successive raid, but for the dead themselves. There was a sadness there, far too deep for words and still so deep that it could hardly be felt. The pathos of the father who mourned the loss of his young children – one boy had been blown by the explosion onto an outhouse roof twenty-foot high, another tiny baby had been shattered – this was something I could understand, something to be felt, but the sadness for the boy as we carried him down from the roof was so great that it made a numbness and a blank. It was too deep for anything but cold, revolted bitterness.

It is hard to write of these things and of my own thoughts when some three months have gone by, but they are as important a part of this record as anything which actually happened to me. It is made harder still by the sense of unreality I feel now. Did these things actually happen? Gaping holes in the line of houses in Geylang, and the drain in Joo Chiat Road where I found a child's arm, show that they did. But even these grisly reminders cannot — and I thank God for it — bring them back as more than fantastic unrealities. Even the days at the General Hospital at the very end, with long hours by the communal grave, have a dream-like quality about them, and I remember that this was true then. But I am again anticipating.

AIR ATTACKS INTENSIFIED

Wednesday, January 21st, the day of the Beach Road raid, saw the beginning of the attack on the Island in all its fury. On most mornings we knew that we must expect one, if not two raids and, although the advent of Hurricane fighters, bringing relief to the hard pressed Buffaloes, meant that many attacks did not materialise, large formations of bombers still got through.

There was one morning, at a time when Kallang was having an almost daily visitation, when the planes had found their mark on the aerodrome, and on Geylang and Katong beyond it, as was usually the case. Stopping in the town to pick up four soldiers, we drove out to see if there was anything to be done. I turned the car into the lane at the back of the Happy World, where bombs had been dropped in the first raid. No sooner had we bundled out of the car than we saw another formation of twenty-seven bombers flying in very high towards the aerodrome — and us — from the south west. We dived for cover behind a surface shelter and waited. Would they overshoot the mark? If so, we were for it. The bombs began their journey with that extraordinary and quite inde-finable sound. The nearest comparison is that of a high wind through a tunnel. Still we waited, and there was more waiting after they began to burst, coming nearer and nearer, each interval between the explosions enlivened with ribald com-ments from one of my companions, as he bellowed a sangui-nary running commentary! But the explosions stopped when they were short and to the left of us, and we got to our feet, thankful that we had suffered no greater inconvenience than usually comes to those who lie down, as we had done, on a large ant heap!

COURAGE OF THE YOUNG

A young Chinese warden, he can't have been more than seventeen, had clambered into the car with the rest of us on this morning in Geylang Road. He was a bit shaken after the raid — and small wonder. His brother had been killed the day before. I saw him again later, after yet another raid on Geylang. He ran up to tell me, almost with pride, that a bomb had dropped only twenty yards from his A.R.P. post.

Seeing these wardens — and some of them no more than boys — standing by day after day, knowing full well that before the day was out they would be near, and unpleasantly near, danger, if not actually engulfed by it — and seeing, too, the prompt way in which they did their job, made one wonder about so many things which are often said to the discredit of the Asiatics here in Singapore. They could never again be accused of lack of initiative, of loyalty, of any developed sense of fellow feeling.

These were exceptional circumstances, as I have said before, calling out the best or the worst. It had to be one thing or the other, no one remained quite the same as he had been. This was sterile soil for the grey flower of mediocrity. The smallest seed of selflessness blossomed as the rose and the rank weed of egotism threw up lank, scraggy stalks — lifeless and unbeautiful. The flowers — pulsating with life and goodness — were there for the seeing in the part of the garden where they had been least expected. Yes, and there were herbaceous borders which should have been a blaze of colour but were not. One passed them by and made for the quiet and unobtrusive corners. One hopes the day will come when there will be a gardener to clear the patch and help the flowers to blossom and be seen as they deserve.

THE JAPANESE ADVANCE

During the whole of this time — almost from the very first moment of the landing at Kota Baru — the Japanese drive by land had been continuing. There was hardly a day when we did not hear of fresh advances and new successes. First, of course, the fall of Penang. We were back this side of Taiping before Christmas. Ipoh and Kuala Lumpur followed, after the landing of an out-flanking force at Kuala Selangor on the west coast. Then Seremban and, after a grimmer struggle, Gemas and Segamat.

On Tuesday, January 27, we were cheered by the arrival of extensive reinforcements. At the same time the Local Defence Corps was brought back — they were classified as civilians and were handed, like the proverbial baby, from one foster parent to another until they reached the long suffering bosom of the billeting officer. Tanglin Club and the Cathay Restaurant were filled to capacity, and they were all housed somewhere. By Friday, January 30, our troops had come a long way through Johore. Further resistance on the mainland must have seemed hopeless and on Saturday, the 31st, we heard that a gap of 160 yards had been blown in the Causeway, the Argylls marching across last, with pipes playing after a series of magnificent achievements. For weeks they fought their way back from the Thai border without relief until the Australians were sent up to a front near Gemas. They were brought back to the Island for a much needed rest and had another spell in the line before they finally went out to cover the retreat to Johore Baru. They, the Leicesters and the East Surreys, probably saw more fighting than any other units and yet it was the Argylls who had the last word on the mainland before the siege of Singapore began.

LAST LETTER HOME

On that last day of January I wrote a long letter to my mother. A friend was leaving by boat. I asked her to post it for me. In it, only days after the events of which I was writing, I said:

> 'I have never seen anything like the patience of the wounded. They, whoever they are, really are the salt of the earth. Our worst attack was in a day-light raid, when Japanese planes bombed right across a very congested area. There were about a thousand casualties in all, killed and wounded. I was able to get there fairly soon afterwards and helped move some of them to hospital. There was one Chinese boy of about twenty, badly wounded. He grinned and talked all the way there. And in the hospitals, too, there is the same uncomplaining

patience. The young auxiliary nurses, most of them with very little training, are doing wonders.

As for me I am quite extraordinarily quiet in my mind. Thank God for it, as I do. There is nowhere else it can come from. Don't imagine for one moment, in spite of the rubbish which we hear has been appearing in the press at home, that any of us are complacent. The danger is much too real for that. There is a quietness and a calmness in spite of, rather than because of, the situation . . . There is such a lot of quiet strength and courage amongst all sorts of people here.

When you read this think that, for myself, though not for you, I am glad to be here, glad to be somewhere I can be of real use to God and man, needing all the prayers which I know you are saying . . . to keep me faithful and to help me stand firm . . .'

BRITISH RETREAT – THE SIEGE OF SINGAPORE BEGINS
Friday, January 30th, 1942 to Sunday, February 15th, 1942.
Now we knew it was a straight fight. The issues were narrowed down to the minimum, and were clear cut. Much of the conjecture, fed and nurtured by rumour during the two months which had gone before, was now superfluous. We knew that we had to hang on as long as we could and at that time we were confident that we could hang on. The Island's defences were said to be the strongest in the world, equal even to Malta's. There were over eighty thousand troops on the Island and we could not believe that Singapore could fall, at any rate for some considerable time, even without the air support which was made impossible by the shelling – and bombing – of Seletar, Tengah and Sembawang airfields. Kallang was beyond the range of their guns, but not of their bombs and was made practically untenable, although it was still being used to within a few days of the end.

With the narrowing down of the issues involved came also, for most of us, a new simplicity of emotion. Feelings which had been falsely buoyed up by almost blind optimism were stripped of what covering they had and awoke to a steadier, deeper and more controlled life in the face of greater and more pressing danger.

The Asiatics, on the other hand, were hard pressed both mentally and emotionally. Their bewilderment was tragic. So many times each one of them moved from one place to another only to find that the 'thing' which was pursuing them had followed them once again. One particular Chinese house-boy was typical of so many. He stuck the bombing splendidly and had developed his own routine, bounded by his quarters, the house and the trench, to such a fine art that, unless he had been killed in the shelter, nothing could have touched him. He was, at times, infuriatingly cool. He was prepared to face any amount of bombing — you knew when to expect it for one thing. But shelling was too much for him. It was not playing the game; the shells came when you weren't looking. The damage and the number of casualties they caused were probably negligible, but the moral effect was very great and there was hardly one amongst us who was not affected by it.

The first week of the siege began with a little sporadic shelling of the Balestier Road area. Tan Tock Seng Hospital had more than one salvo in the grounds and dangerously near the hospital. One shell fell between two wards, but they never had a direct hit and carried on there until the possibility of infiltration by the Japanese made a move imperative on Friday, February 13th.

CONFUSION AT THE DOCKS

The bombing became more intense and from then until the end they concentrated almost entirely on Kallang aerodrome and, more particularly, the Docks, which had already had a good deal of attention. Even so ships, and some of them large ones, came in and got away again loaded with many hundreds of women and children. Not one of these ships was hit when alongside, although it certainly was not for want of trying. There were near misses in plenty.

I drove one party down to the Docks after a frantic rush out to Changi, where they had been living in army married quarters. We arrived to find a big fire blazing — the Railway Station too had been damaged — and clouds of smoke hid the greater part of the upper works of a large ship lying along-side with several others. It was impossible to tell whether the ship had been hit or not — it certainly seemed as if it had, but with relief we found that half the blaze came from a godown only a few yards from the edge of the wharf and the ship eventually got away with every available inch of room occupied. There were well over a thousand on board.

The same number should have gone on another ship, the *Felix Roussel,* which sailed on February 6th, a day or two after the Japanese had got Johore Bahru. Because of a succession of blunders and confusion she had to sail without upwards of three hundred of her passengers. To avoid any congestion at the Docks, which would have been an appalling danger in the event of a raid, the Collyer Quay car park in the centre of the town had been fixed as an assembly ground. Cars were to arrive there at hourly intervals between six in the evening and eleven. The Bishop with Miss Carpenter, and I, with a family from Changi, were there at six and, although we eventually got away in the second batch of twenty cars which were being escorted to the Docks, it was already 6.40 when we left Collyer Quay. Forty or perhaps sixty cars left in the first hour, instead of about three hundred. It was the arrangements on the wharf which were at fault, with no control whatsoever. Husbands came in cars, parked them everywhere and anywhere, helped their families on board and, very naturally, I suppose, stayed there saying their goodbyes. The result was chaos.

I was to go down again at nine with Miss Pring and Miss Murray, and we arrived at Collyer Quay in plenty of time to find a complete jam. The chances of getting through that mob in anything under a couple of hours were so small that we decided to go straight to the ship without waiting. Fortunately I had stopped some way short of the rest of the cars at Collyer Quay and managed to sneak back onto the road through a gap in the railings. At the wharf there were about thirty cars — no more — parked all over the road, holding up everyone who was coming behind. But we managed to worm our way through and parked the car some way beyond the gap between the godowns, then up a most dangerous gangway into a small vestibule crammed with people, luggage and French sailors. The noise was deafening, but I got them both settled, Miss Murray in a cabin by herself and Miss Pring down on one of the mess decks, after wandering through seemingly endless corridors. That mess deck was one of the most cheerless sights I have ever seen. It was the nautical equivalent of 'Hommes 40, Chevaux 10' of the 1914–18 war, but it was 'Femmes et enfants' and not hard-bitten soldiery who were having to sleep on bare steel plating. I helped another family on board and then back to the car.

The pathetic thing was that away to the left was this solid block of cars, with hardly anyone getting through it to go aboard. At 11.45, already three quarters of an hour behind time, with cars three abreast along Keppel Road, the ship could wait no longer and had to get away, leaving a great many behind. At that time we thought there could be no more sailings, which would have made things worse than they were already. Practically all those who should have gone did actually leave Singapore, but many were on small ships which were sunk by the Japanese.

EURASIAN EXITS

One encouraging thing about that shipload on the *Felix Roussel* was the sight of so many Eurasians leaving. We had, it is true, heard of Indian and Chinese Committees arranging ships and passages, but the Eurasians hardly seemed to be getting a fair deal. [Conversations with Eurasians in Sime Road years later indicated that this was the case.] Encouraging to see them go? Yes, perhaps in one sense, but terribly saddening too. This evacuation meant so much more to them than it did even to the European women because of the ties, far deeper and stronger, of Malaya itself. This is their home, the country of their birth, and most of them have never known any other. Ahead of them was an unknown world, largely friendless, and a very uncertain way of life. Theirs was almost completely a journey into a void and a journey in the company of a gnawing, aching loneliness. 'Parting is such sweet sorrow'. Nonsense! It's unadulterated vinegar! And those of us who stayed behind, even without the pain of a darkened wharf, the black mass of a ship's side and a precipitous and slippery gangway, drank great draughts from the cup of bitterness during the last eight days of the attack.

THE HEAVIEST BARRAGE OF THE WAR

As day followed day during the first week of February and
the Japanese were able to bring up more and more guns along
the Johore Straits, the barrage from both sides increased
until it reached its climax on Sunday, 8th. The firing began
early in the evening and increased as the night wore on. The
noise was indescribable. Hour after hour with never a moment's break in the deep roar of the guns away to the north,
the only change coming in a terrific crescendo at intervals
throughout the night. It was obvious that this bombardment
and our reply to it — it was described by the B.B.C. as the
heaviest barrage of the war — must be the prelude to an
attack. And so it proved.

On Monday morning, February 9th, we learnt that the
Japanese had landed on the north-west corner of the Island.
That in itself was not unduly alarming. The wiseacres went
about muttering 'Mangrove swamps. Impossible!', and the
rest of us were confident that they would be pushed back.
But the day dragged on; men, plastered with mud and dog-
tired, began drifting back into the town and the official
communique could give us no greater comfort than the
statement that 'the landing forces had been contained'. Even
so, we thought that after the regrouping of units on the
Island, this threat, dangerous as it was, would be more than
counteracted.

On Tuesday, the 10th, we were cheered by the rumour
that Wavell had been here, but more men came back from the
line and, although news of the actual fighting was obscure, it
was clear that things were not going well. Our guns came
back. They seemed towards evening to have been able to push
forward again, but on Wednesday night, the 11th, they had
come right back and were scattered all over the Tanglin area.
That night was one of the most unpleasant I ever remember.

The Bishop and I had been out all day and got back to
Bishopsgate in the early part of the evening to find the whole
area completely deserted, except for Ismael, the Bishop's
driver, Ah Din, the gardener, and their families. It was a
desolation of eerie stillness, a deserted city. Jack Bennitt's
house was shut up and there was no trace of him or of anyone else in Bishopsgate. It seemed as though everyone save us

must have had orders to move. Should we go too? But where
to go? It would be dark in an hour. No, we would not go.
Just after we got there a crowd of Australians arrived, hot,
tired, dirty and blasphemous. We had a quick remedy for all
four of these states; cold showers, and for six of them beds
and mattresses. But it was after nightfall that the stillness became almost unbearable. It was a quiet not of this earth,
leaving us both with a sense of overwhelming loneliness and
depression.

'OH, PEACEFUL ENGLAND!'

I've known quietness in so many places — the Downs above
Lancing with the shimmering moon-paving leading away
across the sea into the distant shadows; Sussex again, the
shepherd's cottage in the very heart of the Downs above
Jevington; King's and Magdalen; the cliff path from the
Valley of Rocks to Hunters Inn; London City in the early
hours of the morning; Russell's cottage at Merston just outside Chichester; home at Thatchers, at Upper Basildon above
the Thames Valley; but in each of these there was the breath
of life in and beyond the stillness, the life of one's own
imaginings, the living breath of the Spirit, giving shape and
form to the solitariness and the quiet. Then the silence was
peopled with a myriad of voices. The sunlight and the
shadows thronged with a host of memories, of joys and
pleasures shared and of the friends who shared them. But
here there was a great emptiness, a gaping void, cruel, baffling
and overwhelming. Life and loveliness had been torn from
the world, leaving behind the stillness of death, purposeless
oblivion.

What followed was even worse. From ten o'clock right
through the night until the morning we were never free from
the thunder of our guns on all sides of us. The noise was
staggering. It went on for so long and so loud that it hurt
physically. Perhaps it is easy to make too much of these
things. We had only had such a little of it to bear. The
men themselves had had it for nearly two months. To our
untutored ears it sounded worse than it really was. It was
only with the coming of daylight that we were told that the
noise came from our guns alone, and that no Japanese shells

were coming over. But all through the night the two of us lay on mattresses under the back stairs, the torrent of sound pouring over us, lashing us with its fury.

Then, as at so many other times, inactivity increased the unpleasantness of it. To be able to be up and doing something, anything, it didn't matter what, would have been better than this feeling of impotence. For me, too, there was the additional annoyance of knowing that the Bishop was sleeping through a good deal of it! Before dawn two Australians who had spent the night in the house advised us to get the servants away before the full light of day brought machine-gunning and dive-bombing. I was keen to get them off, but I panicked them a bit. Anyway we carted Ah Din, his wife and all their traps off to Jervois Road, Ismael's wife and family to the Great World corner. The gardener insisted on trying to get through to Lermit Road, and the Bishop certainly tried but could get no further than Tanglin Road. All that bother when they would have been perfectly alright where they were!

Thursday, February 12th. We locked the house and moved off into town — a town even more bedraggled and deserted than before, anxiously expectant and tense. Up to nine o'clock there had been no raids, but, as we had given up all hope of air support — we heard later of the capture of Palembang in Sumatra by Japanese parachute troops — our fighters could have operated from there — we knew that we must expect more and heavier raids with an increasing number of casualties.

The General Hospital seemed to be the place where help would be needed most. I found both the Graham Whites there. The Archdeacon was going round the wards, crowded with wounded soldiers and civilians, while Mrs. White, as cheerful as ever, was carrying on in her Red Cross Comforts Store. She sent me into town for cigarettes, razor blades, soap and anything else I could scrounge.

By this time the sirens had no sooner sounded the all-clear than we heard a fresh alarm. It was impossible to wait. The only thing was to drive on and hope for the best, keeping a close watch on pedestrians, who were as good an air raid alarm as the siren itself. I had barely gone a quarter of a mile from the hospital gates when people began to run for shelter. I stopped, looked out of the car and saw the familiar formation of twenty-seven flying in very high from the northwest. There was still some time before they would be overhead, so I raced on the rest of the way to Hill Street Police Station, a strong concrete building. The planes flew over, duly dropped their bombs and we were able, for a short time at any rate, to go on our way.

DENSE CROWDS AT THE CATHAY

Robinsons in Raffles Place were able to give me about eight hundred razor blades. From there I hunted high and low for the Red Cross Comforts Store, eventually tracking it as far as the Cathay after about an hour's search, driving through the desolation. There are so many pictures of this last week which remain vivid and detailed in my mind, and even now, as I write three months afterwards, I can remember almost every detail of that morning in the Cathay. It is Singapore's nearest approach to a skyscraper, built into the southern side of a hill, so that the ground level at the back is four or five floors higher than in the front. All of those floors, as well as the three sub-basements, are protected from the north by the hill. It was probably the best protected spot on the whole Island and an obvious place for a hospital. In every available corner men were lying. So many of them were there that it was hard to pick one's way between them. Passages and sometimes the space at the turn of the stairs were thronged. After a long search, I found Vic Saunders, an Australian Padre whom I had known before, right down underground slaving away in the Red Cross Store. He gave me as much as he could for the General Hospital and I started off to get back to the car. It was a terribly saddening business picking one's way through those hot and crowded passages. The men were as cheerful as their depressing disillusionment allowed. The orderlies and the doctors were doing amazingly good work.

Before I eventually reached the car, I had to go up four flights of stairs in another part of the building and this was almost worse than the other. Here the townspeople had crowded in and were packed tight. In some places there was no passageway at all and one had to step over and between those who were sheltering there. How long they had been there and how long they stayed I do not know. There they sat, whole families, wedged tight together. It was so full of pathos, but on all their faces there was a look of patient resignation, which the Chinese amongst them must have worn many times in their nation's history. The capacity to absorb suffering, to take it into themselves, is their great strength. What can persecution and oppression achieve against such strength as that? The Jews in the west have known the sufferings of persecution for centuries, and in the east the Chinese have faced famine and disaster repeatedly, yet in both cases their solidarity has increased rather than diminished. Each of them seems to be an unconquerable people.

The rest of the day I spent at the General Hospital, going round the wards, talking to the men, toning down the many rumours which were flying from mouth to mouth. 'The Americans had landed at Port Swettenham and were in Kuala Lumpur.' This was the most prevalent and the most cruel of them all, so much worse because it was reliably reported, though albeit as an unconfirmed report, to have come from San Francisco. The men seized on it as a last ray of hope. Most of them accepted it fully, and the pity of it was that some who should have known better helped to spread it.

THE CATHEDRAL AS A HOSPITAL

Towards evening I went out to Bishopsbourne to try and persuade the Bishop to come away, but he was adamant and stayed. The men on the guns in Bishopsgate were glad he was there and he was able to do a lot for them. While I was with him, two senior R.A.M.C. officers came and it was arranged that they should take over the Cathedral as a hospital on the following day.

I knew that, if I was to be of any use, I should have to get some sleep, and with a mattress and pillow I drove down to the Supreme Court. I had hardly arrived before a shell, the first in the centre of the town, overshot Fort Canning and landed at the junction of High Street and North Bridge Road. It seemed that night, though, as if they were feeling their way, trying to get the range, as little more came over. At all events I heard little. After some food, I slept.

One of the worst and most depressing things about the last few days was the pall of smoke which hung over the town, most of it caused by our own demolition of oil stocks. It had started with a blaze at the Naval Base at the end of the previous week and all through the last week other fires were raging. One afternoon — Tuesday, I think it was — I climbed up to the base of the dome above the Supreme Court and spent some time with the roof spotters. Pulau Bukum and Pulau Sambu, the two big Asiatic Petroleum Company installations amongst the islands to the south-west, were infernos. There were at least two big fires at Tanjong Rhu, the other side of Kallang aerodrome; others further east towards Changi and still more northwards in the middle of the Island.

THE DEATH OF A PILOT

There were still one or two Hurricanes operating from Kallang. While I was up there at the foot of the dome the siren sounded and the first of five planes took off soon afterwards. We watched through glasses as the pilot came off, apparently down wind. I had no sooner commented on this than we saw him catch his wing tip on the topmast of a junk lying two or three hundred yards from the edge of the aerodrome. There was the flash of silver as a piece of wing tore away, a sudden twist and a downward plunge into the sea. Death must have been instantaneous, but oh, the pity and the waste of that life. It made the whole show seem so futile. It must have been ghastly for the other men who were already moving across the aerodrome on their take-off.

The raid which followed this alarm was made by three groups of nine planes following one another at close intervals. We saw their bombs bursting along the heights above Pasir Panjang about four miles away, probably trying to put gun positions out of action. It was a strange sensation watching from up there, the whole town spread out below us. In spite of the bombing there had been up to that time, although it was nothing compared with what was to follow, it was hard to pick out any material damage in the town. But this is really a digression.

NEAR MISS IN AN AIR RAID

Friday, February 13th. As soon as I woke on the Friday morning I made my way to Amber Mansions, to Talbot House Club for a bath and shave. Jack Bennitt arrived at the same moment from the Cathedral, where he had made his head-quarters. A number of troops back from the line were sleeping in the Chapter House and he spent a good deal of time looking after them. It must have been eight o'clock, some time after the siren had wailed, when the trouble started. I had just finished my bath when we heard the crack of our own A.A. fire, with the slowly increasing drone of a large force of bombers. Soldiers resting in the Presbyterian Church compound opposite showed us, by their dash for shelter, that the planes were coming our way. A few moments later we heard the shuddering roar of falling bombs — falling unpleasantly close it seemed. The building and the whole air shook as crash followed crash. It was impossible to tell where they were falling until the shattering explosions gradually grew less violent and we were able to pick ourselves up. We saw from the dust clouds along Selegie Road that we were less than two hundred yards from the bombed area and hurried out, past a large crater at the corner of Selegie and Middle Roads, where a woman had been killed.

From there I turned up Sophia Road where there seemed to be a good deal of debris and on, higher up the hill, to Upper Wilkie Road. Although a good many bombs had dropped, with some superficial damage to a few houses, the whole place seemed to be deserted.

It was up there that I found something which seemed quite inexplicable. A small fire was burning on the grass by the side of the lane running down to Mackenzie Road. I ran down the slope and found a heap of soldiers' kit on fire, open haversacks with socks, boots and shirts spilt from them, gas-proof capes and other paraphernalia strewn all over the place. Just on the edge of the fire were two wooden cases, one of 6" shells and the other of .303 ammunition. The cases were both beginning to burn, particularly the latter, and it looked as though there would be a nasty mess if anybody happened to be going by when they went off, as they un-doubtedly would have done. It only took a moment to haul them clear of the fire and, although there was no immediate danger, I couldn't help being glad as I dumped them in the drain. But who had started the fire and why was a complete mystery.

From there back into town, where the M.A.S. had cleared all the wounded from the bombed area, and then on to the General Hospital, where I spent the rest of the day, collecting books and taking them round to those wards where they were scarce, stopping to talk to the men whenever I could. They were in the main cheerful, but hungry for news. Rumours were flying from mouth to mouth, growing as they went. The more fantastic and improbable they were, the more comfort they gave. Many of us had stopped wondering what the outcome would be, but events had moved so rapidly that most people were quite unable to adjust to the new possibility. For so long we had been told that Singapore was impregnable. When the time came we could not believe anything else.

The Graham Whites left Cathedral House this, Friday, morning. They had been there on the north slope of the grounds of Government House, ringed about with shells falling short. On Thursday night they had a direct hit at a point about fifteen yards from their place of refuge under the stairs. They were both shaken, but not very far below the surface was a lot of their usual buoyancy.

Later in the day the Bishop came to the Hospital. He decided to leave Bishopsbourne and that we should both go to St. Andrews Mission Hospital, where Dr. Elliott, Muriel Clark and Miss Sherman were still living. They put us into the old children's ward in the front of the building on the ground floor and there we slept well and long, after listening for what seemed hours, to the scream of shells going over and landing on the wharves half a mile to the south. It was as well for our peace of mind that we forgot, or deliberately overlooked, the presence of the gasometer within a hundred yards of us! It was because of that that the building was not being used as a hospital.

ANALYSIS OF A RAID

It was only shortly after we got there in the afternoon that we had one of the worst of the many raids on Chinatown.

The familiar drone of planes was followed by the sound of the falling bombs and then hell broke loose. The air was filled with the sound of a whirlwind so loud that we had to shout at one another to make ourselves heard. How to describe it? Even when the bombs begin to burst it is still impossible to distinguish individual sounds. The whirlwind is intensified, the whole earth shakes, heaven and earth seem to meet in chaos. And then, the wind dies — there is an endless moment of stunned, agonised silence. When will it end? When will the world start moving again? When? The start, when it comes, is so pitiful that one almost wishes it could have stopped for ever. The frightened screams of children, the shouts and cries of the wounded, the terror-stricken barking of dogs, the sound of running feet, the blast of whistles — and in the hearts of many, a wildness of fear, hatred, loss and despair.

Clouds of dust were hanging over the hill at the back of the hospital as the Bishop and I hurried in that direction. Halfway up the slope there was the distant crack from one of the many snipers who were all over the town by this time, followed by a sharp ping as the bullet struck the path just in front of me. We made good speed for the rest of the distance and after scrambling down the other side of the hill came to a street which had been badly hit. The M.A.S. arrived soon after we got there and we split up searching for casualties. One house I went into had the full blast from an explosion on the opposite side of the street. One boy on the ground floor had a small flesh wound in his buttock, and pitiful wails from the higher floors drew me there, to a small front room, past narrow cubicles and dusty dark corners piled high with personal belongings. A young warden, off duty, was lying by the window, covered with blood, dead.

There seemed little more we could do there so we went back to the Hospital. I soon went out again, across the Maxwell Road junction, now a tangle of dangling trolley-bus wires, into the maze of narrow streets between South Bridge Road and New Bridge Street where the damage from this last raid was far greater. The five foot way on both sides of Sago Street was littered with dead, terribly mutilated. Crowds were surging through the streets, aimless and inquisitive, and since the system of air raid warnings had completely broken down there seemed to their numbed brains no reason why they should not be there. 'No sirens, no planes.' In all that dense crowd, there must have been many thousands in an area no more than two hundred yards square. There was only one official, an auxiliary policeman. I did what I could to help him clear the streets.

Soon afterwards another large group of planes did come over. In a matter of seconds the street was empty. I scrambled down into a drain and it was then that I felt the only moment of near panic during the whole of these days. Anyone who has never experienced it can have no idea of the loneliness which comes when you are on your own during a raid. I had known it once before — in the 'Happy World', during one of the Kallang raids, when I left my private shelter in a small crater and ran off to join the others who had come there with me. Only iron control can prevent all consideration of safety being completely set aside. Anything for companionship, and it was this which drove me out of my splendid isolation in the drain into the middle of one of the sweating, frightened mobs which packed every doorway and the stairs leading up to the first floor. If bombs had fallen in that area, the casualties would have been appalling. But the planes passed over and we could hear in the distance the crash of the bombs in the Raffles Place area.

THE SIRENS STILL DUMB

The sight of the crowds in Sago Street between the raids drove me almost frantic, and I made a confounded nuisance of myself in the A.R.P. control room. I went there straight away to try and get someone onto the question of the siren. Instructions had been given that the siren was to remain silent and that there should be a perpetual alert. But the people in the streets were not rational and needed some sort of reminder, however inadequate and superfluous it might seem. I probably made myself very unpopular with people already sorely tried, but I had come fresh from the sight of mangled bodies of people who need never have died at all and the crowds in the Sago Street area were typical of thousands in real and pressing danger. One of the reasons for their careless indifference may well have been that this was almost the first experience of heavy bombing which China-town itself in the western part of the city had had to face. Geylang and Beach Road on the other side of town had learnt their lesson when they had their baptism of fire several weeks earlier.

After stirring up as much mud as I could in the Control Room, I went back to St. Andrew's Hospital, where the Bishop and I both slept well on mattresses on the floor of the store-room at the back of the building. But the sirens were still silent!

APPOINTMENT WITH THE DEAD

Saturday, February 14th. One of the factors which seriously affected the eventual outcome of the fighting, though by no means the deciding one, was the serious risk of widespread disease. By this time the lack of water had become a very serious problem. Several of the mains had been hit and by the evening we had lost the McRitchie reservoir in the middle of the Island. Transport facilities in the town were interrupted by incessant bombing and shelling which meant that the removal of the dead, even where they were not covered by debris, had become almost impossible. But everything that could be done was done, and a great many bodies were brought in. Bidadari Cemetery was actually in the firing line, with the result that a very severe strain was placed on the improvised arrangements at the General Hospital and at other places.

MASS BURIALS

Before the outbreak of war, plans had been made for the construction of two large water storage tanks, one on the Sepoy Lines golf course in front of the main block of the hospital, the other amongst the trees behind the maternity hospital. The first of the two, which was to prove invaluable and saved what had become a desperate situation, had got no further than the excavation of a trench about eighty yards long, twelve feet deep and ten yards wide. This had been left in its natural state, with the earth which had been removed still heaped around the edges of the trench. On Friday, a

great many dead had been buried and many hundreds more
were to be laid there before the General Hospital was removed to the old Mental Hospital in Yio Chu Kang Road on
the Wednesday after the surrender.

When I got to the Hospital on this Saturday morning, I
went over to the trench where Sam Hall and David Coney of
the Customs were working, with a group of about twenty
Indian soldiers and two of their officers, assisted by six
R.A.M.C. men. That morning and most of the afternoon was
one long horror. The mortuary was full, many of the bodies
had been there for as long as four days, and it had to be
cleared. Two lorries were being used. At the mortuary, which
was quite indescribable, a party of Gurkhas were doing
magnificent work piling the dead onto the lorries while we,
at the other end, were unloading and putting them into the
grave. There seemed to be no end to it. No sooner had we
finished with one lorry than the other was ready waiting for
us. Soon, numbed and almost overwhelmed by it all, we
developed a routine and began to make headway. At all
events, by the evening the crisis was past and things were
fairly well in hand. But it was all a nightmare. Chinese,
Europeans, Indians and Eurasians, British and Indian soldiers,
young children, babies even, young girls and young men, old
men and old women, blameless, peace and pleasure-loving all
of them, not one for the loss of whom someone's life would
not be the poorer — all flung into a pit! Overhead at intervals,
planes roared, near and far the crash of bombs, the heavy
thud of anti-aircraft fire, shells winging their destructive way
to the docks away to the south of us, and over it all a dense,
impenetrable pall of smoke, a symbol of the cruelty and the
despair of our crumbling world.

THE CATHEDRAL BECOMES A HOSPITAL

Early that afternoon I drove the Archdeacon down to the
Cathedral to arrange the Sunday services. Along Outram
Road and River Valley Road we drove at speed — there
seemed less danger from shell fire that long way round. The
Cathedral was an astonishing sight. If only an artist could
have captured the picture of the wounded lying row upon
row in the nave and in the aisles, now emptied of their

furnishings. Doctors and orderlies moved quietly about their work, the stillness broken only by the tread of their boots on the stone paving and the low murmur of voices.

As I stood by the west door and gazed into the shadows studded with the glow of many cigarettes, with the occasional flare of a lighted match and then, beyond the choir, to the altar with the dull gleam of the cross catching the fading light, a great gladness came to me that those four walls, the symbol of love and peace and strength, were sheltering those to whom Christ Himself would then have wished to be most near. Perhaps there were some who felt this closeness. There must have been many whose thoughts turned to some other church, with memories of their own childhood, their marriage and all the associations of earlier, well-loved days. The small churches of the Fens, the grandeur of a Lavenham, a Thaxted or a Romsey, the peace of some great town church, heightened by the noise of the world outside — perhaps there were some who walked again in fields and streets once known and loved, and loved the more by separation. That day the Cathedral was peopled in the fields of memory by a great company of friends and loved ones, and for that I was glad. In spite of the ever present menace of crashing, tearing death outside, here there was a great peace.

One of the first people I saw was Gerry Chambers, Vicar of Nursling on the outskirts of Southampton. I had known him when I was at Romsey. The Revd. G. B. Thompson, Jack Bennitt and Bashford were there too, and to them we left the arrangements for the morning's services and drove straight back to the General Hospital through lonely and deserted streets.

There was still a good deal of work waiting at the grave. Soon after I got back a young officer called Hirsch came there with thirty men. I was overjoyed to see them. He looked a good chap and they an excellent lot. Their coming meant we were able to dispense with a party of Indian soldiers and their officers. They had been extremely useful shovelling the earth down from the sides, but their reluctance to handle the bodies or go down into the grave was so obvious that the six R.A.M.C. men, Coney, Hall and I found it easier to get on with it by ourselves. I had a word with the newcomers before they started, to try and buck them up a bit, and then divided

them into two shifts working in turn, whenever there was
work to be done. For the rest of Saturday and on Sunday and
Monday they stayed and were magnificent. It cheered me
enormously to have them there, as by this time I seemed to
have assumed, or drifted into, command. They gave real help
with extraordinary readiness. Some of them needed time to
get over the first reactions of nausea and disgust. I helped
them as much as I could. One boy, he was hardly more, was
just about done after no more than a quarter of an hour. His
heart was sick and revolted by it all. Only a very little needed
to be said before he was able to carry on and I was glad I
was there to say it.

   After about an hour I started in the car for St. Andrew's
Hospital. The shelling had started again and about ten minutes
before I left outhouses adjoining Outram Road School had
been hit and a small fire started. Every building of any size
in the town area had been turned into a hospital — the
Victoria Memorial Hall, Fullerton Building, Outram Road
Gaol, the Government and Municipal Offices, the Cathay,
the Cathedral and many others were packed with wounded,
civilian and military. Outram Road School was another. As
I drove out of the Hospital gates I saw the pathetic sight of
Indian troops hurrying, anywhere, nowhere, most of them
bandaged, some hardly able to walk, let alone run, driven
only by a panic of fear. One of them stopped me and pleaded
to be taken into the car. I was only able to take him a quarter
of a mile, but even that satisfied his numbed brain.

   I drove on to St. Andrew's Hospital and there, waiting in
the gathering dusk, was the Bishop with a glad — and relieved
— smile of welcome. I had not seen him for the greater part
of the day, and there were many things to tell each other. He
and Jack Bennitt had left the hospital in the early afternoon
only a few seconds before a salvo of shells hit the building,
one in the operating theatre and two in the soft earth immediately below the theatre window, just outside the ward
in which we had slept the previous night. They had felt the
blast as they drove off.

THE BISHOP BEHIND JAPANESE LINES

They had had an eventful day. A puncture had left the
Bishop with no spare wheel for the car, but Jack remem-

bered having seen a deserted Vauxhall out on the east coast at Siglap and they had driven there to find things completely normal and peaceful. Shops open, people moving about freely, no bombs or shells, but this quiet was only short-lived. Within a few hours Japanese tanks, part of those which had driven a wedge into our lines, were in East Coast Road, having effectively split our forces in two. They had advanced through the jungle east of Yio Chu Kang Road, were in Serangoon by Friday evening and from there carried straight on down Paya Lebar Road, across Geylang Road, into Still Road and then right-handed to Tanjong Rhu, where they were in position with direct command of Kallang aerodrome early in the afternoon of Sunday. An hour later and the Bishop and Jack would have been caught.

All that Saturday night shells were coming over, but we both slept soundly, tired out.

Sunday, February 15th. One of the greatest thoughts behind the Eucharist is the offering to God of all that is best in man, his courage, love, ideals of service, sacrifice, and, too, the offering of all that is worst, his sufferings, cruelty, self-interest and greed — the one as an offering in the service of God, the other to be cleansed and redeemed. God is always waiting, drawing from men the offering of their love and service, giving Himself in return. In the Cathedral on this Sunday morning I felt most strongly the quiet simplicity with which Christ comes. Outside, the crack and roar of guns and exploding shells, here quiet and peace in the hearts of those to whom He came.

Many were at the service in the choir and chancel, which we had kept as a chapel. Others who could not leave their 'beds' received the Sacrament where they lay. I shall never forget the reverence of those who came to that service, and the contrast between the peace there and the brute beast raging outside, the patience — and pathos — of the wounded, and the sad disillusionment written on everyone's face. How long, oh Lord, how long?

After a hurried breakfast we went back to the General Hospital to find little change during the night. The shelling had left them unharmed, but more had died and there was still much to be done at the grave. Hirsch and his men were waiting there when I arrived and we soon got to work again, but not without a good many interruptions. The Japanese planes were by this time throwing off the last vestige of caution and were coming absurdly low, their machine guns blazing. Several times we had to down tools and climb into the grave. Once machine gun bullets spattered round the top of the grave and we decided to peg out a large red cross with sheets and red blankets.

In the early afternoon the Japanese guns opened up a big barrage on the docks and suddenly shells started falling dangerously close to the hospital. I was inside the building when it started and it sounded as if the shells were exploding amongst the burial party. I raced down the corridor to an open doorway, from where I could see the grave, half expecting to find that the first salvo had fallen right amongst them, but there were none of them in sight and all seemed to be well.

CHILDREN UNDER FIRE

From there, with shells still falling dangerously near the Hospital, I went under cover to the Dental Clinic, which had been turned into an emergency ward for children from our Orthopaedic Hospital. They had had an adventurous time. Just before the war, when hostilities seemed a possibility and preparations were being made for landings on the east coast of Singapore, they had been moved from Siglap to the other end of the Island, beyond Tengah Airfield opposite Johore Bahru. At the beginning of January they were brought back into town to the Tan Tock Seng Hospital, evacuated from there under shell fire on Friday 13th, put for one night in the former Maternity Hospital at the General Hospital and then transferred to the Dental Clinic in the main block.

Shells had just fallen on the road outside and one large jagged splinter about eight inches long smashed its way through the bunding, ricocheted off a window frame to one of the walls and then down again amongst the children. Although they were all over the floor, only one child got a very slight graze on the forehead. This must have been at about 2.30.

As soon as the shelling stopped, I went out to the grave

and found the soldiers all safe. They had managed to run into the deserted sisters' quarters when the first shell fell. Little more remained to be done there. The mortuary had been cleared in the morning and, with all bodies coming from the town area being taken straight to the grave, I was able to go round the wards for a bit.

At about three I heard the first rumour of the surrender and within a very short time the news, although as yet unconfirmed, was all round the hospital. Some said it was to take effect from eight, others earlier at four or thereabouts. Everywhere I went that was the one topic of conversation. Had I heard? Did I know anything? Most of them were incredulous. They couldn't believe it, but time went on with no official announcement. At four there was a definite lull in the firing, and by half past six there was a complete and ghastly silence. Nothing stirred anywhere. The last planes had been over a little earlier and dropped their bombs in the centre of the town. Seven fell in the Roman Catholic convent compound, where they did a great deal of damage, but with only small loss of life.

THE END – AND THE BEGINNING

Apart from an occasional explosion in the distance, hardly a sound broke the stillness. It was eerie and unnerving after a week of ceaseless noise, and we all knew it could mean but one thing. When I got back to St. Andrew's Hospital, the Bishop was standing in the dusk waiting for me and he told me of the surrender. He had heard from the Colonel at the Cathedral just before the service at about four and had designed the service as one of praise and thanksgiving. He had been very deeply moved. I wish I could have been there to have shared it.

Now we had to decide what to do. There was not time to think yet of anything but the immediate future. It would probably be some hours at least before the majority of people would hear of the surrender. They would soon draw their own conclusions from the silence, but there was no knowing what their reactions would be. Rioting and looting might start at any time and it seemed best to collect as much stuff together as we could and get up to the General Hospital.

There was, however, the chance that the R.A.M.C. unit at

the Cathedral might be glad to move to St. Andrew's Hospital now that there could no longer be any danger from the nearness of the gasometer next door. While the Bishop stayed at the Hospital, I drove Dr. Patricia Elliott through pitch black streets, strewn with debris, trolley bus wires trailing dangerously all over the road, wondering whether we might not at any moment be stopped by Japanese troops. As it happened, however, no troops entered the town until the next morning and then only very few, but we did not know that then. Dr. Elliott seemed quite unmoved and we got to the Cathedral to discover from the C.O. that all troops had received instructions to stand fast, which meant that they too had to stay where they were.

We got back to St. Andrew's Hospital at about 8.30, loaded up the cars and drove up to the General Hospital. I took Dr. Elliott on the first trip, left her with the Graham Whites and the Nelsons and went to the Hopkins to see if they could give the Bishop and me a corner. In spite of a large crowd of doctors there already, we were told to come back when we had done all our fetching and carrying.

The news of the surrender had only just come through when I arrived. Lights were on, crowds thronging the passages, at one spot soldiers had already started handing in their equipment, on the faces of many a look of resignation, with some mixed with anxiety, with others relief, still others bewildered and hurt. At all events the noise, the bloodshed and the torture were over now, and in that there was comfort. The grave would no longer be fed with bodies mangled and torn. The long line of ambulances filled with the maimed and wounded would not form up again — we would be spared that. But what new sufferings, what fresh cruelties would war bring before it could be said to have ended? At 12.30 we had made our last journey and we slept.

Monday, February 16th. But oh, that awakening on Monday morning; not only the silence, but the realisation that we had lost, that it was all finished and that from now on we should be, at best, no more than onlookers, cut off from the world, prisoners in enemy occupied territory.

The following week seemed as though it would never end.

Section Two

———————•◦•———————

Living in Enemy-occupied
Singapore

HOW THE BISHOP, SORBY ADAMS
AND THE AUTHOR
SPENT THIRTEEN MONTHS IN FREEDOM

February, 1942 to March, 1943

Some parts of this section were written long after the diary entries. Where these occur a ¶ has been placed in the left-hand margin at the beginning of the item, at the head of each successive page and at the end.

Living in Enemy-occupied Singapore

MOVE FROM THE GENERAL HOSPITAL

Wednesday, February 18th, 1942. The Bishop and I had become part of the Hospital community and shared in the mass evacuation of the General Hospital to the buildings of the former Mental Hospital to the north-east of Singapore in Yeo Chu Kang Road. The numbers of those who could be moved had to be drastically reduced and very many who were totally unfit were discharged. One young Indian was typical, not too many days after the amputation of his leg below the knee. I saw him, still in hospital clothes, propelling himself down the hill on hands, backside and one good leg.

Instructions had been issued by the Japanese that no equipment was to be taken from the General Hospital in the evacuation, which explained why, in the afternoon heat of Singapore, lines of trolley-born patients on stretchers were draped in thick hospital blankets! Very senior surgeons were judiciously stationed thrusting all manner of drugs and theatre and ward equipment under the folds of blankets. It was just as well they did. Arriving at the Mental Hospital we found nothing but the floors and walls of wards and corridors. On Wednesday, the first day, there was not even any piped water. From one fresh spring a handful of us, with a bucket each, and a tin for a mug, made endless journeys backwards and forwards. We 'watered' all the patients. By the following day things began to improve. Supplies of all sorts started to appear. Some of them were acquired legitimately. Many were not.

BISHOP LEONARD THE LOOTER

On Thursday the 19th, the second day at the new Hospital, the Bishop with a driver set off in the morning in an ambulance. In the late afternoon he returned, the ambulance loaded with food of all kinds, with medical supplies and drugs and all sorts of equipment which he had acquired from many different sources, most of them best described as 'loot'. For three days he carried on these nefarious escapades, never running into any sort of trouble and always enjoying himself enormously. There was no doubt in anyone's mind that the Bishop's brigandage added greatly to the speed with which the Miyako, as the new hospital was called, was able to get some sort of order out of the initial chaos.

DIVINE INTERVENTION?

It was on Sunday, February 22nd, that there happened the 'Great Coincidence' or the 'Intervention of the Holy Spirit', whichever way one prefers to look at it. Early, the Bishop went to the Cathedral to celebrate Holy Communion. Arriving there he found the doors were locked and no one was available with the key. The R.A.M.C. had left several days before. In spite of the fast-closed doors the Bishop held a Spiritual Communion for the twenty and more people who were there as they stood together in the porch outside the west door. In fact, total continuity was preserved at the Cathedral. No Sunday between 1942 and 1945 was without a service.

The Bishop had already decided that it was time to put to the test his plan to obtain permission to go back to his house, with two clergy. He needed to move about freely, looking after the Church, its services and its people. In the Municipal Offices he found the Japanese Mayor. By dint of a long wait and much persistence, he got an interview and was received with courtesy. After putting his case, with the answering of many questions, he received passes giving permission for himself and two others to return to Bishopsbourne. They were to be allowed to move at will on Singapore Island, but not on mainland Malaya, and to have the use of two cars. He had only asked for one!

In the middle of the afternoon he was back at the hospital to an extraordinary development in his absence. A notice had been posted at the hospital stating that all passes issued before that day, Sunday, February 22nd, were cancelled and no longer valid. Only those holding a pass dated Sunday,

February 22nd, would be freed on the morning of Monday, February 23rd. All without valid passes would proceed to Changi for internment in the Gaol. That was the one day when a pass could have been any good.

THREE GO HOME

With three permits to remain free and not to go into internment, the Bishop consulted with Archdeacon Graham White as to who should be with him. Although he knew and was known by a host of people, the Archdeacon was not in good health. He thought it wiser to go into Changi, where in fact he exercised a remarkable ministry.

He also agreed with the Bishop's first choice of the Revd. R. K. Sorby Adams. An Australian, Sorby had already been in Singapore for fourteen years, first as Chaplain and then as an outstanding Principal of St. Andrew's School. Under his influence it had developed as one of the leading boys' schools in the Colony. His knowledge of generations of boys and their families and the affection in which they held him were phenomenal. He would be a perfect choice to go with the Bishop.

As the youngest of the clergy, who would hopefully be

Figure 2:
The Revd. R. K. Sorby
Adams, drawn in Changi
by W. R. M. Haxworth.

best able to cope with conditions, which were totally unknown, I was chosen as the third member of the trio.

By the middle of the morning of Monday, the Bishop, Sorby Adams and I were back at Bishopsbourne. It was a strange drive through streets almost deserted, with very little traffic, and not even many Japanese about. To our great relief nothing had changed at Bishopsbourne. There had been no looting, nor in fact any sign that anyone had been near the house.

It was a curious homecoming. We had no idea what was likely to happen. Would we be able to move about? What was the attitude of the Japanese likely to be? How would we get on for food and the money to buy it? The decision to lie low was easily made. Tragic news of how wise we had been soon ¶ began to reach us. Time began to prove the truth of the appalling rumours of male Chinese being assembled at special points, one in ten of them being driven away by the Japanese. None of them survived.

MASSACRE OF THE CHINESE

However much the Japanese Military High Command may have been commended for immediately withdrawing their fighting troops from centres of population in Singapore after the fall of the Island, the calculated horror tactics which followed were utterly inexcusable and totally to be condemned. They may have induced fear amongst the population, but they also aroused their bitter and lasting hatred.

In the words of one commentator, Dr. L. S. da Silva, 'A week or so after the fall of Singapore the Japanese made a round of Singaporeans whom they thought had some association with the British. These included many of the Chinese Singapore Volunteers. They were taken in groups to the Changi beaches where they were made to dig ditches into which they were tossed after they had been shot.' Dr. da Silva's younger brother and nephew were amongst them.

The experience of Elizabeth Choy, a Chinese girl in her twenties at the time, was typical of thousands of families who suffered from the indiscriminate arrest of one or more of their members. She has written: 'My eighteen year old brother being taken by the Japanese has still been a mystery until now. I walked the streets trying to find out what had happened to him. I ventured into "lion's dens" trying to find and rescue him, but in vain. There were so many others like me, wandering, looking for lost sons, husbands and brothers. It was hell.'

Another Chinese, Doris Palmer, has spoken of her brother, who was in the Singapore Volunteers. After the fall of Singapore in February, 1942, his unit had been disbanded and he was staying with friends. The Japanese authorities issued an order that all former Volunteers should report. If any failed to do so those who were housing them would be liable to arrest. He duly reported at the Y.M.C.A. and was instructed to return a week later when, he was told, he would be given work. Friends tried to persuade him to let them smuggle him to Johore. Not wishing to put them in danger he refused. He duly reported on the appointed day. He was not seen again. Some days were to go by before we could begin to realise the full tragedy of the massacre. It was to be some time before we recognised the hideous features of Japanese domination.

In no time at all, at the opposite extreme of human values, we had an example of the unfailing kindness and thoughtful generosity of hundreds, thousands even, of the members of our Christian community.

BISHOP'S VISTORS, BEARING GIFTS

I doubt whether any one of the three of us would ever forget the sight which greeted us at Bishopsbourne in the middle of Tuesday morning. Three men, one of them K. T. Alexander, the Indian Diocesan Secretary, were walking the few yards up the drive, bearing gifts, amongst them a tin of pipe tobacco (episcopal!) and a tin of meat. Word had reached them that we were back. They were the first of a queue of people, of all ages and races, who came to our door for more than thirteen months, until we went to Changi in March, 1943.

RETURN OF AH SING – THE BISHOP'S HOUSE-BOY

An event which transformed our lives at Bishopsbourne two or three weeks after our return was the arrival of the Bishop's 'house-boy', Ah Sing. He would, he said, have come back sooner, but in the hope of preventing him, his aunt had hidden his trousers! We were relieved that we could now put the cooking into more expert hands than ours. The low point of our skills was a tin of pilchards, cooked in flour from the kitchen at St. Andrew's Orthopaedic Hospital. Something curious had happened. The Bishop and I both woke in the small hours feeling very uncomfortable. 'Do you think', he asked, 'that flour could have been plaster of paris?'. 'Very possibly!', I replied.

Thinking of the forbidding number of tasks ahead of him the Bishop's first objective was to get in touch with the clergy in Singapore. They had all survived and were working in their churches. He also made contact with the clergy up-country and found out what was happening there. The Cathedral became our main concern and very soon full services were being maintained. Congregations increased rapidly as confidence grew and movement in the city became easier. In the strains and uncertainties, and frequently the personal tragedies of life under the Japanese, more and more people found their strength in the Church, in its sacraments and in its life, while many were brought into it for the first time.

The Bishop, Sorby Adams and I gave most of our time in the first instance to the Cathedral. Very soon the Bishop became principally involved with the latter and with other urgent matters of Church policy, while Sorby spent his time in Serangoon, at St. Paul's, and I carried on at the Cathedral.

THE CAMPAIGN AS SEEN BY AN OBSERVER

Written in May, 1942. Before leaving the immediate events of the Japanese attack which began on December 8th, and lasted just over two months, something, however brief, must be said about the campaign.

Some time before the outbreak of war all was not well in higher circles. Duff Cooper came out from England with Cabinet rank and strong powers. Immediately Malaya was split in two. On one side Duff Cooper, with Seabridge of the *Straits Times* as his chief supporter. On the other were the greater part of the Malayan Civil Service. Seabridge seemed determined to find a scapegoat. It was Stanley Jones, the Colonial Secretary, who had to go, although no one was quite sure on what grounds. Others would almost certainly have followed if it had not been for the outbreak of hostilities.

The general impression shared by most of us, both before and during the war, was one of jealous preserving of individual interests and very little ease of cooperation. During the war itself I may have shown a little of the apparent confusion both in the civil and the military areas.

We who immediately suffered because of it could not see the fall of Singapore as anything less than a major disaster of gigantic proportions in the pages of British military history. We wonder now how carefully it will have been whitewashed, even so soon after the event. Allied propaganda will most probably have started already showing it as 'a glorious defeat'.

In fact it was complete and inglorious. The preparation for war during the years before it came, and even more in the months which immediately preceded it, were shown to be inadequate. There were not enough troops, there were not enough planes. Aerodromes there were in plenty, but where were the planes to operate from them and where were the men to guard the mainland aerodromes? There were guns enough. Tanglin R.A.S.C. depot in Singapore was full of them at the time of the surrender and ammunition was plentiful, though with communications so disrupted there may have been times of temporary shortages. The whole strategy of the campaign seems to have gone astray.

Already stories are circulating of heroic actions and individual acts of heroism from many parts of the Malayan Peninsular and from the fighting on Singapore Island. Many people will be far better able than I am or ever could be to weigh up the military side of the campaign, but for some of us the scales of judgement are weighted with bitterness.

¶   THE CHURCH RECOVERS

Gradually, after our return to Bishopsbourne, the Bishop could see that the Church's work in all the Anglican centres in Singapore was continuing. In some cases it was beginning to prosper. People were moving about with greater confidence. Their clergy reported real mutual concern for one another within the fellowship of their Churches, sometimes in tragic and heartbreaking circumstances.

¶ There was one particular area of Church life in which the Bishop's help was much valued. With the internment of their expatriate missionaries the Methodists, the Presbyterians and the Brethren particularly, rose to their new responsibilities. At the same time, deprived of their former leadership, many who were now leaders turned to the Bishop, for comfort and reassurance more than anything, and it meant a great deal to them that he was there. He was not offered, nor did he ask for, anything approaching even an unofficial position with them. Perhaps his role can best be described as a 'Father Figure'.

Conditions of Church life at that time in Singapore did provide most fruitful soil in one area — the Reunion of the Churches. Christian Unity had always been a major concern of Bishop Wilson's. On June 3rd, 1942, he called a meeting of the Anglican Clergy, four Chinese, one Indian and the two of us who were with him, joined later by eight of the laity. The greater part of the two and a half hour meeting was given up to the Bishop's plans for a 'Federation of the Churches'. Its foundation had a large bearing on the relief of sometimes horrifying poverty, but the Bishop's starting point was from the absolute necessity of a United Christian Church in some form or another.

A letter which he sent to the leaders of the Churches ended with this emphatic declaration — 'Our aim is a Universal Church in Malaya, not uniformity of worship but a united faith and an agreed order of ministry. One of the steps to such a goal is a Federation of Christian Churches.'

There was an immediate welcome for the Federation within and beyond the Anglican Church. In particular it became responsible for an extensive scheme of relief and welfare, with well organised case work. This received the encourage-
¶ ment and support of the Japanese.

Writing as I am in May, 1942, the needs of innumerable people are desperately urgent and immediate. The Christian Church is the only institution which can organise relief on the scale on which it is and will be needed here. A great deal is going to depend on those who have the direct responsibility for organising schemes for the relief of suffering. A great deal, too, is going to depend on the capacity for service of individual dedicated Christians in Malaya. It remains to be seen whether they can remain 'awake', or whether the pressure of circumstances — and that pressure will often be very great — will prevent them from looking beyond their own sufferings and their own anxieties.

THE SCALE OF HUMAN SUFFERING — NOW

Even now some are going into the streets to die. Others are being carried there by their friends when they are dead. Of the deaths recorded at Bidadari Cemetery 80% are from dysentery or enteritis. Beri-beri is increasing. Unemployment and poverty, as they are the first cause of undernourishment, will mean more cases of beri-beri, more dysentery, with perhaps worse to follow. Typical was the perfectly formed body of the young baby Sorby and I found on the steps of the now empty St. Andrew's Hospital. We buried it in the wood at the back of Bishopsbourne without telling the Bishop. It would have saddened him too deeply.

In the days that are to come may we all, clergy and laity, 'walk worthy of the vocation wherewith we are called'. The crisis is here already. Many are starving now and we, the people of Singapore, have been told by the *Syonan Times,* the Japanese newspaper, that the remedies, if any, are our responsibility entirely. The Japanese do not, they say, hold themselves responsible for feeding the people of Malaya.

¶ THE FEDERATION OF THE CHURCHES IS BORN

The first immediate steps of the Federation were to organise relief work, for which the Roman Catholic Bishop, as well as the Japanese, gave full support.

All the non-Roman Churches met for groups of discussion and a United Service every month was becoming a central feature of the life of the Federation.

Writing of it later one can see that, in one way, it may have been too successful. The Kempei-tai regarded it with great suspicion. It was falsely accused of being involved in the Double Tenth's so-called espionage plot in October, 1943, and was closed down. There is, however, little doubt that the cooperation achieved during the brief life of the Federation

¶ was responsible for the speed with which Singapore's Trinity
College was founded so soon after the war as an interdenomi-
¶ national centre for the training of Church leaders.

One of the Bishop's constant difficulties was to gauge
correctly Japanese reactions in any given situation. There was
a story he frequently told against himself. Soon after the
Japanese occupation he approached a senior officer to have
something done about the damage from shrapnel to the roof
of the Chapter House at the Cathedral. He thought he had a
trump card. He pointed out that a considerable amount of
sugar had been stored there by the British. This was being
damaged by the rain coming through the roof. Receiving no
immediate reply he stressed again his worries about the sugar,
to be told firmly, even sternly, by the officer 'I am not
concerned with the sugar, but with the dignity of the House
of God'. Collapse of one Bishop!

THE TORTUOUS WAYS OF JAPANESE PROPAGANDA

Steering a course between truth on the one hand and the
distortions of Japanese propaganda on the other could be
perilous, as this letter shows, written much later by the
Bishop to the editor of the *Syonan Sinbun,* the Japanese
replacement of the *Straits Times.* The letter itself explains
how it came to be written.

'In the issue of the *Syonan Sinbun* on December 15th,
1942, I expressed my sincere gratitude to the authorities
for the generous treatment of the Christian Church, not
only in Syonan, but in the whole of Malaya. I believe
Christianity to be a universal religion which emphasises
the greatness of loving service to humanity and I feel
that the permanent greatness of Japan is to be measured
in these terms. It is here that Christians can be of service
in developing the spiritual qualities of human nature.

Christianity is essentially cooperative rather than
competitive, but the desire to serve rather than domi-
nate has not always been a characteristic of so called
Christian nations, but I have not noticed in recent
history any evidence in British policy of religious
intolerance.

Of my own treatment by the authorities I write with

great appreciation and gratitude. I have received both courtesy and kindness. Naturally I have not been allowed to move about my diocese, which extends from Thailand to Timor, but most of my work is within Syonan-to, where I have enjoyed full freedom for my pastoral work amongst the Eurasian, Chinese and Indian Christians and occasionally the privilege of ministering to war prisoners and internees.

It was on this point, and also on the considerate attitude of the Japanese authorities to the Christian Church in general, that I said that I would not object if my statements were used as propaganda, as I consider that truth of fact has both a scientific and spiritual value which is universal.'

While the Bishop wondered how the letter might be received by those who read it in the newspaper in Changi, he did not in any way modify what he wished to say, feeling that it was important to give credit where credit was due. As it happened we did not hear of any adverse criticism from the Gaol.

Early in June a problem of manpower arose at St. Hilda's, Katong. The Bishop decided that I should take over from the Revd. Yeh Hua Fen, who wished to return to government service. I was also to continue helping at the Cathedral, while Sorby carried on at St. Paul's, Serangoon.

¶ THE STORY OF ST. HILDA'S CHURCH, KATONG

It was in 1934 that the Archdeacon, the Venerable Graham White, had a vision for the Church in Singapore. The handbook, beautifully produced, to celebrate the Golden Jubilee of St. Hilda's in 1984, speaks of his 'dream to bring the Church of God to the people — to build "extension centres" in Katong and Serangoon. In a spirit of self-sacrifice he bought the building of Bethel English School and the land on which it stood in Ceylon Road. This is what he called "the planting of a grain of mustard seed".'

The area served by St. Hilda's stretches for about four miles along the south coast, from Tanjong Rhu through Katong to Siglap and inland for about a mile. It consists of suburban houses, mainly, but not exclusively, of Chinese families.

¶   Originally 'services were held in a lower room of the old building, while lessons were conducted in the Girls' School above. The contagious enthusiasm and dynamic interest shown by the Archdeacon, Miss Chia Ah Moy, who was the first Head Mistress, and by Mrs. Stanton Nelson influenced a band of devoted, far-sighted Christians, who gave time, energy and money to the purpose of creating a centre of religious life in Singapore'.

The handbook carries the story still further when it says 'What distinguished St. Hilda's from other churches was that it was a family church', adding that 'Visitors have always referred to the homely atmosphere of the church, a compliment to those who have throughout the years welcomed strangers and visitors into the congregation and have accomplished much by their friendship and interest in their neighbours'.

What follows in the Jubilee handbook will strike a chord of gratitude and gladness in those who were a part of St. Hilda's more than forty-five years ago. 'During the war years St. Hilda's proved to be a beacon of Faith and Hope to many a lonely and fear-stricken heart . . . There was a sense of fellow-feeling, of comradeship, of oneness that held us together in the face of adversity and danger . . . The Church came nearest then to the principles which our Lord preached and practised'.

¶   That was totally true of St. Hilda's in 1942 and 1943.

THE DIARY CONTINUES

Sunday, June 14th, 1942. First whole day in Katong. The departure of the Reverend Yeh Hua Fen from St. Hilda's in Katong was necessary, since there was no money to pay him, but it throws a good deal more work on the three of us and means a loss of concentration on the Cathedral. I bicycled out to Katong in pouring rain. There were fourteen communicants. Mrs. Olsen of East Coast Road is feeling the pinch badly after years of comparative affluence, but she's putting a bold front on things. She's being helped considerably with food by Japanese Army Officers. 'They seem to like old people and children'! One of the occasions when prayers in the house before leaving seemed really meaningful. Over the road to Lebroy, a crony from the early A.R.P. days. Like many others, making the·best . . . Evensong with about twenty there. Back in the rain.

Monday, June 15th. Up early and bicycled out to Bukit Timah Rifle Range P.O.W. camp. The Singapore Volunteers are there. No service. Too much work to be done. Stayed talking. Back for late breakfast. In all the morning.

In the afternoon to Middleton Hospital to see Ivy, one of our Orthopaedic Hospital girls, with a bad go of typhoid, but she would be worse if it weren't for injections some time since. Trouble with her and with all our orthopaedic children lies in their low resistance. To Kandang Kerbau Hospital and cheerful talk with three of our girls who are nurses there, one of whom is quite sure she's going to Hell! Looking forward to seeing Cleopatra there!

Mrs. Karasu, Champion's daughter, is very ill. He was there looking after her. He is an impressive looking man, thin with a fine bearded head of white hair. It's touching to see his devotion.

Got home, to find the Bishop's driver, Ismael, safely back after a spot of bother. The Bishop had to bail him out for $50. The Police accused him of receiving two blankets, which in fact he had bought in the market. A bit shaken. The Bishop had offered to go to court with him, an offer which was courteously declined with — 'No, Tuan. Best you stay here pray Tuan Allah!'

Bridge in the evening. Bishop down!

RECREATIONS AT BISHOPSBOURNE

References to bridge and golf appear here from time to time, the latter on an intricate miniature pitch-and-putt course we laid out in the small garden of many gradients at Bishopsbourne. For me bridge was much more complicated. It was my misfortune that I shared a house with two bridge maniacs. On top of which I was the junior partner! I knew enough of the rudiments of the game to make up a three at three-handed cut-throat bridge. Their trouble, and mine, was that they never knew when to stop!

Tuesday, June 16th. In all the morning. The Reverend John Short, Army Chaplain, turned up from River Valley Road P.O.W. camp on one of his visits with a Japanese escort. Mrs. Karasu worse. Being treated for typhoid. Champion still there nursing her, is very anxious. He had been there all night.

I was caught in pouring rain at the Chan's. Evelyn and I took Man Pui and Soon Chew down about a thousand in a rubber of crazy bridge which lasted only three hands! The excuse was the rain, but I rode on home in spite of it. Back for usual Tuesday golf in the garden and preparing for to-morrow in Katong.

TYPICAL PARISH DAYS

Wednesday, June 17th. Early to the Cathedral, John Lee celebrating. The Bishop had a meeting with a Japanese officer whom he met yesterday about possible permits for visits to camps, so our fortnightly Chapter Meeting had to be put off. Good to see the compound cleared of all the junk which had collected there in its days as a Japanese car dump. Breakfast of coffee and biscuits with Sorby at the Meyer's and then on into 'my parish'.

The Moss's at Lorong 34. He getting over an attack of malaria, Betty not fit, Bill still out of a job, Zoe, and Coral, the baby. Horace turned up just as I was leaving.

I've heard so much of the Chuas and the meeting with them was up to expectations. Eng Cheng and Peter at the house, and Mrs. Chua at the Clinic. They have got a household of twenty-one, looking after two complete families whose husbands are missing. Offers from both Eng Cheng and Mrs. Chua of help at St. Hilda's.

A word with old Champion. His courageous faith is amazing. His daughter has died and her body rested for a short time in the church, where we had prayers.

Ran into Miss Allen, in a state of furious excitement, bristling. Some trouble at the house, but impossible to get anything out of her, so I went to see for myself. Daniel Defoe and his wife in tears. Mrs. Gill storming and bridling after a visit to the Municipal Building, where she had been told to get out of her house. Apparently not till Friday, but moving things to avoid distraint. Daniel has nowhere to take his stuff;

gave him $5 and a chit to Mitchell to let him house them at St. Hilda's.

Thursday, June 18th. Early to the Engineers, near Bishops-bourne, for communion. They are a group of Europeans from Changi living under Japanese guard. About thirty were there, twenty-two of them communicants. They suggested a weekly Evensong or Matins, with a celebration weekly. Possibly a better arrangement. There is certainly a demand for a service every week, as a good many come, and there is place, in view of spiritual awakening on so many sides, for a communion service.

Completed lists and took it easy in the afternoon. Choir practice at the Cathedral. A case of six mortar bombs in the compound was *most* unhealthy looking. Reported at Central Police Station. To the Red Shield Club, where about twenty-five of the Municipality are messing. They seem quite pleased at the change. Stayed some time. Back by dark.

Friday, June 19th. Celebration at Bishopsbourne. Sorby's eldest boy's and his mother's birthdays, and the anniversary of his father's death. Poor S. rather distrait all day. Too many nostalgic memories and thoughts. Looked in on Jervois Road for a short time. More questions asked by the Japanese guard than usual. Norman Coulson came for bridge. Bishop back from a meeting with the Church's Federation Executive. Raised Cain because of slackness of Relief Committee. Late to bed.

LT. ANDREW OGAWA – A GENEROUS ENEMY

Saturday June 20th. Late up. Bishop out to see Lt. Ogawa about various things.

Within days of our moving back to Bishopsbourne we met Lt. Andrew Ogawa, a Japanese officer, who was to have a decisive and lasting influence on Church life in Singapore.

After war service in Manchuria, Saigon and Northern Malaya, he arrived in Singapore from Kuala Lumpur on the day after the surrender. He served for a few days on the staff

*Figure 3: The Bishop with
Lt. Andrew Ogawa, a generous enemy.*

¶ of Changi Internment Camp and was then made Director of Education and Officer in Charge of Religious Affairs. He did not continue beyond the latter half of 1942 in that vital role, but the foundations of tolerance and protection for the Church which he laid were to last for the whole Japanese occupation.

A member of the Nippon Sei Ko Kai, the Anglican Church of Japan, he became a regular visitor to Bishopsbourne and a firm friend of the Bishop's, of Sorby Adams's and of mine. In fact, Andrew Ogawa and I still exchange letters more than forty-five years later. He immediately became a member of the Cathedral congregation. From the outset he and a fellow officer attended the services at St. Andrew's, making a point of arriving in a military staff car with a blue flag flying, establishing in the mind of the authorities that Japanese officers were using the building, so securing a measure of additional protection for it. It was also largely due to his persistence that an order was issued that no churches or their compounds should be used for military purposes. This remained in force for the whole of the Japanese occupation.

Lt. Ogawa was able to continue his official cooperation with the Bishop for much of 1942, particularly helping him to set up the Federation of the Churches, which led to close links in many fields between Anglicans and the Free Churches, as I've already described it.

That the Bishop was able to visit Changi Gaol and some of the P.O.W. camps for confirmations was due to Ogawa. We were fairly certain that more than once he resisted attempts to have us interned. It was he who frustrated a move by the

84

¶ Kempei-tai to make us live at the Cathedral when we were ordered out of Bishopsbourne in September, 1942. We knew that it was because of his intervention that Sorby Adams was released after he had been arrested by the Kempei-tai for throwing a packet of cigarettes over a fence to Australian P.O.W.s. When Japanese 25th Army Headquarters were moving into Raffles College, to save the books of the library from probable destruction Ogawa had them moved to the Museum.

These were some of the things which we knew made up a part, not only of our debt to Andrew Ogawa, but also that of the Church in Singapore. He did convey to us indirectly that the Kempei-tai had warned him that he was being too friendly and so his visits to us were discontinued. Before we were interned he had, for whatever reason, been moved to other work and was no longer responsible for education and religious affairs.

There is another story which seems to be typical of Lt. Ogawa's thoughtfulness and compassion. Days only before the outbreak of war in the Far East, the Dutch ambassador to the Philippines and his wife travelled to Shanghai from Manila on a shopping trip. Their three children, a girl of nine and boys of seven and five, were stranded in Manila and separated from their parents. The Japanese sent them to Singapore to be interned at Changi. As Lt. Ogawa said of himself and another officer, 'we felt too much pity to send the kids there and so took them to our residence in Tanglin Road. They were very nice children and spoke English well.' On one occasion, while he was away from the house at his office, the children went out of the garden. Ogawa has reported 'The Kempei-tai came again to question me, but I managed some way to keep them in our house till they were to embark on the exchange ship *Asama Maru* for East Africa'.

On May 1st, 1943, Lt. Ogawa was posted to Sumatra, having already been transferred to other work in Singapore ¶ some time before.

Saturday, June 20th, continued. Corner arrived with the news that Mrs. Arbens had been killed in a car crash in Orchard Road, going head on into a lorry turning across into Cairnhill Road. She must have been killed outright.

A good deal of thought about confirmation classes begin-ning on Monday, and again after lunch. I had an hour's lie-off.

Out to Kandang Kerbau Hospital to see Sheares about books for Changi. There are difficulties in the way of direct supply. When I got there I saw Guy Vaz and three others just admitted. Working out at Raffles College on anti-malarial work with quite a lot of stray hand grenades still lying about, they found a strange bakelite variety. Guy, trying to extract detonator, dropped the thing. All four were plentifully peppered, but none seriously, although liberally blood-spattered. Found young Ebert there too. Poisoned knee and fever after cutting off a wart! Amy Chan wanting to be married in Holy Trinity Chinese Church rather than the Cathedral, because of nearness to Japanese in Adelphi Hotel! Tried to reassure her. Back in the dusk. Preparation for tomorrow.

Sunday, June 21st. Early to St. Hilda's, in Katong. Glorious morning. Better congregation, but still a good many non-communicants. To Mrs. Hackett, her son Denis looking very washed out after dysentery. No more trouble, but the Kempei-tai called after I was there last time, having seen me visit the house. Quite a good crowd in church and many children at Evensong.

Monday, June 22nd. Early to Bukit Timah Rifle Range, the Singapore Volunteers P.O.W. Camp, for a celebration. The rain held things up a bit, but I was able to carry on. Forty there. On afterwards to see Mrs. Pearse. She is in a pretty bad way leading an almost completely Swiss Family Robinson existence in a hut at the back of beyond. Found Pat, her son, there too. He had the day off. She's very worried about his schooling, but as he is over standard five nothing can be done. She has a terribly lonely life, alone all day.

Back for thought about this afternoon's confirmation class at the Cathedral. Out to Serangoon for Boys Choir practice after lunch. Confirmation class of fourteen at the Cathedral. Rather a mixed bag and they may have to be sub-divided later. Liked the look of Fook Yuen, a non-Christian, who had come on his own as an enquirer.

Tuesday, June 23rd. Celebration early at St. Andrew's Hospital and breakfast with the doctor and his wife. Long talk and tea with Wee Chye Eng. She has magnificent heart, knowing as she must that her husband won't come back. She has been told as much by a visitor, that he was amongst those caught up in the massacre, and yet forcing herself to talk naturally of him. Pity she will not have at any price. She gets enough of it from those around her and it maddens her. The one and perhaps the only thing which keeps her going is the background of her time at school in England and her religious experience then has a large place in those memories.

The Bishop and partner staged a magnificent come-back and beat Sorby and me one up at golf in the garden, although it went to the 19th! Sorby and I had our revenge when the Bishop came bottom of the Bridge Poll! Unfortunately hilarious Evensong at Bishopsbourne, when we all three got the giggles!

Wednesday, June 24th. St. John Baptist. Celebration at St. Hilda's at 8.30. Eight of us there. Breakfast and then out to 8th mile to Hill Top. Glorious view over to the islands. These visits do remind people of the existence of St. Hilda's! Five minutes sea gazing on the beach at the bottom of Siglap Road. One of these days I shall take a picnic lunch and get sand into the sandwiches! Shades, blessed shades, of Seaview in the Isle of Wight!

Found dear old Mrs. Misson. After seeing the ruins of her house in Joo Chiat I had thought she was dead. Cheerfully told me how she had sold her meat safe — her last possession — to pay the rent. Most impressed that I should have turned up after a vivid dream she had had about Archdeacon Graham White the night before!

Heard of books in old Police mess. Must try and get them for Miyako Hospital and thence into Changi.

Thursday, June 25th. Service at Jervois Road Camp for civil engineers. Atmosphere a bit strained, but a very good number there. Arranged to have morning service followed by celebration on alternate Thursdays.

Friday, June 26th. Slight discord at breakfast, but such are very rare. It is amazing how well the three of us, the Bishop, Sorby and I, get on. For over four months now we have been together. Sometimes we have had good cause to get a bit nervy, but our relationship has not been affected in the least. On the contrary, I think it has become deeper with the passing of time. There has had to be patience often enough — perhaps more has been needed with me than I know! Even so, our fellowship is something for which to be very thankful.

Desultory reading in the morning. Sorby with Ogawa in the afternoon. Good deal of talk these days about post cards which we are to be allowed to write home through the Red Cross. Their anxiety for us all at home must be almost unendurable. The *Syonan Shinbun* speaks this morning of the coming of the *Asama Maru* en route for Lourenco Marques with returned American nationals. Will they, I wonder, allow some of the women and older men to go?

THE CHURCH GROWS

St. Hilda's, Katong. I have had a fortnight at St. Hilda's as Priest-in-Charge. Things are beginning to take shape, especially as I am able to be more mobile than Yeh Hua Fen. There are a great many loose ends lying about which need picking up, Committee, Choir, Sunday School, Youth Fellowship, Communicants Guild and some sort of Membership or Electoral Roll.

Committee. St. Hilda's has always seemed to have a strong sense of fellowship and a great deal of hard work has been put in to building up a good corporate spirit there. There are several who have, in the past, played a useful part in the life of the Church and, in spite of altered circumstances, are capable of doing so again. The formation of a committee would mean the possibility of an exchange of views on all manner of points. It should be something more than a purely business, i.e. a financial, committee, and there should be possibilities of showing them that they have a wider responsibility. They would be the representatives of a fellowship and not just of an institution. It would probably have to be elective, with the hope that the right people got on!

Figure 4: St. Hilda's, Katong, drawn from photographs by Mary Marshall. A new church was built on this site in 1947.

Electoral or Communicants Roll. Something of the sort is essential apart from my own visiting list. The fact that they have 'signed something' is for many people salutary. It helps to give them a sense of responsibility towards the body of which they are members.

A purely practical reason is that we — the Bishop, Sorby and I — can never be quite sure how long we are to be free. We may go to Changi any time and things must be kept going even though we are not here. There is too much goodness among them for it to be allowed to go to seed. The more orderly things are now, the easier it will be for them to carry on if we are interned.

Choir. Even without the immigrants from St. Paul's, Serangoon, most of the old choir are still there.

Sunday School. There are a good many children in the immediate neighbourhood who might be able to come, and with the East Coast Road bus service back, that might make it easier for those out at the far end. The problem of teachers would not be great. Champion, Ken Armstrong, Jane Albert and Elsie Handy are still available. Violet and Myrtle Wilkins would probably come back [they did!], and Chua Eng Cheng, who has had a good deal of experience at St. Paul's in Serangoon, is anxious to help.

Communicants Guild. I am certain there is room for it and there are many whose lives would be enriched spiritually, and that, in its turn, would mean an enrichment of the whole fellowship. But it must be more than a spiritual cult for religious women! It would have to be balanced by some sort of outward expression. Possible that they should be asked to do some of the case-work for the 'Universal Church' Relief Committee. Bit awkward, though, if some of their own number had to be investigated!

Youth Fellowship. This had got under way last December on the social side. Scope is rather limited at the moment, but it's worth bearing it in mind as a possibility for the future.

Confirmation Candidates. Only one so far as I know at the moment.

All things considered, it looks as though there are a great many opportunities at St. Hilda's and a good deal of work to be done. Certainly more than can be crammed into two days a week. The trouble is to get as much as possible done there without entirely neglecting Cathedral visiting.

Sunday, June 28th. Another fresh morning for the Katong journey, as always by bicycle. About forty-five there, but many non-communicants. Breakfast with some of them. They are all so kind and generous and yet they need all their extra food and money.

Visits do bear fruit. One of them thanked me for going. 'My husband's begun to read his Bible'! Did the round of Ceylon Road.

Not many at Evensong. I always enjoy the friendly chatter in the compound afterwards. Persistent rumours that school and compound are to be taken over lock, stock and barrel. It will be hard if they are and we shall have to look elsewhere for somewhere to have our services. But beggars can't be choosers.

Mrs. Codd at church. Short of milk for baby. Promised to take some out on Wednesday.

Monday, June 29th. Early to 'Taylor's', saw thirty of them and was able to hold a service. Arranged for confirmation next week.

¶ UNDER-COVER POSTMEN

For obvious reasons there could be no record in the diary of the nefarious activities carried on by the Bishop, Sorby Adams and me during 1942—43. The comment 'Early to Taylor's' refers to the Bukit Timah Rifle Range P.O.W. Camp, composed largely of Singapore Volunteers, of whom Taylor was the Commanding Officer.

The Rifle Range needs a note on its own. I've mentioned elsewhere one of the acute problems which arose for so many married couples and their families separated from one another after the fall of Singapore. There were no official channels of communication of any kind. Nobody, husbands, wives, parents or sons had any chance of knowing who had and who

¶ had not survived. It was important to try and find a way of communication between the P.O.W. camps and civilians in Changi. Norman Coulson, as an engineer doing work in Singapore recognised by the Japanese, had access to a lot of the camps, supplying pipes and other essential equipment. Doing the same kind of work he also went freely to the Gaol at Changi, so having totally illicit contact between P.O.W.s and internees. He did a heroic job, as also did Mervyn Sheppard in the Gaol, of whom more in a moment.

To a limited extent we were fortunate in being allowed into some of the P.O.W. camps. Others we never penetrated. However, with entrance into one it meant that information we gave them could be distributed amongst all the others in the P.O.W. network. So, there was our link with the P.O.W.s. We also had links with Changi through the Miyako Hospital, to which internees were brought if they could not be dealt with in the Gaol. We had unlimited entrance to the wards. The combination of access to the P.O.W. camps and to the Miyako was something we were in a position to use.

More than once, riding out to the Rifle Range on a bicycle, I took a gas-cape rolled round the column of the saddle. I'm not sure what I should have done if it had rained, for hidden inside the cape were about fifty small notes from Changi, which we had picked up at the Miyako. Somebody at the Rifle Range was tipped off when I arrived, the gas-cape discreetly unwrapped and the notes were on their way.

We had been doing this for some time and through the Bishop's visits to several camps by car, besides paying our regular visits to the Miyako. This was all fairly straightforward. But then the load of the traffic seemed to be growing heavy and we realised the risks might be getting out of hand. We decided to check one or two of the letters to see if they had in them any indication of how this 'postal service' was being carried out. It was alarming to see specific reference made to the way in which letters were being ferried backwards and for-wards. I can remember one of the letters, and there were others in a similar vein, which said quite clearly, and I quote, 'If you will reply to this I am sure the Bishop will arrange for it to come back to you in the same way that your letter came to me'. If that had landed in the possession of the Japanese, there would have been serious repercussions long before the Double Tenth.

So, with great regret we decided that this had got to end. There must have been many people who were mystified and disappointed that their contact, which was so valuable and so valued, had finished. We had to end it without any explanation, and so it just stopped.

ILLICIT POSTAL SERVICE AT CHANGI

Meanwhile in Changi Gaol a much more thorough-going and extensive postal service was being operated by Mervyn ff Sheppard, now Tan Sri Dato Mubin Sheppard. In his book, *Tamin Budisman — Memoirs of an Unorthodox Civil Servant*, Sheppard describes how, in May, 1942, he was approached by a member of the Central Committee. 'I was', he said, 'given an opportunity to be of service to both internees and Prison-ers of War by operating a one-man secret postal service between the internees in Changi Gaol and the P.O.W.s nearby, who had access to all the other P.O.W. camps on the Island. Notes from individuals, restricted in size to two inches square when folded, were collected in the camp office and passed to me the night before I went out. The Japanese wanted us to grow vegetables, mainly spinach, inside the prison walls, but the soil was sterile and I was given permission by the Japanese Camp Commander to go out three times a week carrying a scythe and two large sacks and to return ninety minutes later with the sacks full of freshly cut grass, for use as compost.

'The notes, some containing cash, were squeezed into empty cigarette packets, which were then closed and placed in the bottom of one of my empty sacks. I had to locate a P.O.W. party on its way to work, scything my way up to the edge of a road along which they passed. The exchange with the leader of the other party of three or four "cigarette packets" needed careful timing, and was made when the Japanese sentry's attention had been diverted; but for three months postal deliveries continued without a break. When my sacks were full of grass, with the notes from the P.O.W.s hidden near the bottom, I walked back to the prison, rang the bell, was admitted, bowed (a must) to the sentry on duty

¶ and passed into the exercise yard to unload the "compost".
I was never once searched.'

All went well until a day in November, 1942. The location
and the extent of Sheppard's activities had now changed. With
five other friends he went out twice a week with two hand
carts. The Japanese Camp Commander had been persuaded
that the black earth of a particular field was even better for
spinach beds than cut grass. The fact that it was alongside
rubber trees being cut down by P.O.W.s was, of course,
purely coincidental! On one occasion the exchange of cigarette packets, now converted into match boxes, went wrong.
'The sentry accompanying the party must have been watching and he saw the P.O.W. officer fumble and drop the box.'

The consequences for Sheppard were grave. For more than
a month he was put through excruciating tortures by the
Japanese Kempei-tai, first at Changi and then in the Y.M.C.A.
building, the Military Police Headquarters in Singapore. In
spite of pressure, both persistent and severe, Sheppard held
out, maintaining that he had been caught in an isolated
incident. Nor did he involve any of the P.O.W.s who, with
him, had for months carried on this interchange of hundreds
of letters. When set beside Mervyn Sheppard's the efforts, as
illicit postmen, of the Bishop, Sorby Adams and me were as
¶ nothing.

Monday, June 29th (continued). Back at about eleven to find
a telephone message from Bidadari Cemetery. Mitchell had
died at Miyako. His sons had not confirmed the time of the
funeral. Swallowed breakfast and pedalled out there arriving
at about 12, two hours late! — to find two sons and Stefan.
In afternoon preparing for confirmation class. Sorby back
from his weekend in Serangoon in great form. This Monday
reunion is always good. Bishop with news from Dr. Chelliah
of raising of preaching ban, although he is a little alarmed at
condition that he must be personally responsible for us all!
As well as his work at the Cathedral Dr. Chelliah has a senior
job in the Education Department.

Tuesday, June 30th. John Short failed to turn up from River
Valley Road P.O.W. camp where he is Padre. He usually

comes on Tuesdays. Sandy Hope took me off to Rochore Canal Road in a hunt for silver cups for chalices. Several requests for them from P.O.W.s and from Changi. Some of the booths we poked about in might well have been in the back streets of Salisbury. Odd bits of china, old and decayed tennis balls, tattered novels, faded prints and photographs, car pumps, a weighing machine and some beautiful old pewter. Two large quart pots, a pint pot which once belonged to 'Thomas Watts. Eight Bells' and another from a pub in the Mile End Road. But the prices on this Oriental stall would differ hugely from those of their Anglo-Saxon brother. If the whole lot could be bought for £1 in England it would be a bargain. Here in Singapore, if they cost more than $2 [in 1990 currency values — 25p!] it would be robbery! The search for suitable cups produced one in plated silver for 50^c and two handleless pewter at 50^c the pair. They should serve the purpose.

Met Miss de Silva on the way back in great distress. Sonnie had been taken off on a charge of selling cigarettes. What should she do? What could she do? Sandy and I followed her down to the Central Police Station where she discovered nothing. Persuaded her not to go further and that a mistake must have been made.

Back to Bishopsbourne with Sandy to tea. Usual golf with Mistri, a very generous Indian friend of Sorby's. Glorious victory for Sorby and J.H. by 5 and 4, but Bp. rather disconcerted by a strange female, who kept popping up out of the bushes just as he was going to play a shot! Fairly successful bridge. Improving gradually.

Permission to preach granted yesterday, withdrawn today as premature, under instructions from Kempei-tai.

Wednesday, July 1st. Celebration at Cathedral followed by Chapter Meeting. Fairly good discussion on a good many points. Back to Bishopsbourne to pick up odds and ends of stuff for Katong and lunch there. They were most kind — even broached one of their last bottles of Guinness! Met John Handy on the way back, after one of the rare Japanese requests for my pass, and sat in the shade with him for a bit. Told him of the Bishop's hope that every member of every congregation would be a regular subscriber and discussed ways and means. To St. Hilda's for Sunday School Meeting. No news of persistent rumours that the St. Hilda's school buildings are to be taken over. The Wilkins, the Champions, Eng Cheng, Juliana at meeting. Decided to start with Childrens Service on Sunday 12th. If all goes well, Sunday School two Sundays later. Back for cool evening. Week's A.R.P. brown-out has come to an end.

Thursday, July 2nd. Bishop's application to go to Changi P.O.W.s for confirmations. Padre Short seemed to think there must be a good many amongst the Military, and we have heard, from those who have been released for jobs in town from Changi Gaol, that there are some ready there too. We hope permission is given. Down to the Cathedral for choir practice. Seven women there for the first time. Did a bit of work on new gardening project in the compound.

Friday, July 3rd. Large scale move to the Customs House of British engineers and others still free. We rather wonder whether we may not have to go there too, but it would make things extremely difficult. We have to be on tap here at all hours. News of P.O.W. post-cards, but we have not had ours as yet.

Saturday, July 4th. Into town to try and get news of post-cards. Twice to see Ogawa and Chelliah, but without result. Middleton Hospital have had theirs and sent them in. Tele-phone Co. have sent in their own. People seem to think a ship for Lourenco Marques leaves soon. We must catch it with cards somehow. They have all been waiting so long for news. It's nearly five months since the fall of Singapore and they've heard nothing.

Sunday, July 5th. Trinity V. Early as usual to Katong. Forty there; still only a proportion made their communion.

Monday, July 6th. On the way down to Cathedral saw a large crowd gathered on the pavement near the Stamford Road, Dhoby Gaut corner. In the middle of the crowd was a head on a wooden platform. Eight Malays had been arrested and beheaded for attempting to steal petrol. They were spotted and shooting followed, during which a Japanese soldier had been killed. I did not see the placard which was put up at each of the eight places where these heads were exposed, but this was the generally accepted version (or rumour) of the incident. It was a grisly enough sight to act as a deterrent to any other would-be looters. This was the only one I saw, but I heard there were others in front of the Municipal Building, at the Post Office, Kallang Bridge and elsewhere.

Tuesday, July 7th. Anniversary of the beginning of the China Incident five years ago. At Bishopsbourne. Drew up letter for Katong congregation about almsgiving and the need to accept their responsibility for the maintenance of the Church and also for a part of the Priest's salary. As it is they are not even paying all the Church expenses.

Norman Coulson in for bridge. I gradually improve! News that post-cards to be written to relatives at home does not apply to civilians. This was a bitter blow and hit us hard. The only hope is that full lists are being sent and that the post-cards are not the only record. If not, then the word is bound to get round at home, either in the press or on the B.B.C., that news has been received and then those who have heard nothing will believe the worst.

What misery is stored up for mothers — the women of all nations. What a picture. Armies in the field, armies in the factories. We hear plenty about them. But what of the army of women in the homes? What spokesman have they got in the affairs of and between nations? And yet they are the people who suffer more than any others. What a depth of understanding and sympathy Michelangelo has put into his 'Pieta'. Standing at the west door the huge magnificence and bold colouring of St. Peter's at Rome is almost staggering. Perfect in proportion, but none the less massive, one forgets the beauty and delicacy of the small things until in a quiet corner one is faced by the exquisite figure of Mary supporting the body of Jesus. And it is in the small quiet corners that all the mothers are to be found, almost unnoticed, nursing their sorrow alone.

Wednesday, July 8th. Early to the Cathedral for celebration. Much gunfire and drone of many planes. Probably a salute to the exchange ship bringing Japanese internees. Breakfast at the Green Spot and out to Katong.

BEHIND THE JAPANESE SCENE

Thursday, July 9th. In the evening to the Engineers in Jervois Road for weekly service. Went into the Guard Room to report as usual, but was stopped. Curtis, the interpreter, came out and did his best. Apparently they had had word that nobody was allowed to go in and the sergeant of the guard was adamant, as of course he had to be. At any rate I was allowed to go and see the C.O., who was most courteous. He took my name and address and said that he would apply for permission for us and let us know the result. I mentioned Ogawa's name so we shall probably hear through him. It will be a blow for them if we are stopped. A lot of them always come to the services. It may be possible for Short to get to them from the P.O.W. Camp in River Valley Road.

If only there were a means of finding out, I think we would discover that there are a good many Christians in the Japanese Army and a still larger number who have had some contact with Christian influences. One of the two sentries who marched me off to the C.O. had been at a Mission School and was a baptised Methodist. Huge delight amongst the three of us at the discovery of this common bond. The other sentry exclaimed 'Ah, Christian!', still marching stolidly up the hill with his rifle at the slope, crossed himself very violently with his free hand and capped it all with a resounding 'AMEN'!, completing the performance with a loud bellow of laughter!

I had heard a good deal about the easy relations existing between officers and men and it was interesting to see an example of democracy in practice. The Colonel was sitting at one side of a long table, a junior officer on his right and a private opposite him. Two other 2-star privates were sitting in easy chairs. It is, of course, a completely different system and has obvious advantages. It means that each military unit really is a unit. That there was no loss of discipline was obvious from the bow which each man gave as he entered or left the room.

Friday, July 10th. Another large draft to Changi, amongst them Mrs. Nairn from the Middleton Hospital — we shall miss her cheerful philosophical Scots self — John Odell, who had taken over the replanning of the Cathedral compound, Clubley and Skipper from St. James's Power Station. They both of them came to the Parsonage in Kuala Lumpur on their way down from Butterworth after the power station had been blown up there. Matthew Patterson and Swan from the Gas Company have also gone. Fifty of them in all gathered at the Municipality. I dashed back to Bishopsbourne to pick up two mattressss for Clubley and Skipper and got back with two minutes to spare just in time to hurl them into the back of one of the ambulances.

Saturday, July 11th. All the Britons still out, except us and two others, are down at the Customs House. St. James's Power Station and the Fire Brigade carry on where they are, under house arrest. The Customs House lot have elected Norman Coulson their Chairman. From all accounts he has blossomed out to a very marked degree since the surrender.

Sunday, July 12th. Celebration in the Cathedral at 8. First time for me for over a month. It's good to be back there, although I am more and more drawn to St. Hilda's. Cathedral congregations have improved almost 100 per cent. Full round of visits in Katong. Mrs. Chua, pleased as punch to have the washing soap. How can these people manage at 30^c a bar and prices at the level at which they are standing now?

Extraordinarily vivid ride home, full of small intensely living pictures. People thronging the streets, rickshaw pullers sitting in a huddle gossiping, small boys kicking a tennis ball against a wall, a Chinese girl in black riding a bicycle with much solemnity and little certainty, faces at windows, one turning to talk to someone in the room behind, faces laughing and solemn, carefree and haggard. In some the light shone out undimmed, in others there was a brooding darkness. In many an infinite pathos. Riding amongst them, close to them,

I can't help feeling, in spite of the enormous gulf between us, a strength of affection and an intense admiration for their patience and their amazing courage. They live hard, but they do live bravely.

Monday, July 13th. Bicycled the six miles out to Reformatory Road to see Mrs. Pearse. Her isolation, with her son Pat away all day, presses on her very heavily and she is getting very unnerved. I had already had a celebration with the Volunteers at the Rifle Range P.O.W. Camp and had all the things with me. We had a short service in her little shack and I gave her her communion. The dignity and simplicity of the sacrament, especially in out of the way places, I always find very moving. There have been celebrations in many strange corners since the surrender — the Customs House, Outram and Jervois Roads, the Miyako Hospital, the Rifle Range, Bishopsbourne, the Middleton Hospital, and in many quiet rooms, some small and barely furnished, others comfortable and orderly. 'Out of the everywhere into the here', wherever the here may be.

Amy Tan and Seng Poe married at Holy Trinity in the afternoon. Very late — but Seng Poe only returned from a shopping expedition ten minutes *after* they were due to be at the Church! Confirmation Class followed and then back to the wedding feast.

Tuesday, July 14th. Private celebration and breakfast for Mrs. Jones and the two Scotts. To the Cathedral to see Mrs. Page and give her some money to help her on for a bit. Then to Kandang Kerbau Hospital for a long talk with Dr. English and Lady Heath, who had been brought from Changi to have her baby. Dr. English, too, had come with her, very well and quite unchanged.

I looked in to see Stack. It is astonishing how standards of living have changed. He is a man who was getting $400–500 a month before the war. I asked him how much longer he would be able to carry on. Two months — he said — but if, as he hoped, he sold his car for $500, that would see him through for two years!

Bridge with Max Cochemé, a French doctor with a British passport, who is still free.

Wednesday, July 15th. Late to Katong to see the Wees. Large family, non-baptised, but the three boys and three girls all with very definite Christian background and they care enough about the religion, which is not theirs, to study it. This is another of the families where Sorby has been a real friend and evangelist.

The strangest thing about him, and it is an invaluable asset, is his complete lack of self-consciousness in the fullest sense of the word. It never accurs to him, in his personal relationships, to ask himself whether he is liked or not. But this could only be said of one who is as universally lovable as he is. It would be hard for anyone not to like him. When I went back to the Wees with him in the evening, I saw just how much he meant to this family. There was a welcome from all of them, more perhaps from the younger generation than from their father and mother. Although they, too, were obviously glad to have him there. Specially glad were Helen, Swee Lian, Swee Geck, Bin Hock, Bin Chye and Bin Whatt. I am going there next Wednesday, but as a poor substitute for Sorby.

Saw Lim Chuan Boon. It's very hard for a boy of about eighteen, as he is, who desperately wants to become a Christian against strong family pressures. He's got what looks like glandular fever — still with a high fever, but as cheerful as can be expected. Back to St. Hilda's for Andrew Ho's baptism. The whole Ee family there, Lily, Nancy, Ruby, Jessie, May, Pearl, Doreen, John Tan and Malcom Ho, Nancy's husband.

Thursday, July 16th. Celebration for old Mrs. Angus and her daughter.

Choir practice. Returned Hackett's watch to the Engineers Camp in Jervois Road. Fond farewell through Hylton. It's sad to think we shall go there no more, but we've had a good spin.

Friday, July 17th. Sudden news that the Telephone Company have been whisked off to Changi en bloc, why nobody knows.

Allowed to take no extra food with them. In all day reading
and compiling lists for Fellowship until Bishop's Reunion
lecture at four o'clock. Very few there, but St. Hilda's
represented.

NO FEARS OF INTERNMENT

Friday, August 7th. Three weeks and we are still here at
Bishopsbourne with no immediate sign of a move. More of
our already reduced company have gone to Changi. Those
who remain, with the exception of ourselves and about half
a dozen others, are at the Customs House under guard, but
with free movement during the day. Max Cochemé is with
them. It is still hanging in the balance whether he should
go to Changi or to French Indo-China.

We three have no reason to think that our days are numbered. On the contrary, we are less disturbed mentally than
we have ever been. The strain of life has diminished in ratio
to the responsibility. Our own work has no limitations imposed upon it other than the ban on preaching, but there
seems to be no restriction on the teaching of the faith as
long as it is given at other than service times through the
Churches. For example, the Bishop has been giving Reunion
lectures followed by discussion for the last six weeks and the
Cathedral Fellowship is allowed to meet at the Cathedral.
One of its functions will be definitely instructional.

Our own three-cornered fellowship at Bishopsbourne is as
firm and full of affection as ever. As Sorby himself said last
night, 'I am years younger than I was six months ago. Then I
had the whole responsibility of St. Andrew's.'

The Bishop is sometimes anxious and asks himself repeatedly whether he is doing all that he might. There is no doubt
that it is difficult and sometimes impossible to gauge the
best moment for making any specific request and with the
right amount of persistence. Importunate widows commend
themselves to the Almighty. It is not quite so certain that
importunate bishops are as welcome in the courts of the
mighty Japanese. He cannot get up-country, we cannot
preach — but many of the clergy are coming down here next
week when he should be able to settle much. But in spite of
his misgivings he remains as cheerful and as good a friend

and companion as I could hope for. This, in spite of my many impertinences which may try him! We continue to have gifts of much love lavished on us. That has been one of the most joyful discoveries of this time — the value in which people hold us as their clergy.

Thursday, August 20th. The Diocesan Clergy Conference has come and gone. For two days all the clergy were here. From all over the diocese came nine Indians, six Chinese and, with the Bishop, three Europeans. They are a very mixed bag — the Indians certainly saying more than the Chinese. A great many practical difficulties were cleared up by open and frank discussion of personalities. If two of the former are not more reconciled now, they never will be!

We ourselves are just as we were, all the other houses in Bishopsgate still being vacant. The three houses opposite have been cleared for occupation by the Japanese, which means that we may not be as solitary and quiet as we have been for the last six months. *Laus Deo* for the quiet which we have had.

The Governor and others are reported to have been shipped off somewhere. Much fighting in the Solomons. The *Syonan Times* reports heavy Allied losses, amongst them ten cruisers. Gandhi, Nehru and others have been arrested. Big convoy action in the W. Mediterranean making towards Malta.

PROGRESS AT ST. HILDA'S

St. Hilda's congregations are good. The Bishop was there last Sunday evening with about fifty. There had already been between thirty and forty in the morning. The time is ripe to start St. Hilda's Fellowship with a four point programme of worship, work, study and play.

Worship must be kept at the centre. The whole idea of the Fellowship is to bind them closer together so that they worship as a unity, which will mean an enrichment of both Fellowship and Worship.

On a personal note we have still had no postcards to send home. A further list of next of kin has been sent in to the authorities.

Thursday, August 27th. A few days ago we had the long
awaited postcards which we have been expecting. I wonder,
though, if we should have had them yet had it not been for
Norman Coulson's persistence. Minute instructions as to the
amount we could say and the manner of saying it. I wrote –
VERY WELL AND HAPPY. NO NEED TO WORRY –
followed by fifteen words of special messages. It is on its way!
In two to three months time Mother will have the first direct
news of me for nearly nine months. Perhaps it may be the
first news of any kind. I hope against hope that they may
have had some word.

JAPANESE UNDERMINE EDUCATION IN MALAYA

This is an example of the kind of propaganda being put out
by the Japanese as part of their attempts to build what they
call the Co-Prosperity Sphere.

'Education in Malaya and a new national consciousness.'
Syonan Times

'All the evils of those particularly carefully thought out
and employed "European Christianized" and bureauc-
racy planned and controlled systems of education . . .
have to be destroyed . . . The mind of the child will have
to be gradually cleansed of all its old shibboleths, super-
stitions and loyalties and slowly won over to the new
beliefs and new loyalties . . . The parents and teachers
should seek only those influences which will awaken,
reinforce and sustain the desires and dutifulness that
will be essential to the success of such a vast undertak-
ing. Only such as reach the innermost personality, stir
the highest motives and foster the exercise of self
discipline will do. Apart from the new national . . .
religion of faith in the future salvation of the community
. . . there are no other means that can lead local peoples
to their own social, economic and political salvation
beyond which we need not bother to go . . .
    Faith is the essential spring of human and intellectual
progress. It is the only means by which the gains of
education can be effectively carried out beyond the
school to the entire sphere of human life in which

today's children will have to play an ever increasing active part. Their ability to do so will depend upon the inner faith which inspires their personality and is moulding their character. Faith is the inner energy which can carry the influence of the school out to the home, to the family, to the community and from the community to the nation.

First an abiding faith in the ability of the Nippon Empire to reconstruct the East and its people into one great Sphere of Co-Prosperity. Secondly, faith in the future of the whole Malayan nation as a co-member of that Co-Prosperity. Thirdly, faith in the destinies of each community as units in such a Malayan nation; and finally, faith in the part each community, each individual will play eagerly and gladly for the happiness and welfare of all, the individual contributing to the prosperity of the family, the family to that of the community and the nation to that of the New World Order, of which the Greater East Asia Co-Prosperity Sphere will be but a part.'

Friday, August 28th. The wireless has been sealed.

We have begun to build up the community life of St. Hilda's. I had already sent out a letter, with an explanation of the ideas behind the Fellowship and yesterday we had the first meeting. There is always in our job the danger of being too easily satisfied, but it is impossible not to have some glad and thankful appreciation of signs of progress as they appear. The number of those who came was more than I had dared hope. There were fifty-one of us and even so there are others who will come later. But more than the actual numbers, and far more important, was the enthusiasm with which so many greeted the whole idea and made suggestions. So far we have only just cleared the first hurdle, but a good many things have been set in train. Games are provided for, library, choir, and the idea of adult classes was received favourably.

So there it is. We have got our committee of seven. Next Sunday we shall have a bunfight after Evensong. We shall soon have the whole of the floor above the church for our own use. This *is* only a beginning, but it is at least that.

REPATRIATION – OR NOT?

Endless talk of repatriation which is disturbing and unsettling. Our lives the whole time are in a state of suppressed emotional excitement. Will there be repatriation at all? I don't think there can be much doubt on that score – some are bound to go. The women and children and the older men, which will mean the majority of those who are in Changi, where the average age is about forty-five. On the other hand, will everybody go en bloc, which, according to one interpretation of International Law, is what should happen. The three of us are in an odd position though, and it's conceivable that we may be given the opportunity to stay. The Bishop would only consider it justified in his case, apart from his care of the Cathedral, if there were a slackening of some of the restrictions which have been and still are imposed, chief of which is his inability to get up-country. Unless he is given that permission his work is reduced to the barest minimum.

But the needs of the people here raises quite another point. Unless it became quite obvious that our continued liberty was to be only short-lived then we ought to stay for as long as we can. So much is being done and remains to be done that any sacrifice would be repaid. But then I have fewer ties and fewer sacrifices to make than Sorby or the Bishop. Our one hope is that we shall be given no option and that we shall be told what we are to do. It is of course possible that they will make a hard and fast age limit and stick rigidly to that without recognising the clergy as non-combatants, in which case I would stay anyway. One thing of which we can be farly sure is that the time may come when it will be an embarrassment to them to have any of us out at all, whoever and whatever we are.

If we do go it will be terribly bitter-sweet. We have known such love and affection from everybody that it will be hard to leave them. And it will mean that much which has been done will be undone. Even so, there are many who, in these last few months, have gained something in conviction and understanding which, under God, will never be lost. So there it is. We can only wait as patiently as we may and see what happens. If we stay there will still be the satisfaction of the work which we are able to do, and if we go there will be freedom and a heavy load of anxiety lifted from us and from our families.

THE TALE OF A TREE

Tuesday, September 15th. 6 Dyson Road. In just over a fortnight our whole mood has changed, principally because the violent uprooting of this last week has left little or no time for nostalgic brooding. Our story is really the 'Tale of a Tree', most of it absurdly small and petty. This was the way of it. During a night of storm about a month ago a tree, one of the Flames of the Forest variety of a great height and with very shallow roots, crashed down across the road about a hundred yards up the valley. The sloping wood at the back of Bishopsbourne had several similar trees, one of them not thirty yards from the house and directly behind it. If that had come down there would have been little of the house left and almost certainly nothing of us. As a precaution, the Bishop asked the Municipality to have a look at it to make sure that it was safe and that was the end of his part in the affair. After some time, without any warning, a squad of tree cutters arrived and work was begun. Apart from a natural interest in their simian antics, we thought no more about it.

BANISHED FROM BISHOPSBOURNE

Then came a telephone call from Dr. Chelliah. Captain Ogawa had been told to order us from Bishopsbourne, having fought and won a battle against our going to Changi, which was the original order. He maintained that the Bishop was of considerable assistance as long as he remained free, but the unknown 'assailant' insisted that expulsion from Bishopsbourne must be the price of freedom. The Bishop went straight off to the Military Police to try and discover details, since Chelliah knew nothing of the reasons for this sudden and totally unexpected move. The M.P.s were as much in the dark as we were and seemed to be most indignant that they should have heard nothing about it. They even advised the Bishop not to do anything until he was ordered to go in writing. On the whole they were surprisingly sympathetic, but we were still without any tangible explanation. Further telephone conversation with Chelliah brought no enlightenment, except that the Diocesan Office in the annexe at Bishopsbourne was also to move and that we had to be out immediately. If we were not, then steps would be taken to put us out. There seemed to be little argument in the face of that!

All this took place on the Monday (September 7th) and we began, on the following day, to hunt for another house. Nothing came to light until the Wednesday, which brought an offer from Paul Samy of this house, 6 Dyson Road, just off Thomson Road, not far from MacRitchie Reservoir. [Paul, an Indian judge, by his kindness and great thoughtfulness gave us six months of comfortable and very convenient lodging.]

On Thursday we had the first real news of the reason for the move. The Bishop and I drove out to Katong to see Paul Samy, who confirmed his offer and said that we could come here, at any rate for the time being. We got back to Bishopsbourne at about four to find that an officer had been down from the General's house at the back of us. He ordered work to stop on the tree and came into the house, demanding angrily by what right the Bishop had ordered the tree to be cut down, quite certain in his own mind that the Bishop was not really out and that Ah Sing was concealing him. Before he left he said that the Bishop was to go up to see the General at 10.30 on the following morning. Well, that was that! We at least knew what all the fuss was about, but it was obvious that, if we were to get everything away, no time must be wasted.

The next morning two lorries arrived early and we began to move all the office stuff. The Bishop and Sorby went off to see the General, only to be told that they were to return at 4.30. Then came another complication. A message from Ogawa came to the effect that we were to live at the Cathedral, which was later toned down, mercifully. If permission could be obtained from the Military Police, we would be allowed to go to Dyson Road. Even at the meeting in the evening, the General's A.D.C. still maintained that it was a question of the Cathedral or Changi. 'Chapter House', to them, seems to indicate a palatial and well appointed residence! Not only is the Chapter House filled with the Church Book Shop, but there are no conveniences at all and no room.

Now there is not a spare inch of space. Every available corner is crammed with books, files and every conceivable article of furniture. We bundled things onto the lorries as fast as we could. Files falling to pieces and spilling their contents all over the place, books belonging to the Bishop jumbled up with the Archdeacon's, Bernard Eales's and Middlebrook's. This went on for the whole of Friday and for most of Saturday.

In the evening the Bishop and Sorby again tramped up the hill to the General's house. They were received by the A.D.C., who insisted volubly and repeatedly that the Bishop had written to the Municipality ordering them to cut down the tree. Repeated assurances that no such letter had in fact been written were at long last successful, but not until the A.D.C. had tried every conceivable explanation. His information on the point seemed quite definite. The gardener would have been flattered had he known that it was even suggested that he had written it! When at last he was quite convinced that there had been a mistake, he became more genial and shifted his ground, pointing out that Bishopsgate was in the middle of a newly created military area.

At last we had got at the real reason for the move. If that was it, then it was possible to feel reconciled to going. Eventually and at long last, tea was brought and the meeting ended on a note several degrees more cordial than when it had begun. The Bishop put in a Parthian shot to the effect that he hoped we had not disturbed the General by our near presence. To which came the astounding reply, 'On the contrary, the General has been very pleased that you were able to live as his neighbour!'. But we suspect he must have strong animist views and the laying on of an axe is more than he can stand!

The meeting over, we finished clearing up one or two things and were just going off to friends for an evening meal and a rest when a harassed Alexander arrived. The house which the Bishop had got for him, for Ismael, and for the gardener and their families five miles out at Adam Road was being stubbornly defended by an irate Malay who had had no instructions to let anybody in and refused to budge. Sorby soothed him down and he eventually yielded and we were able, at long last, to get back into town. Dyson Road, when we got there, was in a state of chaos. The Bishop's bedroom and mine filled with trunks, stores, cases and whatnot. Ah Sing and Amah had nowhere to sleep and no electric light. Eventually all was peace and we flopped into bed dead beat.

The next morning we were still loading stuff onto the lorries at Bishopsbourne and the Cathedral's available storage space was getting less and less but, just as we were congratulating ourselves on driving the last load away, a real crisis developed. The Bishop had gone up to the house to see the last load out and had no sooner arrived than five Japanese officers appeared. Two lorries were standing outside almost ready to go. The sight of them loaded right up seems to have caused no little concern and many questions. Why were these things being taken away? Very wrong! Even wronger when they went into the house and saw two fans dismantled and ready to be removed! Jap to the Bishop: 'You are a British subject and all the furniture is enemy property.' Bishop: 'But this is Church property.' Jap: 'You are the Church.' Bishop: 'No. The Church is made up of Indians, Japanese, Chinese and British.' Jap: 'Oh!' More questionings, but eventually relations became more cordial, much to the Bishop's relief.

'TZT! TZT! MR. BISHOP'

One of the more coherent utterances of the early outburst was to the effect that he was under arrest. As he was not given his discharge, he assumes that he still is, ten days afterwards! The furniture, by this time, had all been taken off the lorries again, bringing to light yet another fan. The finder lifted the corner of a rug, saw it, shook his head and more in sorrow than in anger murmured 'Tzt, tzt, tzt! Mr. Bishop, Mr. Bishop!'. There was also a frig. on the lorry — not a very good one, as they were assured by the Bishop — the good one had already been removed! — but they insisted on keeping it. The long and short of it was that everything was allowed to go except the fans, the refrigerator, two wardrobes, two hideous hat and clothes stands which they made a special point of keeping, a sofa and armchairs, none of them with cushions. Eventually the Bishop bade them farewell and left them in possession, but not before the interpreter, who had been to see us several times before, patted him on the shoulder and said 'I am very sorry this had to happen to you. Very sorry!' A striking example of the contrast between the official and the individual, since it was he who had previously been shouting the odds!

Taking it by and large, the few bits and pieces which we had to leave behind more than made up for all that we had carried away. Even the pot plants from the front porch were transferred to the Cathedral where they adorn the west entrance. Back to Dyson Road, much more orderly after Ah Sing's efforts, for our first real meal in the new home.

A later development arising out of the move came on Monday, September 14th. The Bishop and I were both in the Cathedral when a Japanese officer arrived to inquire where we were living. We discovered from him that the wireless which we left at Bishopsbourne had been removed and they thought that we had got it. Firm denial from the Bishop. The Japanese insisted that we had it, to which we could only laugh and point out the danger involved. He still was not satisfied and said that, if it was brought back, nothing more would be said! While thanking him for such unprecedented munificence, we said that we still had not got it, but it seems that Bishops are no longer trustworthy after the 'deceit' of the fans! A search was insisted on, but when they got to Dyson Road with the Bishop they only had a very quick look round.

P.O.W. CONFIRMATIONS

Friday, September 18th. The Bishop was due at the old R.A.F. H/Q in Sime Road for confirmations in the two P.O.W. camps there and took me with him as his Chaplain. There is a strange inconsistency about the regulations governing the various camps. For about two months now he has had a letter from Ogawa which explains fully, not only who he is, but also the nature of Confirmation. It goes even further than that and requests that he should be given opportunities of going into the camps 'to cheer the spirits of the prisoners'. Until now he has had access to five of the camps which form a group under the direction of a Colonel Nakajima, who has been most anxious to help and has made visits possible to the two camps at Sime Road, and others at 4th Avenue, Bukit Timah Road, Caldecott Hill and Adam Road. When we visited the two hundred Singapore Volunteers at Bukit Timah Rifle Range, we went there every week for a service. Official permission was never even asked for, since the guards allowed us in without question. But since their move to Pasir Panjang our only attempt to go and see them has been foiled by the guards. Havelock and River Valley Road camps have so far proved impenetrable and at Tanjong Pagar we have been able to do no more than send in Bibles and books of various sorts.

The most productive single visit of the Bishop's was the one to the P.O.W.s in Changi with Captain Ogawa in June, when Sanday was ordained priest and there were over two hundred men confirmed. But, even with such limited facilities, a great deal has been done, largely through the enlightened attitude of Nakajima. At all events a total of about fifty were confirmed at the two camps at Sime Road. Both chapels, although complete contrasts in style and design, had been put up by the prisoners themselves since they had been in the camps.

Figure 5: A model of St. David's, Sime Road showing 'The Adoration of the Magi' and 'The Descent from the Cross', drawn by Stanley Warren when he was a P.O.W. there. The model is in the museum on the island of Sentosa, a holiday centre linked with Singapore by cable car. (The endpapers show these drawings in greater detail.)

THE STORY OF ST. DAVID'S CHURCH, SIME ROAD

Very many of those who spent part of their lives at Sime Road Camp, either as P.O.W.s or later as Civilian Internees, had reason to be grateful for the first of the two, St. David's Church. Prominent among their memories would be the striking, almost life-size figures drawn on panels behind and on either side of the altar, representing 'The Adoration of the Magi' and 'The Descent from the Cross'.

Stanley Warren, of the 135th Field Regt. R.A., in 1942 a young man in his early twenties, has written of how they came to be made.

'My regiment arrived in Singapore on January 12th, 1942, and was sent immediately into action in Johore. My particular job was O.P.A. (Observation Post Assistant) and I had to assist in directing artillery fire onto the enemy. The regiment acquitted itself bravely but suffered heavy casualties in artillery duels with the Japanese. Our last positions were near Bukit Timah and from there we marched to Changi on the 16th February, the day after the surrender.

We spent about a month at Changi before we were moved to Sime Road, where our allotted task was to cut roads to the Japanese War Memorial . . .

After a week or two the Chaplain asked me if I could do something about those screens which enclosed the sanctuary area of the otherwise open chapel. We searched the camp for materials and found only one tin of dark grey oil-based vehicle paint and arc lamps shattered by machine gun fire, from which I took the carbon rods. These when scraped yielded a coarse gritty charcoal, which gave a bluish grey tone when rubbed onto the whitewashed surface of the asbestos. The pencil drawings were quickly produced and approved by the Padre. I must have begun work early in April, 1942.

Surprisingly the drawings were readily accepted by the men, apart from one or two minor changes in poses which were incorporated. Since we ourselves are participating in the great events, some portraiture crept in, not in any deliberate self-conscious way. (The figure holding the head and shoulders of Christ is a self-

¶ portrait of the artist.) Most of the detail was taken from life. The tessellated floor I saw in a wrecked villa and there is the universal army tea bucket beside the Virgin and Child, who are in front of an open structure like the little church itself.'

'The message was simple enough', wrote Stanley Warren,
¶ ' "These things are happening here and now. Join in!".'

St. David's was very different from the second of the two chapels. This was larger with a delightful sanctuary. A sloping roof, bright riddle curtains and frontal, with a mediaeval window design painted on the east wall on either side of the altar. They were done by the man who produced the heraldic heading for the menu, with which we were provided at dinner.

The Bishop's visit was obviously one to which they had been looking forward for a very long time and was a red letter day in the life of the mess, when any excuse for a beano is snatched at. 'Beauty and the beast' was a masterpiece on the part of the cooks. Bully, with an egg on top, baked in a tin mug!

They were a delightful crowd. Col. Baker, Camp Commandant, and Knight, C.O. of one of the Norfolk Battalions; Col. Harvey, R.A.M.C., formerly in Hong Kong; Pusey, a Staff-Captain, and one of those who had been confirmed earlier. ('Dr. Pusey was the last Churchman in our family!') and the two Padres. Two Japanese guards who had seen the car outside came round at about 7.45, long after dark. The letter from Ogawa worked wonders.

Monday, September 21st. Heard of former Malayan Japanese just arrived back from internment in New Delhi, who said that conditions had been excellent. Men and women allowed to mix freely during the day and given small allowance. Consular officials were on parole and allowed six rupees a day. The food was good and they were quite satisfied and glad to be back for the sake of the wider fellowship. What a contrast!

Sunday, October 4th. St. Francis Day. A joyful day — over

thirty communicants at St. Hilda's early, nearly fifty there in all.

In the Cathedral for Evensong. The first time for many weeks. It's good to see so many of the European 'remnant' there. I took the Bishop's adult Sunday School before the service and talked about St. Francis, his ideals and the Anglican Order of Franciscans.

Monday, October 5th. It's now 9.30 p.m. (11.00 p.m. Tokyo time) and there is, as yet, no sign of Sorby and the Bishop. They went out early to a confirmation at the P.O.W. camp in 3rd, 4th and 5th Avenues, Bukit Timah Road, and should have been back about one and a half hours ago. The car has been misbehaving lately and that may be the reason, but it's getting late even for that now. Can't help being rather worried. So many things may have happened.

9.45 p.m. and all's well. The wanderers have returned after having a long evening's baptism, confirmation, food, boxing and wrestling, finishing up with the towing of the car by P.O.W.s along Bukit Timah Road in pitch darkness!

Friday, October 23rd. Large shipment of comforts a fortnight ago. The three of us and all those who are out were given a small share of them. Between us cigarettes, sugar, milk, cocoa, and about thirty vitamin caramels — vile! Largely composed of sawdust! The troops and those in Changi are in much more need of stuff than we are and we counted ourselves lucky to have as much as we did. The cigarettes are most welcome. Ten Virginian which used to be about 15^C are now 75^C–85^C. Max Factor lipstick is selling in the Black Market at $40 a stick. Parker fountain pens round about $50, tobacco $4 an ounce. A letter in today's paper speaks of M & B 693 selling at 50^C a tablet — probably more. Bicycles of any sort are unobtainable under about $70–$100. Luxury buyers nearly all Japanese. No one else has any money.

Gala night on Tuesday. An excellent party at the Schweizers, (he is Swiss Consul) to celebrate their 14th wedding anniversary. All the Swiss and Danes there, mostly male. A very cheerful crowd. We ran into a picket on the way down. They were at the Rochore Canal Road — Serangoon

Road junction with fixed bayonets. We had to go through
with our hands on high to be searched. Apparently they were
having an arms hunt. Eventually left at about 11.30 and
cycled brazenly home. Felt rather like debs. after our first
ball!

Life at Dyson Road as quiet and tranquil as ever and in
other respects just as busy. The confirmation has come and
gone — a glorious service last Sunday with the Cathedral full.
Unfortunately it poured with rain and many could not
come. About a hundred candidates — twenty of them mine
from the Cathedral congregation.

St. Hilda's becomes more and more a whole time job, or
should be, and there is much joy in it, although a sense of
how much remains to be done. At last the quarters at the
back of the church have been got ready for the Mitchells,
with fresh distemper everywhere and the asbestos roof sheet-
ing, shaken out by the near bomb misses, replaced. That
means that the whole of the upstairs will be free for our use,
with services in the church on the ground floor.

Ever since we started the Sunday School, three of us,
Violet and Myrtle Wilkins and I, have had breakfast at St.
Hilda's after the eight o'clock communion service. For the
last few Sundays others have joined us and it looks as though,
before long, we shall have developed — spontaneously, that's
the best part — a regular parish breakfast.

Friday, October 23rd. The financial position is extremely
good. It is fairly certain that we shall be able to give the
Bishop $60 a month, probably more. Our policy is to carry
a reserve of $30. At the end of September we kept back a
further $28 to offset the cost of repairs and renovations to
the quarters into which Mr. Mitchell is moving. The work has
been done for $16 and he will be moving downstairs in a day
or two — not before time either! I estimate our average
monthly income as being $100–$120, which should mean a
balance of $70–$90 a month.

It astonishes me how they are able to do it, but apart
from the satisfaction of knowing they are giving from a sense
of responsibility towards their Church, it also means there is
more money.

Sunday, October 25th. Thirteen of us for breakfast after Church this morning with the idea of discussing plans for the Fellowship.

The Sunday morning programme will now be: 8.00 Celebration; 8.45 Breakfast; 9.30 Study Group; 10.45 Sunday School; 4.30 Choir Practice.

It means a heavy morning but, with transport as difficult as it is, the only way to fit everything in is to have things following one another. More and more I come to love the place and the people. There is so much of God for them to learn, so much of the life of love for them to live, with its joy and comradeship. O Master, Friend and Brother be with them to guide, defend and cheer them. Build up in them that life of love. May Thy life be their life, Thou in them, they in Thee.

Saturday, October 31st. Bunting Potger and Birdie Mitchell married at St. Hilda's, the first since the surrender.

CONFIRMATION AT CHANGI GAOL

Monday, November 2nd. A day long to be remembered. After many months the Bishop has been allowed to go to Changi Gaol for a confirmation, and, as the pass allowed him to take one other as his Chaplain, I was able to go with him. We passed the guards at 2 o'clock, the time allowed on the pass, and immediately were under the gaunt grey shadow of the Gaol. High walls, massive blocks of buildings, the severity of the lines increased rather than broken by the long rows of narrow slits high in the wall of each cell. So many times before I had seen it there and always — perhaps callously — with no more than a passing thought. But now — what were we to expect?

We had heard so much of life there, of block and yard and stairwell, but still imagination baulked at reality. Past a returning wood gathering fatigue we arrived at the main gates guarded by two armed Sikhs. After whispered injunctions from one of the wood fatigue that we were to bow right and left, we went in across a narrow space between the outer walls and the buildings and then into the entrance

117

courtyard. A Sikh guard took us to the Commandant's office, where the Bishop's pass was examined and from there back into the entrance yard, where we were greeted by Bernard Eales, Jack Bennitt (both looking well) and Archdeacon Graham White (not so well). Arthur Worley, the Judge, had told us some time ago that he had aged and was very tired. He is a good deal thinner than when I saw him at Bidadari some time ago and I began to see the reason for the fears for him, if he were to go down with one of the prevailing ailments such as dysentery.

Dr. Eleanor Hopkins was waiting to take us through to the Women's Camp. Most people are loud in their praises of her as their Commandant and say that she has done and is doing a difficult job extremely well. She looks well enough, though tired. People began flocking round us as soon as we arrived, with a real warmth of welcome. Mrs. Graham White looking better and more rested than I have seen her since I came to Singapore, and Mrs. Nelson as charming as ever. They had prepared the three candidates and made all the arrangements for the service held in the dining room, with its long concrete tables, concrete benches on either side, with a short cross table at the top where the altar had been arranged with much love and care. About eighty people had come, so many of them I knew, exchanging broad grins. There were three candidates, one adult and two children.

All the Harris children, Eurasians who had come in with their mother from Katong about six weeks before, looking very much fitter than when they were interned. There is no doubt that children are much better looked after at Changi than they can ever be outside. Special food and care had certainly done wonders for Helen and the others. It was after the service that the greetings really began, Mrs. Millard, dewy-eyed and a little thinner; Dr. Elliott, our Missionary Doctor, looking wonderfully well in spite of her years and her health; Muriel Clark and Beatrice Sherman, both Missionary Nurses of ours; Miss Josephine Foss of the Pudu English School in Kuala Lumpur; Mrs. Burgess, Mrs. White, Mrs. Allen and Mrs. Keet, who were all at the Customs House in Singapore with their husbands for three months after the surrender; Molly Bell and her baby, born two months before in Kandang

Kerbau Hospital. Mrs. Harris, Helen's mother, looking quite settled. Her baby had died at one o'clock in the morning of the day when, seven hours later, she was interned. Mrs. Symons and her daughter were both looking very well. Mrs. Macmarine came and shook me warmly by the hand. Her story is one of quiet fortitude. Mrs. Goodridge, Lydia Edge and Mrs. Mackintosh-Whyte came up. She was delighted to hear something of her husband whom we used to see regularly when the Singapore Volunteers were still at Bukit Timah Rifle Range P.O.W. Camp. Several of the General Hospital Sisters spoke to us and finally Mrs. Williams, with her daughter, Pat. She was most anxious that we should tell her son, Brian, still free in Singapore, that we had seen her. Just before we were going Dr. Worth took me off to see Dr. Smallwood, who was very concerned to have news of her husband in the Volunteers. Word seems to have got round that many of them have left the Island, but what can one say in the absence of definite news. That is the only thing which is any comfort and I had none for her.

Time was all too short and there was much to be done in the Men's Camp, so back we went into the entrance yard and from there past the kitchen, through a maze of corridors to a small grassy yard where we were to have the confirmation. The twenty-four candidates and the congregation were already there, about a hundred and fifty altogether, while more kept drifting in. The altar had been erected against one of the walls, with a most striking reredos of the Nativity painted by Walker, head of Singapore Schools Art Department. To one side were the choir, numerous and well drilled, led by the Cathedral Choir Master, E. A. Brown, now a thin man after losing five stone, but he still looks erect and fit enough. Denis Soul, as of old, was the organist.

The Bishop, I felt, both here and in the Women's Camp, was not entirely happy in his address. There had been the difficult question in his mind as to the right note to strike. Whether to speak to the point with counsel on the way in which the restrictions of confinement should be met but, apart from the presumption of this from someone who was not having to undergo these restrictions, probably everything that could have been had already been said on the subject.

Another course would have been to have enlarged on 'The Lord looseth men out of prison', which the Archdeacon had had printed on the Confirmation cards, speaking of the prison of the closed mind, but he felt too strongly about this to be able to trust himself. He finally decided to talk on the three-fold question for Peter with the emphasis on the meaning of personal allegiance to Christ.

Those confirmed were John Burnham, Maxwell Russell Holgate, W. A. Gibson, W. Annesley-Young, J. R. Skipper, Eric de Broise, W. J. Duncan, T. H. Dutton, A. J. Hathaway, A. H. L. Lamman, C. G. Mawson, Val Murie, E. W. Mumford, A. W. Pinnock, H. W. Reid, Norman Symons, J. L. Woods, A. F. Carter, A. F. Greig, C. J. A. Haines, L. W. King, J. E. Prewett and H. G. Turner. The ages of those confirmed showed fairly clearly the average age of those at Changi. In their case it was 40.8, with only six who were below that. For the whole camp I believe the average is rather higher.

All through the service I was seeing more and more people whom I knew — Norman Jarrett, Horrocks, Paul Verdayne, Evan Powell Evans, Keet, Amstutz, Harris and many others.

It was during the service that we saw evidence of the first essential of Changi equipment. Some sort of stool is a must. Seats don't exist, and if you want to sit it is either on the ground or on concrete, unless you have your own seat to carry about with you. The only other essential seems to be a pair of shorts, though even they might be dispensed with! Everywhere we went people were either coming from or going to a lecture, with note-books under their arms. It is this continuous moving throng which remains as the most lasting impression. The Bishop summed up the effect of the whole place in four words — 'Busyness, noise, boredom and bustle'. Everybody seemed to have something to do and seemed to do it with the maximum amount of noise, but it was all busyness for its own sake as an escape from boredom.

It was in 'D' yard, one of the two smaller yards, though quite a good size none the less, that we realised for the first time the enormous number of people in the Gaol. The word had gone round that we were to be there after the service and for half an hour greeting followed greeting without a break. I was amazed to find how many people I knew and even then

*Figure 6: ' 'D' Yard before a Church service' by W. R. M. Haxworth.
He was particularly struck by the cross on the altar standing out against
the grey wall.*

there were numbers I didn't see. The general impression
I got was of their fitness. A great many, like so many of the
women, had put on weight, others, though in the minority,
had lost. But the most encouraging thing was to find people
like 'Bird' Nelson and Pendlebury, of whom we had had bad
reports, looking better than I had been led to believe. Perhaps
the day when we shall go there ourselves may not be so far
distant, so there will be ample time to speak of people individually. But this day of sudden revelation and the people
whom I saw will always remain clear in my mind.

Just as faces flashed before my eyes and were gone, so do
names — and faces — run through my mind now. Chris
Windle, and Hughes of Kuala Lumpur,who, afraid that I
would not recognise him, grasped his beard firmly at the chin.
Others were Jenkins of Oxford's St. Edmund Hall and of the
Customs, John Burnham, newly confirmed, Captain Maddox,
eight-five and the oldest inhabitant, with messages for
O'Loughlin, Charlie Maddox of Katong, as thrilled to have
news of his wife, Doris, as she was of him afterwards, 'Hock'
as courtly and delightful as ever, Walters, looking fitter than
when I saw him last, Mervyn Sheppard, Colin King, Harris the
warder, Mervyn Manby and several others I had met when

they were at the Miyako, Keet and Spinks, both former Lay
Readers at St. Hilda's, delighted to hear of everything happening there. Alan Ker insisted on taking full particulars for
Civil Liability of my car which I *haven't* lost. We are still
using it! Others were Dr. Allen, Bill Vincent, Jack Hill, Eddy
Upton, Peter Ellis, as bronzed as a Malay, Haines and
Osborne,Barnett, Robertson of the A.R.P., Rendle of Toc H
and 'Tiny' Richards, who pressed me to take a little Balkan
Sobranie for the Bishop. Like a mutt I didn't reward the
generosity of the thought and persuaded him to keep it,
forgetting that it's sometimes more blessed, and gracious, to
receive than to give.

David Coney of the Customs was another I saw, but the
person who impressed me most deeply was David Molesworth,
with a thick close-trimmed beard as a frame for the most
astonishing peace and calm in the blue of his eyes. The sight
of him gave me an impression that here was the one quiet
place in Changi. David, I think, has always been like that.
His spiritual depth is rooted in and fed by his love of the
small things of God's world and of an interest in and concern
for individuals. His ministry as a doctor could never be anything but blessed, especially when it is backed by such a keen
sense of the ridiculous and a delightful subtlety of humour.

At last the time came for us to go. I had seen practically
nothing of the Gaol itself. I still do not know what the
inside of a cell looks like! The time we had was all too short
and, after the Bishop had had a hurried consultation with
the Archdeacon, we were off again, grateful, far, far more
than that, for our greeting from so many friends, cheered by
their cheerfulness, depressed by the sordid and close-thronged
condition of their lives, bewildered by so many new impressions, exhausted physically, mentally and emotionally.

Another sorry sight greeted us as we joined the Changi
Road — hundreds of prisoners from Java — Dutch, Eurasians
and Javanese, standing by the side of the road, looking
puzzled and disconsolate. Many have been brought here in
the last few weeks.

Slowly we drove back along the Changi Road trying to
recover our balance and sort out our impressions. At the top
of rising ground far away in the distance we could see the

spire of the Cathedral. But was it? Might that not be St. Mary's, Oxford? And surely that dome was the Radcliffe Camera and the hill on which we stood beloved Headington? Would that it were! Do I wish that though? There is a large part of me that does, but another part would not be anywhere else in the world but here. There is a stark quality of life for so many people that, for the first time in their lives, they are forced to be real. So much artificiality has been stripped away that there is a longing for solid ground and firm foundations, however incoherent that longing may be. I shall always remember in Kuala Lumpur when I was so anxious to get back here to Singapore, one of the Roman Catholic brothers saying 'Don't worry where you are. Do your job, God's work, wherever it may be.'

In the evening on our way back from town we called in to see George Cessford, who gave us news of more postcards, this time with an unlimited number of words. This was much more to the point and meant that we should be able to give a much clearer idea of our real circumstances and of the life which we are living. Well over two hundred words were crammed on to mine, all of them legible. It is an enormous comfort to know that, however long it may take, they will be learning something of me. That is my only fear — that they will be anxious.

It is strange to think that being in Singapore at the time of the siege was probably safer than the voyage out here with the threat of submarines and surface raiders in the Atlantic and Indian Ocean. Those who suffered most were those who left Singapore by sea in the last week when, from all accounts, the casualties were appalling. Those who did survive had, in a great many cases, ghastly experiences. Bombing, shelling and fire, with all that they mean on board ship. Hours in the water or in open boats, sometimes days on small deserted islands — so many stories are current that there must be some foundation for them.

FIRST ANNIVERSARY OF THE OUTBREAK OF WAR

Tuesday, December 8th. A year ago today war started and what a year of new experience, changes, fresh responsibilities

Figure 7: The baptism of Diana Macnab in Singapore Cathedral in 1942. Her mother, Sandy Macnab, had been brought from Changi Gaol for the birth in Hospital. Those present were (top, left to right) Brian Williams, Bishop Leonard Wilson, George Cessford, Norman Coulson; (bottom) Dr. Cicely Williams, Sandy Macnab with Diana, Catherine de Mowbray, and the author.

and new friendships made. For me a year of growth. No one with the greater part of his effective life before him could have gone through it and be quite the same at the end of it as he was at the beginning. The fellowship of St. Hilda's is the first of its kind that I have known and I find that I have been able to respond to it at least in some measure. These months and all that has happened have given me a sense of Christian urgency and also, through the way in which we have been allowed to share in the sorrows and sufferings of so many, a new understanding. So many vital personal problems have arisen, crying out for a solution, in many cases the fundamental problem of the means of existence. Doors have been opened to us which might always have remained shut. One of the best things in our life is that we are looked to for help and guidance. The satisfaction is so much the greater when we are able to leave help where before there was none.

Some of the young have problems demanding solution, problems which affect the whole family. Often trouble is caused by an obstructive tyrant of a father, who hasn't the wit to see that it is impossible to give his children freedom with one hand and to take it away with the other. In the past, when children had few opportunities of mental development — especially girls — the parental claim to absolute and complete obedience was reasonable enough. But parents themselves have brought about a change. They send their children to schools where some, if not necessarily all of them, begin to think for themselves. From there they may go on to Raffles College, where the process is continued and enlarged. New ways of thinking, new ideas and, for some, a completely new outlook on life, a new life even, as a result. Parents, most often fathers, are sometimes surprised and even resent the freedom they themselves have given their children.

Friday, December 11th. Yesterday evening the three of us were due at Seton Close with the Swiss crowd. After six days of continuous heavy rain there was bad and heavy flooding. In the morning a high tide prevented the water coming down from inland from getting away. This caused floods three-feet deep in the centre of the town. At the far end of Whitley Road we found that the big open drain, twelve-feet deep and twenty-feet across, which runs between Bukit Timah and Dunearn Roads, had overflowed. There was three-feet of water at the Stevens Road crossing. Right plumb in the middle of the floods there was a loud phut and the wheeze of escaping air as my back tyre collapsed. With best trousers well up above my knees I waded through with Sorby while the Bishop ploughed his way through on the 'pink peril', his resplendent machine, a present, like so many other things, from the Jews. He and Sorby went on and on with their bridge and it was 2.30 local time before we were home!

The floods did a good deal of damage in the low lying districts. Poor old Mrs. Ganno, in the Improvement Trust houses down by the river, was swept off her feet by a sudden rush of water and for most of the rest of the night she was walking about in three-feet of water, salvaging what she could. The next morning, as though she had not had enough with the household goods packed away in boxes all sodden, she had to deal with a cobra which she found in her back yard! And all that at the age of seventy-five or more!

THE WONDER OF CHRISTMAS

Tuesday, January 5th, 1943 A.D. Christmas and another year, with many thoughts of the old and hopes for the new. What a fantastic year it has been. It started badly enough but, in spite of all that has happened, there has been much of real personal happiness to offset the loneliness of separation from home. Opportunities of work have been boundless and I wouldn't have been anywhere else if I had had the opportunity.

One picture stood out in my mind during all the talk of possible repatriation — the agonising moment when, if it had happened, we should have looked our last on this Singapore which I have come to love. Even the thought of so much which would be waiting for us away from here would not ease the pain of that parting, if it should come. Even now we cannot be sure that we may not go to Changi and quite soon. Bobby Waddle and Philip Sands, both very good friends of ours, went with some others from the Electrical department on Boxing Day, and others have been told that they are to be ready to go. But to go now would be with different thoughts and feelings.

Six months ago our work had hardly begun. St. Hilda's can now stand on its own feet and, if I did go, there would be others who would be able to continue what has been started. John Handy, as lay-reader, could carry a good deal more of the responsibility of things, although he is already of the greatest help. The Wilkins, Nellie Chen and Juliana Chan, Noel Scharenquivel and his wife, Sandy Hope, Humphrey Potger and several others, are in their different ways a really first class nucleus and St. Hilda's owes a great deal to them. The thought of leaving them is hateful, and particularly those who need special training, the dozen or so confirmation candidates and the children, now over eighty of them. But in many respects those who are already leaders there would benefit from the opportunity of leadership. They feel that they have helped to build up something worth maintaining.

Christmas was a case in point. I had, it's true, given one or two suggestions, but they did the work. This was the Christmas programme at St. Hilda's.

Christmas Eve — Crib Service in the evening, the crib a framework intertwined with narrow strips of coconut fronds to form the roof and sides. The St. Andrew's Hospital figures looked really lovely.

The 'gift box' fixed to the back of my bicycle was filling up in Katong as I started home for Dyson Road. All the same it was not so full that I could not make room for the loudly protesting duck shyly handed over for our Christmas by eight-year-old Donald Palmer. It quacked its way across town to join several other birds already penned in our garden.

Christmas Day — Celebration at seven with about twenty communicants, and again at eight, fully choral with seventy-five communicants, the church overflowing with a good many standing outside in the porch. The breakfast afterwards was a terrific success. There must have been about twenty of us there altogether, everyone in very good form. The room was garlanded and looking grand. The Church was full for the Children's Carol Service and how we sang! They *are* such a cheerful lot and I would *not* be anywhere else.

Boxing Day Social — A great success and a completely co-operative effort. There were upwards of a hundred and sixty there — a good many Roman Catholics very impressed. We started off with about half an hour of games which went riotously well and then got down to the serious business of the concert, a scratch programme, much of it unrehearsed. The highlights were the Bishop with a burlesque of 'I was a pale young curate then', Bertie Tan, a conjuror of international fame, who was brilliant, and a really beautiful performance of Drinkwater's *The Travelling Man* by Nellie Chen, Mavis Wilkins and Yahya Cohen.

The simplicity and freshness were most moving. Nellie as

the mother played a difficult part with real sympathy, and overcame two problems which might have been very real stumbling blocks. The part was one which lent itself to burlesque, but there was no trace of it in her portrayal. The far greater difficulty lay in the ending. Within a very short space of time she had somehow to bridge the gulf between the heartless woman who turns the stranger from her door and the mystic who, seeing who it is she has turned away, has seen too late. But she managed the change, principally because she had shown us the mystic so clearly in the earlier part and the vividness of the vision once seen and so eagerly reawaited.

Yahya, too, caught the spirit of the play and, as the Travelling Man, was excellent. It would be difficult to point to any faults in his performance.

It was Mavis as the child who surprised us all. Her gaiety, her enthusiasm and her complete unselfconsciousness were astonishing, and many of us will remember for a long time to come her mock-ride to the Golden Mountains with the Travelling Man, singing a gay lilting tune as they went. It was a beautiful performance and the greatest tribute to the three of them was the complete stillness with which it was received by the audience, who were a very mixed bag.

The social as a whole was a great success and those who were there seemed to enjoy it. Food and drink were plentiful; there seemed to be no end to either. At all events we have set a high standard and have now got a reputation to live up to. I've said nothing about our Christmas tree. It was magnificent — so tall that it was pushing up against the ceiling — tinselled and garlanded and all.

Yes, it was a good Christmas and crowned on the following Sunday evening, when there must have been nearly a thousand people in the Cathedral for a United Service of Nine Lessons and Carols. The crowds were so great that even the sanctuary was full, with people standing two and three deep in front of the altar. In the middle, by chance, was Alexander, the Bishop's Indian Secretary, his wife beside him holding their baby in her arms. It was a perfect Nativity tableau. With the carols and hymns sung in seven different languages, it was a stupendous occasion!

PAROLE FORMS SIGNED

A recent development for us has been the signing of parole forms on December 18th. The three of us went to Count Asahi's office. He is Controller of Enemy Civilians in the whole of Malaya and Sumatra. We had to take this oath:

> 'I do hereby swear in the name of Almighty God that, on being permitted as an enemy alien to live outside the Internment Camp, I will not attempt to escape nor commit any act which may benefit the enemies of the Empire of Japan, nor will I infringe any of the conditions mentioned on the next page.'

Signed.   18th December, 2602
[the year according to the Japanese calendar]

The only difference which this makes to us is that we have to be in by 8.30 local time and wear a badge — a white star in a red circle (first prize in the horse show!). The Bishop has a concession and is not restricted with regard to time in case we are ever called out late at night, so no real change in our way of life is involved.

Tuesday, January 19th. Private letters through the post to be written in Japanese only after July 1st.

There has been a big 'carrying into captivity' during the last fortnight. Weston, O'Toole, Curran, Freddy Hill, George Cessford, Alec Macdonald, Sam Urquhart, Tommy Hodgson, Cameron, Webb and a good many others, more than twenty in all, went in on the 16th. Bobby Waddle, Philip Sands and half a dozen others went to Changi about a fortnight ago and yesterday, Harry Miller, Ivor Salmond, Wade, Smith, Byron, Dr. Cicely Williams and Mrs. de Mowbray went back after their three months in Asahi's office.

Now there are only about twenty of us left. So far we know nothing of any move to intern us. The general impression seems to have been that this large-scale internment was brought about by the direct intervention of the military authorities, so it is possible that we may go at any time.

On January 8th we performed a nativity play in mime at

the Cathedral. So many were unable to get in that we did it again a week later, when the crowd was even larger. There was not an empty seat half an hour before the start. People standing everywhere.

The Bishop has heard from an unknown source that a new English news broadcast to Australia was inaugurated on Friday. Every night personal messages are sent to relatives in Australia. His to Mary, Susan, Tim, Martin and Jennifer Ann (who turned out to be a boy, James!) was the first to go. Mary will cable home that I am with him since he mentioned in the message that Sorby and I were out and working.

About five months ago a list of forbidden books and records was circulated. The announcement was made in the papers a few days ago that there was to be another list shortly of about a thousand records.

Thursday, March 4th. Today's baptism by the Bishop at St. Hilda's was very special. Fifteen-year-old Lee Siat Moy took the name Grace, with Sorby Adams, Nellie Chen, Juliana Chan and Humphrey Potger as godparents.

Monday, March 8th. In spite of feeling periodically that we have been under close scrutiny and supervision and the objects of a good deal of enquiry, we are still at large, with hopes of remaining so, at least for some time. The work goes on, we have still had no news from any of our families, nor have we been able to send any more postcards or wireless messages. Here are the British Europeans still free: Norman Coulson and Bill Ross running the Municipal Workshops, Clarke and Wilgress in the Analyst's Laboratory, Gater running a Malaria Research Laboratory, Green preparing vaccines and anti-toxins, Williamson, opthalmic surgeon at the Tan Tock Seng Hospital, Lander, Blakemore and Canton, health officers, Ernie Sloan and Hylton running the Power Station at Alexandra Hospital, Corner and Birtwhistle at the Museum, Holtum at the Botanical Gardens, Borehill and Turnbull at the Power Station. Auten, Wilbraham and Salter in the Opium Packing Plant, and the three of us, Sorby, the Bishop and myself, twenty-three in all.

As far as we know at the moment there is no suggestion of

any of us going to Changi in the very near future, though warning when it does come is likely to be short.

LIFE AT ST. HILDA'S

Reading through some of the things I have written here, it is good to find how a lot of the early planning at St. Hilda's has already borne fruit. We have built up a really good spirit on Sunday mornings. The breakfast is becoming more and more popular. There were twenty-five there last Sunday morning, more than half of those who attended the service, and for the last three Sundays there have been more than twenty at the Study Group. The Choir is very strong numerically, though not as yet technically. But then most of them have had next to no training or experience. They certainly make up for this by their keenness. Noel Scharenquivel has taken on the job of choirmaster. With three organists, things are quite promising.

Saturday, March 13th. For the first time I am having the satisfaction of building up the 'common life'. Each member of the body is a limb with its own part to play. Rough places have to be smoothed out, co-ordination between one limb and another fostered and nurtured — and all for what? That they may each and together come to know God and that they may each and together build up a small corner of His Kingdom. St. Hilda's has become precious to a great many of them, though I doubt whether more than a very few of them begin to see what is really behind it all. But they are beginning to learn something of the Fellowship of Service.

John Handy is becoming a real pastor. He visits regularly and I have no doubt of his love and the sense of mission which he feels he has. He has changed a very great deal during the last year. He has always, I think, at heart been a humble-minded man, but his shyness and reticence have led him to put up a barrier which has seemed at times overbearing. But now that has gone and he has a new simplicity. If, as the Bishop has half suggested, he were to be ordained to the priesthood in the event of our going to Changi, he will have difficulties I know. They will be nothing like as great as they would have been a year ago. His ordination, if it should come, will only be advancing what would, at any rate, have happened after the war. He has felt increasingly during the last six months that he is called to the priesthood. As far as his ministry at St. Hilda's is concerned, he knows them all a great deal better now and they have more confidence in him.

CHANGI DRAWS NEARER

Tuesday, March 16th. From what I have written, it is obvious that our mood is one of possible change. The position of the Christian Federation of the Churches has become a little obscure. Last week we heard from Watanabe, the Director of Religion and Education, through Dr. Chelliah, that the Federation is to be dissolved. The reasons and implications we have as yet no means of judging. But together with this rather strange decision, which has not actually been implemented, has come a close inquiry of the functions and duties of a Bishop and his clergy. In his report, and at a good many other times, the Bishop has said that he would be perfectly willing to be interned as soon as the Japanese Church sends a Bishop from Japan. But the latest suggestion, almost amounting to a proposal, is that Chelliah should go back to Japan and that he should be consecrated Bishop. The whole project would clearly be dictated and sponsored by government and not by the Nippon Sei Ko Kai, the Anglican Church in Japan.

We have been wondering what Watanabe meant when he told Chelliah that in a day or two he would see why it was necessary for there to be another Bishop here. From another source, supposed to come straight from the Japanese head of one of the Municipal departments, we hear that all those who are still out are staying out 'for the duration'. And another report coming from Auden says that repatriation is still very much to the fore as a possibility. Which, if any, of these is true we do not know. Nor do we know where and/or whether we shall be affected by any of them.

Saturday, March 27th. On Monday morning we go to Changi at forty-eight hours notice!

Sunday, March 28th, 1943. Yesterday was a day of frantic preparation. When telephoned by the Bishop, John Handy accepted with calm and great humility that, on the following day the plans he and the Bishop had discussed against our internment were to be given effect. There cannot be many men who have been informed, and have so graciously accepted, that within twenty-four hours they are to be made deacon and ordained priest.

Word flew round Singapore and, by the time of the service on Sunday morning, the Cathedral was packed. Then and later, in the evening, there was pandemonium after the service, as crowds flocked round us, not only to say goodbye in most touching farewells, but pressing bundles of money on us, either for ourselves or with requests that we take them to their friends in Changi.

I managed a quick dash out to Katong for special goodbyes to one or two families after the evening service at the Cathedral and got home to Dyson Road to find the house full of last minute visitors. Eventually we were on our own, with time to sort out our own packing — what was going to Changi with us, which of our belongings were going to the Cathedral for storage (there hardly seemed time to wonder or worry when we should see them again!), who had given us money and for whom and much else besides. At last we fell into bed, but not for long. It had to be an early start in the morning.

Monday, March 29th. The lorry arrived at first light and the earliest of our visitors soon after it. Eventually we were loaded and the very special farewell said to the faithful Ah Sing, the Bishop's house-boy, who had come with the Wilsons from Hong Kong, and, with him, saying goodbye to all our visitors. First stop was to be at St. Hilda's in Katong. We had told them we would come. It was one of the saddest, most moving moments of this whole miserable business of pulling up our roots and leaving them on their own. So many were there at St. Hilda's of those with whom we had shared so much during the past year. It was, perhaps, as well that time was short. There, outside St. Hilda's, the Bishop prayed and blessed us. With such a heavy load of sadness, theirs and ours, we soon left. It was a silent journey to Changi.

Section Three

---•◦•---

Internment in Changi Gaol

'THE DOUBLE TENTH'
October 10th, 1943

March, 1943 to May, 1944

None of this section was written at the time in Changi but some years later, much of it based on earlier recollections, written and recorded.

With acknowledgement to Archives and Oral Dept., Singapore

Figure 8: An aerial view of Changi Gaol, c.1942.

Internment in Changi Gaol

THREE GO TO PRISON

Monday, March 29th, 1943. The visit to Changi with the Bishop for the confirmation in November, 1942, was some preparation for what was to come At least I knew what the inside of the Gaol looked like. However, it's one thing to come, to observe and to go away again. It's quite another to become a part of Changi as I was soon to find.

We were to live on the second floor of 'B' block. Even on the short escorted trip up the dark metal stairway we saw the acute overcrowding, one of Changi's major problems. Every inch of the floor of the large workshop we passed was carefully measured and occupied. The space at the foot of the stairs, little more than a thoroughfare — that too was allocated and lived in.

Above, on each of three floors, were forty-four cells. Originally designed to hold one prisoner, three were now crammed into every one of them — and they were very small, no more than 11' by 7', with a large concrete sleeping slab in the centre. In every cell, too, was an oriental type water closet, without a pedestal. This restricted space still further. By general agreement this was given only limited use, other facilities in the Gaol also being available.

Arrived at the door of cell B3 40 — (Sorby was housed on the other side of the landing) — it would be an overstatement to say the Bishop and I were 'greeted' by an elderly 'Tommy' Thomson. Hardly a word was said, but this very reserved Scots accountant from a firm of mining engineers in Kuala Lumpur proved a wonderful friend in the two and a half years we spent together.

We had done our best to heed warnings of people from Changi, whom we had met while they were patients at the Miyako Hospital. Remembering limitations of space in the

Gaol we had taken in with us as few essentials as we could. Even so unpacking was a nightmare in so small a cell, which already had an occupant.

However, we had good reason to appreciate the letter which had been smuggled out in the middle of 1942 to those of us who were still free. When our turn came we found it an invaluable 'Thomas Cook's Guide to Changi'. Apart from differences of diet we found that little had changed during the eight months since the letter was written. As a contemporary account it does capture the atmosphere and feel of internment. Albeit, it does show life in Changi at an early stage, a mere shadow of later intolerable conditions.

PERSONAL GUIDE TO THE GAOL

The Cooler.
17th July, 1942.

'This is written to show you the true conditions in this small town. So far we have suffered no feeling of incarceration. Everything, of course, is new to us and naturally full of interest and we wander about like a bunch of rubber-necks, seeing the sights. The food is much better than we expected and we are really satisfied. Heavy fatigues come round twice weekly, mainly bringing in firewood for the kitchens.

Educational facilities are numerous. Every modern European and Asiatic language has its teacher. Latin is taught, so are astronomy, mechanics, hydraulics, higher mathematics, theology and English literature, to name only a few. Debates and lectures are daily occurrences. Concerts are excellent and of a fairly high standard. Vaudeville is remarkable for its variety, not to mention obscenity. The orchestra of eleven professional performers leaves nothing to be desired, while the male voice choir commands both respect and loud applause. Churches of all denominations hold meetings daily, both morning and evening.

In respect of all these activities a stool is not so much a luxury as essential. It goes with you everywhere. Wood is at a premium and canvas unobtainable, so bring one in with you. If you can lay hands on an electric kettle bring it. Extra points can be wired up. Files, a hacksaw, odd woodworker's tools, screws, nails and the like you would find a real boon.

Try and decide the classes you would like to attend and buy the text books you will need. Get hold of a supply of exercise books and pencils.

Bring in whatever food you can. It will help supplement, sweeten or add taste to the eternal rice.

I have never come across such optimism as there is here. Rumours are legion. The accepted time fixed for the end of hostilities is from six to twelve weeks! Rumour insists that Tobruk has been recaptured; we are nearly into Tripoli; the Japanese fleet is finished and there is hardly one of their nationals left in China!'

Equipped with this information the Bishop, Sorby and I realised how much we were better off than we would have been without it.

Looking back to the day of arrival, as we emerged from the chaos of cell 40 on B3 we met people we knew at every turn. Finding our way about we tried to stand back from the four prison blocks and to see them in some sort of perspective. Our judgement didn't match that of Mary Thomas in her excellent book on Changi, *In the Shadow of the Rising Sun*, published in Singapore. 'Aesthetically' she said 'it was a very fine building, even when seen from within the compounds, being beautifully designed and proportioned. Its satisfying appearance, where there was so little that was pleasant to look at, might be called one of the amenities of our lives.'

We were going to be too well aware of its disadvantages to be able to arrive at such a detached view. In wet weather the rain, often accompanied by a breeze, or worse, blew in. In prolonged dry spells there were problems of dust, even though the concrete prison was comparatively new. In spite of being built on slightly raised ground only a mile from the sea the cell blocks were so airless at night that many people preferred to sleep out of doors. That meant a mad rush for overcrowded cover in not infrequent and sometimes heavy rain showers. High on the list of disadvantages were the peculiar acoustics of the Gaol. Every sound was amplified. It could be and usually was indescribably noisy.

By many we were asked then as we have been since 'Why were you interned when you were?'. The question should more properly be 'How did you get away with it for so long?'. Thirteen months was a long time in an atmosphere where the Military Police, the Kempei-tai, were everywhere. We knew we were being watched and that there were several times when strong pressure was being brought to have us interned. We were often very anxious for the safety of our friends. Some of them, who came frequently to the house, told us they knew they were under suspicion. In some ways it was a relief to join the more than 3000 in Changi. My camp number was 3186!

The greatest regret and anxiety was in having to leave behind so many people with whom, for the past year, we had shared so much. In fact we need not have worried. As we heard later the Church, especially at the Cathedral and at St. Hilda's in Katong, grew in numbers and in strength.

In the evening of our first day in Changi, Monday, March 29th, 1943, the last of three performances of Sutton Vane's 'Outward Bound' was given on the open-air stage in a corner of the Main Yard. It was a good introduction to the entertainment world of Changi, although it was the last time the outdoor stage was to be used.

Not long before our arrival Ted Hebditch, Electrical Engineer for the Gaol, had been asked to put up a small discreet illuminated 'V' sign on the middle of the proscenium arch of the stage. Unfortunately it was not discreet enough. The Japanese took violent objection. Not only did they order its removal, and the whole stage with it, but Hebditch and the electricians provided a typical example of capricious punishment given by the Japanese at Changi. They were put under arrest and made to kneel on wooden strips while Sikh guards beat them across the shoulders with riot poles. They were then shut up for twenty-four hours in the cage where lorry tyres were stored. They would have had no food or water had it not been for Mrs. Nixon, of the Women's Camp, who, at great risk, pushed a long-spouted teapot of water through the wire.

From March until October, 1943, in spite of the appalling overcrowding and squalor (nobody who has not fought a daily war against bugs on the scale with which they took over the Gaol can know just how squalid they can be) life was full of interest. Food was tolerable — just. We had a good supply of illicit B.B.C. news, received on secret radios and distributed throughout the Gaol by an elaborate system. This was soon to lead to devastating results in the Double Tenth enquiry by the Kempei-tai, the Japanese Secret Police.

RICHARD WALKER — AN ARTIST FULFILLED

Many hundreds of internees in Changi found it difficult to face each day with anything but expectations of yet another day of unrelieved tedium and boredom. Richard Walker was not one of them. For some years he had been well known in Singapore as Art Superintendent in many of the English schools. From the beginning of internment in Changi his gifts were largely confined, as he has said 'to the full-time painting of signs — scores of them — on teak panels to be posted about the gaol, telling internees what they might or might not do in particular spots'. At the same time for

Figure 9: 'The Adoration of the Magi', a reredos painted by Richard Walker in Changi. It was used there and at St. David's in Sime Road.

several months he was painting an altar piece, at the request of the Revd. G. B. Thompson. For this very beautiful picture of the 'Adoration of the Magi' he used the teak back of a cupboard looted from the Warders' Quarters. We took it with us to Sime Road, where it served with great effect at St. David's.

Twenty-five years after the end of internment, Richard Walker wrote most movingly, 'The human memory is very accommodating, discarding unpleasant happenings and heightening the pleasant experiences. At Changi I was more fortunate than the majority of internees. I was fully occupied during daylight hours — no long afternoons dozing or lying awake with gnawing hunger pains waiting for the next morsel of food — no boredom. There was interest and beauty to be found in the ever-changing cloud formations — brilliant dawns and sunsets — flowering weeds in the exercise yards, king-fishers darting and tunnelling in the sides of the swill pits, tailor birds stitching nests among the leaves of the spinach being laboriously cultivated in one of the walled enclosures.'

As Richard Walker showed, it was always possible to occupy our time fully with lectures, plays, classes, discussion groups, concerts, choirs, gramaphone recitals, playing or watching yard-cricket and a lethal form of six-a-side soccer on a gravel pitch, in which I had the honour to represent Plymouth Argyle! There was, too, all the time anyone could want for reading. The Camp Library, with a painstaking corps of book-binders, had a wide variety of choice. We had been able to contribute a good selection when we were free, 'finding' books in abandoned houses and sending them in on the quiet through Miyako. There was, too, a Religious Library run from their cell on B4 by two American Methodist Ministers, Hobart Amstutz and Tyler Thompson. It was a long haul to get there, but worth the many stairs. In Sime Road they were more conveniently housed.

ENTERTAINMENTS IN CHANGI

I found very soon that I was being involved in all the items listed above, with sermon preparation added. Rehearsals for plays occupied a lot of time. No sooner had one been per-formed than we had started thinking of the next production.

*Figure 10: 'Daily Bathing Parade in the Laundry at Changi'
by Bert Neyland.*

Strangely, the demolition of the stage seemed to accelerate rather than hinder Changi's theatrical life. Some felt there was positive gain in the greater intimacy which came with a move indoors to the Laundry. At all events it did nothing to halt the enthusiasm of producers or players, under the energetic leadership of A. J. W. Hockenhull and M. ff. Sheppard, who formed Sheppenhull Productions.

In the earlier days of 1942 there had been a One Act Play Competition. Not only was it won by the Revd. Jack Bennitt, but he also took four out of the first five places! In 1942 and at the beginning of 1943 there had already been a series of acted readings of 'The Apple Cart, 'The Importance of Being Ernest', and other similar plays. As Arthur Hockenhull has described them, 'They were mostly "Scenes from . . .", tentative but not undiverting and quite forgetworthy'.

However they have not been forgotten, nor have the performances given in the Laundry of a series of full length plays —
'The Wind and the Rain', in which I had the part of Ann
to Kerr Bovell's Charles Tritton, 'Arms and the Man', which
was performed as a reading, 'French Without Tears', and 'The
Amazing Doctor Clitterhouse'.

None of these plays could have been contemplated if it
had not been for the sacrificial generosity of members of the
Women's Camp. With the approach of each production a list
of wardrobe requirements was sent through to Miss Iris
Parfitt. She and her supporters regarded the robing of Changi's
'leading ladies' as a matter of honour. Nothing was too
much trouble. Precious clothes from their small stock, and
usually the best they had, were lent without hesitation,
even though on being returned to their owners seams were
split and garments often stained and damaged. As Iris Parfitt
herself has said, 'All their shows were dressed with much hair
tearing by our Entertainments Committee. We had a few
"glad rags", and those we lent were returned more rags than
glad by the stalwart glamour-girls of "the other side".'

Dorothy Moreton's *An Irishman in Malaya* has a superb
pen and ink drawing by Bert Neyland of the quartet from

*Figure 11: 'Sheppenhull Productions Inc.' by R. W. E. Harper, with
Arthur Hockenhull and Mervyn Sheppard far left and far right.*

DUKE of MANTUA   GILDA   MADDELENA   RIGOLETTO

*Figure 12: 'The quartet from Rigoletto' of Harold Haines, Albert Paley,
Sandy Ross and John Woods, by Bert Neyland. The grand illusion of
'feminine' beauty was created by the sacrificial lending of clothes by
the Women's Camp.*

Rigoletto, where the Costume Department had made the
Gilda and Maddalena of Albert Paley and Sandy Ross visions
of seductive loveliness.

With every production we knew how much our benefactors
in the Women's Camp contributed to an illusion, even a
fantasy. Take for example 'The Amazing Doctor Clitterhouse'
and Daisy, the gangster's moll, played by the Bishop's Chaplain — me! 'She', a dizzy blonde, was dressed in a stunning
black halo hat, a smart white silk blouse, slinky black satin
skirt and broad scarlet belt, with suitable feminine appen-
dages and make-up. The conversation of two young Liverpool
seamen after the performance, as they wandered home to
their lonely cells, was more of a compliment to the Wardrobe
Mistress than it was to Daisy. 'Cor! I shouldn't 'arf mind 'er'
said one. To which his friend very properly replied, 'Yer can't.
She's the Bishop's!' Years later Iris Parfitt, to whom I had just
written the story, replied 'I do hope you've managed to live
down your reputation as the "Bishop's Bint"!'.

We knew that plays produced in the Men's Camp gave a lot of pleasure to players and audience. It was a major disappointment that they were refused a showing for the Women's Camp, in spite of repeated requests to the Japanese.

MUSIC IN THE GAOL

The Camp Choir under Gordon Van Hien and Denis Soul, and John Woods' Glee Singers were also very popular, not only to the singers (of *course* we liked the sound of our own voices!) but also to large appreciative audiences. When we were still free in Singapore in 1942 one of the most productive finds in our scavenging for books for Changi was in a second-hand bookshop in Bras Basah Road. *Song through the Ages* was just what it said, a collection of songs which went back over many centuries, from earliest times through to our own day. John Woods, a solicitor from Ipoh in North Malaya, was a gifted and enthusiastic amateur musician. With tremendous industry he devised, transcribed, arranged for a male voice choir and wrote out music scores for a series of seventeen concerts, using the title of the book 'Song through the Ages'. Hundreds of people who heard the Glee Singers would agree with the internee who wrote and was quoted by Dorothy Moreton in her biography of John Woods, *An Irishman in Malaya*, 'J. L. Woods was one of the most valued contributors to the cultural and artistic life of the Camp'. I wasted no time in getting my name onto the waiting lists of his Glee Singers and of the Camp Choir.

Changi and Sime Road produced many fruitful combinations of talents. Amongst them was that of Lance Jermyn, poet, and Denis Soul, composer. They provided several songs which we sang at camp concerts, amongst the best of them 'The Woeful Ballad', which reads well and sang even better.

Three young men on a time, on a time,
    Rolling, roystering sang this rhyme:
'Scrap all the old things! We have Truth.
    We know everything. We are Youth.'

Three old men, on a time, on a time,
    Wagged their heads as they croaked this rhyme:
'This is wild heresy. Youth must be told.
    We know everything. We are old.'

The moon looking down, on a time, on a time,
  Thinly, wanly piped this rhyme:
'I've seen everything; they've but read.
  I know everything. I am dead!'

CONCERTS FOR THE WOMEN'S CAMP

Though the Women's Camp could not see our plays there were times when, grudgingly, the Japanese allowed concerts from the Men's Camp to be given for them. I was not there for the first, but it must have been a most moving occasion. In 1942 a choir of about fifty were allowed to sing a programme of carols and Christmas music. There was one condition. On the flat roof of the Japanese administration block they were out of sight of their audience below them in the Rose Garden, as the bare yard in the Women's Camp was called, with heavy irony. The only person who could see his audience and be seen by them was the conductor.

A member of the choir, Dr. W. W. Holmes, wrote of this occasion, again quoted by Dorothy Moreton, 'As we finished the second verse of "O Come, all ye Faithful" the conductor signalled to the women to sing . . . All the men stopped singing. The women's voices, softened by the distance, had a strange ethereal quality. There was a hesitancy in their voices too; a faltering which conveyed a sense of pathetic isolation. So might children, lost in forest darkness, sing to dispel their fear . . .

'There was time for our final item. With a great burst of sound we broke into the opening "Hallelujah" of Handel's chorus from "Messiah". This chorus had great significance for us; an exhilarating song of victory over everything we loathed. We put all we could into the final sustained chords . . . The music was suddenly over and we dispersed quietly . . . When should I again hear Christmas music in freedom? But this disturbing thought was quickly banished by cheerful news — 'There will be candied peel in the rice on Christmas Day!'.

Another concert for the Women's Camp, described by Freddy Bloom in her diary published as *Dear Philip*, took place in February, 1943. 'We had a most wonderful treat yesterday. The men were allowed over to give us a concert of classical music — Van Hien's really excellent choir with

147

one outstanding soloist (Woods). Eisinger is easily the best pianist I have heard in years and Eber a satisfying violinist. The whole thing was perfect — that grand feeling of elation so rare in Changi jail. Even the big Sikh guards tried to walk on tip-toe.'

Freddy Bloom also mentions permission having been given for a showing to the men early in July, 1943, of the 'Circus', and 'that takes some rehearsing and preparing'. She should know. She was its producer, but she was later able to write 'It was fun giving the "Circus" to the men. How they did enjoy it. It was really a success.' It was!

THE CHURCH IN ACTION

Our contacts with the Miyako when we were free had given us frequent news of the Church in Changi. The surprise which greeted us was to see how many there were at services, although the confirmation in November, 1942, had already shown us clearly enough that the Church was alive. We had not expected, nor did we find, any widespread movement towards the Church. Even so, through all its branches the Church was making an impression on the life of the Camp and also strengthening its own life in the process.

ARCHDEACON AND MRS. GRAHAM WHITE

Some time before our internment we had heard how valuable, vital even, was the role played by Graham White, the Archdeacon of Singapore. This appreciation of him gives a clear picture of his place in the life and the affections of the Camp.

> 'He was an old-fashioned High Churchman with little previous relationships with the Free Churches; but he soon became loved and respected by all, whether fundamentalists, modernists or agnostics. He worked incessantly for the Church, preparing confirmation candidates, teaching prospective ordinands and others, and every day after lunch he said evensong, followed by a New Testament study group — attended largely by Free Church fundamentalists. He also studied much himself, made a verse translation of Hebrews and a special study

148

of St. Paul. He had a great pastoral sense, was shrewd and humorous and had a quite uncanny sense of his congregation. When he preached the congregations in other yards were small.'

With the internment of the Bishop in March, 1943, the Archdeacon was saved a good deal of the responsibility of leadership, but still he would not rest. Although obviously a sick man he would not give up his daily classes as long as they were allowed to continue.

Mrs. Graham White held the same position of respect and affection in the Women's Camp. She, too, was frail and ill at the beginning of internment, but everyone who went to her with their troubles was sent away with something of her buoyant spirit. It was she who made all the arrangements for services conducted there by clergy going through on most Sundays from the Men's Camp. She too held classes and services for as long as she was able, but the strain of life under those conditions was very great, even for one of her will power.

CHRISTIAN ACCORD

Returning to the Men's Camp there was no Sunday when services were not held, nor had it been long in March, 1942, before Roman Catholics and Anglicans were able to hold Communion services every day. Here, as in so many other ways, I found it took time to get used to extreme limits of space. It was not unusual to have to stop in the middle of a weekday Communion service to move in out of the rain and to rig a miniature altar at the side of a narrow passage which was also a main and busy thoroughfare. Under these conditions no one in Changi could ever be under the illusion that the Church was dormant. They saw the Church at worship under their noses!

With the arrival in Changi of the Bishop with two more clergy it became possible for every part of the Gaol to be under the special care of a priest. It worked out like this — in charge of B Block, Sorby Adams and Jack Bennitt; C Block, Colin King and Bernard Eales; D Block, Archdeacon Graham White; Hudsons Bay and Labrador, G. B. Thompson; Golders Green and Youth Work, Eric Scott, while I was given

149

responsibility for the Kitchen Block. The majority of those who lived there were Police and Prison Warders. All the clergy shared the work in the Women's Camp through visits for services.

For a long time suitable cloths for the altar did not exist nor were vessels other than tin mugs available for Holy Communion, until, still free, Sorby and I scoured the second-hand markets round Rochore Canal and smuggled in through the Miyako, as well as to some of the P.O.W. camps, plated sports cups and pewter mugs, all looted, which we bought for a few cents. In spite of the absence of outward helps to ordered worship, in spite of the many makeshifts and inconveniences, there are many who will have remembered for the rest of their lives the reality and solemnity of some of those services, especially of Holy Communion.

Any Changi churchgoer on Sundays had a wide variety of services from which to choose. The Roman Catholics could be found in Hudsons Bay. In nearby Labrador, another small prison yard, Holy Communion was always celebrated on Sundays and on most weekdays, while full Choral Evensong was sung there every Sunday, with a choir trained by Denis Soul. Services were also held in each of the three main yards, one of them always Methodist or Church of Scotland in form, or a United Service. Even with all these services it could not be said that we, the clergy, were overworked with preaching. There were a lot of us — the Bishop and eight Anglicans, three American Methodists, two Presbyterians, one Brethren and fourteen Salvation Army Officers, four of them in the Women's Camp. We all got on with one another extremely well.

This feeling of close fellowship between the non-Roman clergy made many aware of the need for Christian reunion. It was difficult to avoid being conscious of our divisions, and being ashamed of them, when we were living and working at such close quarters. There was a spontaneous closing of ranks, a new experience for me and way ahead of anything I had met in England. Our co-operation was of very real value. It was not a question of different bodies making, or wanting from others, any short cuts to reunion. The loyalties of each individual to his own Church were fully recognised, but we found ourselves going further than that. There appeared a sense of shared Christian loyalty which rose above narrower divisions.

To express this accord a small group of clergy met over a long period to discuss questions of Christian doctrine and living. In the middle of 1943 those talks expanded and grew into the Friends of Reunion, in which the laity also had a large part. The Friends met every week, with someone talking about an aspect of his own denomination. Groups for discussion then dealt with points raised. These were so organised that all shades of opinion were reflected in each group. At the next meeting the reports of discussions were pooled and talked over.

For a time, as was to be expected, it was the differences between us which became most prominent and the exchanges sometimes tended to become almost heated. However, once that stage was passed, we began to discover the things about each other which we had in common and we found a new and greater understanding of one another.

Apart from anything else, one thing these discussions achieved was to provide a topic of conversation for the greater part of the Gaol. As someone has remarked, 'The question whether the Virgin Birth was a necessary part of Christian belief was discussed in almost every cell in the prison!'. People who did not normally even think about Christian doctrine could be heard arguing hotly for one point of view or another on this and other subjects.

The same could be said of many who heard the Bishop's lectures on the Bible, amongst the best attended series of any in Changi. A large number of his hearers would not normally have thought of themselves as within the organised life of the Church.

Other systems of thought also had their able presenters. Amongst them Harold Hughes, a prominent Malayan business man, gave a course of lectures on Theosophy, which had an enthusiastic following.

'NOTORIOUS CHANGI GAOL' – DEBITS

For most people memory more readily hangs on to what is good than to what is bad. It's the good in people, the things in them that make us laugh or give us pleasure which are more easily remembered. Situations which are frightening or uncomfortable are more easily forgotten. That is why, after more than forty years an account of Changi may tend to make it sound like an austere holiday camp. Where is 'the notorious Changi Gaol' of so much press comment?

It's there alright, let there be no mistake about that, but the worst elements, on which its justifiably dreadful reputation hangs, did not emerge until October 10th, 1943 — the 'Double Tenth . . . . . The major and disastrous Kempei-tai investigation was so called after the Chinese Festival, the tenth day of the tenth month. There are, however, other things which, taken together, make a pretty grisly picture.

Worst of all, and basic to everything, we had been robbed of our liberty. We were imprisoned. We were deprived of the most elementary freedoms — freedom of communication, even for husbands and wives separated in the Gaol at Changi by no more than a wall; freedom to know what was happening to those who were vital to us, our families and friends, whether there in Malaya or thousands of miles away. Some letters did arrive for us, but usually more than a year late. News of us reached our families in brief messages, not only rarely, but more than a year after we sent them. The first news of our survival in the battle for Singapore took a minimum of more than twelve months to reach home and for some it was much longer than that.

Red Cross parcels piled up in the Japanese stores — and stayed there.

Food lacked essential vitamins and, as a result, health problems began to appear. It did not help the doctors when there were people like the man who was given a rare pot of Marmite for a vitamin B deficiency. He could not understand why his skin condition had not improved, especially since he had, as he assured the doctor, rubbed the Marmite in every day!

There are further additions to the catalogue of debits — the Japanese provided no drugs.

Overcrowding and noise were at barely supportable levels at Changi.

The Japanese rule at Changi was totally capricious. Oc-

"Stone walls do not a prison make . . ."
SEZ YOU !!

Figure 13: From Jail Bird Jottings *by Iris Parfitt.*

casional outbursts of unreason could lead them to give several days 'in solitary'.

Japanese guards created serious problems for the Women's Camp by their unwarranted intrusions and invasions of privacy.

– AND CREDITS

On the other hand, beside all this if we *had* to be interned we did, before the Double Tenth, have certain advantages.

The climate was perfect, though some found the high humidity a problem.

Inside the Men's Camp the Japanese interfered hardly at all. The internal administration of the Camp by our own representatives was well handled and ran smoothly.

153

We had a settled existence with all the facilities with which the Gaol was equipped — a central kitchen, good water supply, electricity and sanitation.

There was minimum pressure from the Japanese for the supply of an outside labour force or heavy fatigues at this stage.

The leaders in the Women's Camp worked with the Men's Representative in their dealings with the Japanese, which gave the women some measure of protection.

There were very many things in our programme of lectures and courses of study which served to enlighten and to entertain, and which met all tastes and most needs.

We had complete freedom to hold Church services.

The doctors and dentists in Changi worked wonders on minimal resources. Reasonable hospital facilities were available at the Miyako.

However much there may have been these credits on the Changi balance sheet, they were totally obliterated by the 'Double Tenth'.

THE DOUBLE TENTH DISASTER

October 10th, 1943, seemed at first light as though it would be no different from that other day a short time before when we were all out in the Main Yard for a roll call. We ought to be finished in time for the Camp Choir rehearsal later in the morning. At least, so it seemed, until time passed, quite a lot of it, with nothing happening. The sun was getting higher, we were getting hotter, and standing, especially for the older men, who hadn't thought to bring their stools, became a problem.

That was when the invasion started. Hordes of Japanese soldiers appeared through the door into the yard away to our left. This was more, far more, than the calling of a roll. Before long individuals were singled out. In the late afternoon we were allowed back into our yards, where we saw those whose names had been called separated in a group by themselves. We heard that a thorough search had been made of the whole Gaol and of all our belongings. Several of those who had been detained we either knew or we suspected to be involved in monitoring news broadcasts and supplying a secret information service throughout the Gaol. Even the use of a length of flex as a clothes line was slender evidence enough to give Ted Hebditch, the Camp Electrician, nine months with the Kempei-tai, though without serious torture. Many signs pointed to all this having something to do with forbidden radios. There was, however, much more to it than that.

On that first day and others which followed about seventy people were taken, of whom some were soon sent back, leaving fifty-seven in all. Amongst them was the Camp Treasurer, Yoxall of the Hong Kong Shanghai Bank, in whose cell had been found a tin box full of $210,000, much of it in Japanese currency. Straits dollar notes might have been explained away. It was just possible they could have been brought in at the start of internment. Japanese 'Banana notes', however, (so called from the banana tree in their design) were a different matter. They must have been sent into the gaol. How? By whom? Why? These were questions to which the Japanese were going to need answers. In fact they were basic to the whole Double Tenth enquiry.

THE BISHOP'S BORROWING FOR THE CENTRAL COMMITTEE

Although I knew the Bishop had been sending money into Changi when we were free and had arranged for this to continue after our internment, neither Sorby Adams nor I knew any details of the operation, nor how deeply the Bishop was involved. He had deliberately kept this information from us.

Very early in internment it became clear to the Central Camp Committee that the Japanese had no intention of providing drugs and medicines or additional foods for the children, the elderly or the sick. On the other hand the Japanese officers at Changi had shown that they would be ready to make purchases on behalf of the Committee. This they could do at a very considerable profit. They would have a good rake-off. Clearly the Central Committee were going to need money.

When internment started many people took considerable amounts into Changi with them. Those who wished, could lend to a Camp Fund, repayable after the war. But this money was not enough for purchases over any length of time and somehow the Central Committee had to find extra funds.

In 1942 a message was sent to the Bishop. He borrowed

money, a total of £25,000 or $200,000, from a neutral in Singapore in the name of the Anglican Church. It was then smuggled into the camp. As long as we were free it was fairly simple to arrange this, either by patients, carefully selected, who were returning to Changi from the Miyako Hospital, or through Norman Coulson on one of his maintenance trips to Changi authorised by the Japanese. Not only did he send into the Gaol tons of engineering equipment without their knowledge, from Municipal stores under Japanese control, but on one occasion he hid a large sum of money in a length of piping destined for the use of internees at the Gaol.

HEROISM OF 'K. T.', THE CHOYS AND AH TEK

When the Bishop was interned in March, 1943, he arranged with K. T. Alexander, his Indian Secretary, that, on receipt of a message he was to go to 'Mr. X' and borrow the necessary funds. To get the money into Changi needed the help of others besides Norman Coulson. It called for a great deal of courage and ingenuity, but it was done. Usually it was the same two people who organised the transfer, Choy Koon Heng and his wife, Elizabeth, both of them completely fearless and selfless. From headquarters in a shop they were allowed to operate at the Miyako Hospital they used various methods to get the money to Changi. Ah Tek, a non-Christian shopkeeper, played a major role.

Lorries from the Gaol, driven by internees, called fairly frequently at a neighbouring shop. A Japanese guard brought them from Changi. While his attention was distracted, a package of money was passed to the driver of the lorry, who brought it back into the Camp.

Other methods were also used. I can remember one such. It happened when I was taking the funeral of an internee at Bidadari cemetery. Returning from the grave to the Superintendent's office I found a carton of cigarettes in my robe case. That was what it appeared to be, but in fact it was several thousand dollars in $10 notes slipped into the case at the request of the Choys by Mr. Bracken, the Superintendent.

Once we knew the Japanese Military Police, the Kempeitai, had their hands on the money in Yoxall's cell, the Bishop's arrest could only be a matter of time. Each day, and night, during the following week the Japanese enquiry gathered momentum. Every morning we heard who had been the target of a disturbance during the night, as a group of Japanese soldiers came and left with their prisoner.

... FEAR ...

The atmosphere of fear and dread which hung over Changi was something we shared with thousands in Singapore. It was graphically described at the beginning of the Introduction to the published record of the Double Tenth War Crimes Trial.

> 'To the cosmopolitan city of Singapore the "Double Tenth" case was no small affair. It was a huge and ever-growing spider's web which caught now Europeans, now Asiatics, now Eurasians, within its coils. From the Bishop of Singapore himself to the humblest coolie none could be sure that the next knock would not arouse his household from its early morning sleep to provide another victim for the torturers of the Kempei-tai. For it was by such melodramatic methods that the Japanese Military Police achieved the dread in which they were universally held in the occupied territories. The darkness of night, the sudden swoop, the atmosphere of terror were their agents to impose submissiveness upon a reluctant people. But, as the terror grew, so the popularity of the Japanese diminished and the population of Singapore grew less submissive. It was a vicious spiral descending into ever greater depths of horror. Thus the case of the "Double Tenth" was in effect the story of the occupation of Singapore, of an alien enemy in the midst of a hostile people, of fear on one side breeding fear on the other.'

THE BISHOP'S ARREST

Seven days after the Double Tenth in the late afternoon a message came to the cell, 'Bishop, you're wanted in the front office'. He put on a thin black cassock. He said later that it was taken from him when he arrived at Kempei-tai headquarters. Together we went down to the entrance to the front yard. He walked across the yard to the guard room. Several of us were there watching. It was not long before he came out again and we saw him being escorted to a waiting car and driven away to the Kempei-tai interrogation centre. Ironically it was at the Y.M.C.A. It was a bitter moment and desperately sad.

In the minds of many people was the nagging question of whether and when their own turn might come. In fact, seven and a half months later, when he was released, the Bishop told Sorby and me that he had had to work very hard to protect us and to prevent us being involved in the enquiry.

Two things stand out from this time. One was a tragically depressing scene one late afternoon in 'B' yard. Without warning a party of about eight Japanese soldiers, led by Walter Stevenson, came from the Main Yard through the gap in the wall. He took them to a point in a low bank. He removed a turf resting on a wooden board, which concealed a cavity holding a wooden stool, into which he had built the radio set he had operated with great daring and ingenuity on our behalf and to our immense comfort for one and a half years. It was to cost him his life. He was one of the fifteen who died, either while undergoing interrogation or after being returned to the camp at Changi or Sime Road.

TOMMY THOMSON'S FEAT OF MEMORY

The other incident had a very different atmosphere and outcome. The Bishop had had a private arrangement with Tommy Thomson, our cell companion, that he would act as the Bishop's accountant for all the money he had raised for the Camp Committee, both before and after coming to Changi. Next to the Bishop's arrest there came for me the second most dreadful moment when, early in November, Tommy was ordered to report at the Front Office. He was not young and the idea of him being put through a Japanese interrogation was unthinkable. I waited by the entrance to the front yard with 'Farquie', his great friend. Time went by with still no sign of him, until, after about an hour and a half, he appeared — and turned right, back into the gaol! Unaccompanied, he walked towards us. We could not believe it. He was the only person in the whole Double Tenth enquiry

to be questioned at the Gaol without being removed to
Singapore to one of the two main Military Police enquiry
centres at the Y.M.C.A. or Smith Street.

Tommy and I made straight for the Main Yard, where we
'blued' a precious cigar he had been keeping 'for an occasion'!
He told me what had happened. A Japanese interrogator
brought a message from the Bishop that Tommy was to give
him details of the money in the Loan Account. Tommy was
delighted that he had been able to remember all the items,
except one of no great importance. He felt sure that this list
would have meant confirmation of the evidence the Bishop
himself had given to his questioners at the Y.M.C.A.

That was not quite the end of the story. It had a final
twist which was almost comic. Tommy had a hunch the
matter wouldn't rest there. He felt sure the Japanese would
search the cell hoping to find a copy of his list of amounts
and dates. We decided to plant one which Tommy wanted
them to find. We put it in a book on a shelf with others. He
was right. A young Japanese soldier arrived and with civility,
speaking no English, began a search of the cell. We hardly
dared look at one another as the searcher grew 'warmer'.
Had he known, we were even more delighted than he was
when he found what he wanted.

GRIM CHANGES IN LIFE AT CHANGI

The change in the life of Changi was instantaneous from the
moment of the Double Tenth. All lectures, plays, classes,
choirs, recitals and concerts were banned. Church services
were allowed without interference, though preaching was
not permitted. For me one of the most moving of many
memorable services in Changi was the Sunday service in 'B'
Yard at which the Bishop should have preached. He had been
arrested less than twenty-four hours earlier. I was due to take
the service — which I did.

There were other changes. The Men's and Women's Representatives found the Japanese in Changi increasingly unreason-
able and difficult to deal with. The loss of a reliable source of
news we felt keenly and we saw how much we had depended
on and been encouraged by B.B.C. radio bulletins. For some
time the Kempei-tai continued to make arrests until the total

reached fifty-seven, including three women, Freddy Bloom and Dr. Cicely Williams, both for five months and Mrs. Dorothy Nixon for a shorter time. We still had no news of anything which was happening to any of them.

THE BISHOP'S STORY

When he returned to the camp at Sime Road seven and a half months later the Bishop told us that he had been accused of being the Lawrence of Malaya. It was unfortunate that he had in his library at the Cathedral a large number of books on Lawrence, for whom he had a great admiration. He had also lectured on him in Changi.

The details of the charges against the Bishop were that he had used his position while free in Singapore to organise throughout Malaya a large espionage organisation. At the time of the surrender, the charge continued, he had been informed by the Financial Secretary and the Manager of the Hong Kong Bank of the existence of large stocks of British currency, which he had subsequently used for the paying of agents and for the financing of espionage generally. The money that was sent into the Gaol was to be used for the same purpose and would in due course have been distributed. He had used, they said, the Federation of the Christian Churches as a cover for his work throughout the peninsular. It was interesting to discover that the Federation had been ordered to close down at about this time. The charge continued that he was the head of an organisation which received instructions on short wave wireless sets operated in the Gaol. They were also convinced of the existence of a wireless transmitter being operated from Changi. That was the formidable charge with which the Bishop was faced when he arrived at the Kempei-tai headquarters in the Y.M.C.A.

It took three days of the most extreme torture in his attempt to convince them that all these charges were completely false and that the money was sent into the Gaol for humanitarian reasons. In the evening of his arrival, he was questioned, the interrogation being punctuated with beatings for between three and four hours. It was quite obvious that they already knew the answers to many of the questions he was being asked. They knew, for instance, that the money

had been sent into the Gaol and they knew how it had been
sent in. Beyond any doubt it would not take them long to
fill in the gaps in the story. They already knew it in detail
and in some cases in great detail, but for the first three days
they concentrated on the charges as outlined here.

On the following morning he was again taken to the torture
room, where he was made to kneel down. A three-angled bar
was placed behind his knees. He was then forced to sit back
on his haunches. His hands were tied behind his back and
pulled up to a position between his shoulder blades. His head
was forced down and he remained in this position for seven
and a half hours. Any attempt to ease the strain of the cramp
in his legs was frustrated by the guards, who brought the flat
of their boots down hard onto his thighs. At intervals the
bar behind his knees was twisted or the guards would jump
on one or both of the projecting ends. Beatings and kicks
were frequent. Throughout the whole of this time he was
being questioned and told to confess that he was a spy. He
said afterwards that this was the one time that he lost his
nerve and pleaded for death.

Again the next morning the Bishop was brought up from
the cells, this time to be tied face upwards to a table, with
his head hanging over its end. For several hours he remained
in that position while relays of soldiers beat him systemati-
cally from the ankles to the thighs with three-fold knotted
ropes. He fainted, was revived with warm milk and the
beating continued. He estimated that he must have received
over three hundred lashes.

It is quite impossible to set this down as he described it
when he returned to the Camp and even more to attempt to
describe his thoughts during this time. But the picture would
not be complete without it. The beating, he said, was far
easier to bear than the excruciating pain of the previous day.
It was not long before he lost all sense of feeling. The blows
had lost their power to hurt, so dead were the nerves in his
body. He felt, too, almost a feeling of exaltation on this
third day.

Those of us who heard him cannot doubt the reality of
his experience of the near presence of God. He felt himself
uplifted and supported at a time when his body had ceased

to have any meaning for him at all. Finally he was taken down to the cells and thrown onto the floor. There was no skin left on the front of his legs from his thighs downwards. His flesh was raw and livid from the blows he had received, torn to shreds. No medical attention was provided for him while he was in that state and he said that if it had not been for the help of Walter Stevenson in the same cell, who subsequently died as a result of the treatment he received, he would not have survived.

THE MISSING $10,000

For some weeks there was no further interrogation, but it started again several months later. The Bishop, however, was fortunate in having no further beatings, with the exception of about half an hour of kneeling. Then began the long business of accounting for every cent of the money sent to the Camp. $10,000 dollars more had been sent in, according to the story of the Choys and Alexander, than had been received in Changi. It took seven and a half months to find the explanation.

The tragedy was that the solution to the mystery, when it was eventually revealed, was so simple. The Choys and Alexander had always been right. $100,000 had been sent into Changi. The Central Committee had only received $90,000. At a point when the enquiry had dragged on for months, in whispered conversations in one of the cells, two of those involved realised what had happened. At a certain point word had been sent out to the Choys from the Gaol that no further money was needed for the time being. By ill luck the missing money was already on its way. An internee, who knew of the Central Committee's decision and who was involved in getting the money into Changi, accepted the $10,000 and passed it direct to a group of people who were able to, and did, buy extra medical supplies for use in the Gaol. They had done so, without a word to the Choys, the Committee or the Bishop.

Even allowing for the unremitting fabrication of evidence by the Japanese, it was no longer possible even for them to pursue the Double Tenth enquiry any further. The Bishop was released, and with him K. T. Alexander and Elizabeth

Choy, while for her husband, Choy Koon Heng, a prison sentence of twelve years was ended with the arrival of the British after he had served sixteen months.

THE BISHOP'S ACCOUNT OF HIS TORTURE

In 1946 the Bishop had returned to Britain after joining his wife and family in Australia. In October he preached a sermon on B.B.C. Radio in which he spoke of the depth of his own spiritual experience during his seven months in the Y.M.C.A. He told of the taunts of his interrogators, who, in the middle of torture, asked him if he still believed in God. It was, he said, by God's help that he replied 'I do'. 'Then why does not God save you?' shouted the torturer. 'He does' the Bishop managed to answer, 'but not from pain. He saves me by giving me the spirit to bear it.'

Of extremes of pain which he had to suffer, the Bishop said 'When I muttered "Forgive them" I wondered how far I was being dramatic and if I really meant it, because I looked at their faces as they stood around and took it in turn to flog me . . . By the grace of God I saw those men not as they were, but as they had been. Once they were little children . . . and it's hard to hate little children.'

When he came back to Sime Road the Bishop also told us of several incidents which showed the Japanese Kempei-tai to be adepts at the art of mental torture. There were times when men were taken through the whole drill of an execution, right up to the moment of the order to fire.

While this did not happen to the Bishop himself he was told with all the appearance of complete and utter seriousness that, as he did not seem to be disposed to tell the truth, he was to be placed in a dungeon without food or water and kept there until he died or told the truth. He believed implicitly that this threat would be carried out and when he returned to the cell he gave last messages to a friend of his, who had a position next to him on the floor. He asked him to pass them on to his wife and family.

He was not called up for questioning for five days. He asked whether the threat of death was to be carried out, to which his interrogator replied that that had only been a joke.

The Bishop also said in his sermon, as he had told us in Sime Road, 'There were many dreary and desolate moments, especially in the early morning . . . There was a tiny window at the back of the cell and through the bars I could hear the song of the golden oriole. I could see the glorious red of the flame of the forest tree. Behind the flame tree I glimpsed the top of Wesley's church and was so grateful that the Church had preserved so many of Wesley's hymns. One that I said every morning was 'Christ Whose Glory Fills the Skies' . . .

> Dark and cheerless is the morn
> Unaccompanied by Thee;
> Joyless is the day's return
> Till Thy mercy's beams I see.

'And so', said the Bishop, 'I went on to pray,

> Visit then this soul of mine,
> Pierce the gloom of sin and grief.'

'And gradually the burden of this world was lifted and I was carried into the presence of God and received from Him the strength and peace which were enough to live by day by day.'

Towards the end of 1942 Hugh Walpole's *Herries Chronicle* appeared at our house in Dyson Road. *The Bright Pavilions,* with its gruesome accounts of Tudor atrocities, filled the Bishop with a dark, prophetic foreboding. He was only able to shake it off after several weeks had passed. When he returned to Sime Road from the Y.M.C.A. he and I both remembered and talked about his strong and vivid premonition that somehow he was going to be involved in acute physical suffering.

'DOUBLE TENTH' SURVIVORS' TESTIMONY

Before the end of internment a commission of enquiry in Sime Road Camp took statements from all those who had survived the aftermath of the Double Tenth. This extract gives some idea of the conditions of life at the Kempei-tai headquarters at the Y.M.C.A. and elsewhere.

> 'They were crowded, irrespective of race, sex or state of health, in small cells or cages. They were so cramped

that they could not lie down in comfort. No bedding or coverings of any kind were provided, and bright lights were kept burning overhead all night. From 8 a.m. to 10 p.m. inmates had to sit up straight on the bare floor with their knees up and were not allowed to relax or put their hands on the floor or move or talk. Any infractions of this rigid discipline involved a beating. There was one pedestal water-closet in each cell, and the water flushing into the pan provided the only water for all purposes, including drinking. Nearly all of the inmates suffered from dysentery. No soap, towel, toilet articles or handkerchiefs were permitted and inmates had no clothing other than what they were wearing. In these conditions and this atmosphere of terror these men and women waited, sometimes for months, their summons to interrogation, which might come at any hour of the day or night.'

LIFE GOES ON IN CHANGI

Of all this we knew nothing in Changi, nor were we to know until well into the New Year. In the meantime after the Double Tenth we seized on anything we could find to dull our anxieties, for ourselves as well as for other people. Reading by the hour proved an excellent time-filler. For example, the three volumes of Winston Churchill's *Marlborough* — the fourth was not in the camp library — read at lightning speed did not particularly increase my knowledge of the Duke, but they did help to eliminate the slow drag of time. Another invaluable substitute for both worrying and boredom was bridge. The hard fought battles of three handed 'cut-throat' with Sorby Adams and the Bishop at Bishopsbourne and Dyson Road, often under protest into the small hours, were beginning to pay off!

Some time before the Double Tenth, Stanton ('Bird') Nelson, of Singapore's refugee hotel 'The Nelson Arms' in January, 1942, had a serious mental breakdown. There was no problem about his going to the Mental Hospital at the Miyako and there he remained for some time. Towards the end of 1943 we were allowed to have him back at Changi, when the Japanese gave our carpenters permission to build a small hut for him on a bit of unused ground. A group of us who were his friends worked a 24-hour roster looking after him, with Kathleen Nelson, his wife, allowed over from the Women's Camp every day. He was very ill with dementia, but slowly improved over a long time. He was able to return to camp life when we got to Sime Road.

It was good to be able to help him, but we would all have preferred not to have picked up the scabies he brought back with him from the Miyako. Unfortunately the doctor looking after him at Changi hadn't spotted it before it was passed on to us. It's a foul disease — mites get under the skin with frantic irritation and choose between two and three in the morning as their busiest time!

Many of us who knew him liked the remark of the young policeman who had also had a bad mental breakdown. He came back to Changi proudly claiming that he was the only Malayan Police Officer who had a certificate of sanity!

Christmas, 1943, produced from the Japanese a typical quirk of irrationality. The Men's and Women's Representatives were discussing with the Japanese the services to be held in the two camps. Suddenly out of the blue the authorities decreed that in the Men's Camp there would be two services only on Christmas Day, one for the Roman Catholics and one for non-Romans. No amount of explanation, argument or reasoning would shift them. That's as it had to be. 'But', we said amongst ourselves, 'that's not as it will be!'

SECRET CHRISTMAS COMMUNION

All over the Gaol, in quiet corners very early on Christmas morning, communion services were held in the shaded light of a candle. Our own sentries were watching for wandering Japanese, unusual at that hour. The service I held in one of the cells of the Kitchen Block I found deeply moving. It was the nearest I have ever been to the atmosphere of the Catacombs in first century Rome. Even more, I have never been nearer in spirit to the dim light of the stable at Bethlehem. I stood in the cell on the raised concrete sleeping platform, with about twenty communicants standing round, on either side of the cell, while some stood in or just outside the doorway. The spirit of Christmas lived that morning in Changi.

High on the list of all unusual but wholly meaningful celebrations of Holy Communion must be those, very much abbreviated, held by the Bishop in the Y.M.C.A. Often a Roman Catholic girl gave warning of the approach of any patrolling guard. On one occasion, included with those in the cell who received their communion of grains of cooked rice for bread, and water for wine, was Elizabeth Choy, who was sweeping the corridor. At a word from the Bishop she knelt down and received her communion through the bars of the cage.

WALTER CURTIS AS INTERPRETER

A constant problem for our Men's Representative in his dealings with the Japanese was the difficulty of language. A few of them had some grasp of English but most had none. The whole life of Changi and of everyone in it benefited enormously from the skill and tact of Walter Curtis as an interpreter.

There was one occasion when I had good reason to admire and be grateful for his dexterity. During a spell of characteristic unpleasantness Tominaga, the Officer-in-charge of the Gaol at Changi, had committed Arthur Worley, a senior Singapore judge, to a short spell of solitary confinement. (From December, 1943 to April, 1944, he was also held by the Kempei-tai in Singapore.) The Japanese authorities, on going through his private papers, found a note from me which I had sent to him to Changi when we were still free. It was totally unimportant. There was no reason to have kept it. It said 'I was glad to hear of your move', which I recognised at once. I remembered I had written discreetly to say I was glad he was better and had returned to Changi after a spell in the Miyako. If I admitted to Tominaga that I had had contact with Changi and had sent the note there through the Miyako I was in trouble.

I managed to play the innocent, but it was wearing a bit thin under Tominaga's eagle and evil eye, until Walter asked whether it might mean that it was a note to Worley at the hospital congratulating him on a move from one ward to another as a sign that he was getting better. Of course that was what it meant! In fact, now I had been reminded (by

Walter!) I remembered writing such a note! After further such nonsense Tominaga lost interest and thanks to Walter I walked out of the office.

He was among those who were taken to Singapore after the Double Tenth. Freddy Bloom was in the same cell as him at Smith Street Interrogation Centre. In her book *Dear Philip* she said of him,

> 'Walter Curtis had the advantage of speaking Japanese. He unselfishly used that advantage to the benefit of all of us, with a saint-like devotion and persistence . . . Walter was a Roman Catholic convert. He believed in his religion and he lived according to it. Never in all those trying months was he anything but humble and selfless in his attitude towards all of us. He was a good man who risked, and received, many a beating in his efforts to improve our lot. The Japanese had allowed him to bring his Bible into the cell with him.
>
> His wife and nine children had been evacuated to South Africa. He assured me that he was not worried about them, for St. Joseph would look after them. When I suggested that he was "preying on" rather than "praying to" the saint, he calmly shook his head and said he knew he need not worry. Somehow I felt certain St. Joseph would not let that man down.
>
> It was Walter who thought up our grace after meals. "Thank God, we do not have to eat this lot again." '

There were many times when, without British interpreters, understanding between the Japanese and internees in Changi was hazardous. For example in April, 1944, Major-General Saito addressed the Camp. The rather bizarre instant-interpreting by a Japanese officer was as follows:

> 'May I introduce the new commandant of this camp, Maj.-Gen. Saito.
>
> He says, "You internees have been living in this camp for two years. It has not been possible to change you internees with other countries although we know how long you have been here in this camp. I am awfully sorry you have been living here for so long.
>
> This war is fighting very hard now — General says he does not know what time it will finish. Maybe Japan

army fight for India — for British armies — for going on to India. We will fight for the ocean — New Britain — New Guinea — fighting every day near Australia. English and U.S.A. going to try to smash Japan — but this will be very hard. Japanese army and civilian people going to try their best for this war. Many aeroplanes will be coming over and dropping bombs. Maj.-Gen. went to Japan and looked all over Japan — Japan is a very great country now.

You never can tell about this war — nobody can tell after living here almost two years how many more years you will have to be in this camp. We do not know — nobody knows. Your faces look very well — Maj.-Gen. says you look fine. Maj.-Gen. will try his best for your rice — now all run short — that is why. He will try best for more nice things. Maj.-Gen. says if you feel you want to say or ask for something, try for anything. The Major will try his best for everybody. You folks living in this camp must try best for your health and if you want something about this ask the Doctors and the Health Department. That is all the Major is going to say this morning." '

And that was the last anyone heard of these fine words for a full further sixteen months. However before the day was out the Men's Representative issued a statement from which it was clear that something was pending. He quoted Miamoto, one of the Japanese officials at Changi, who gave him permission to say that 'if we would put up with our troubles for a little while longer — say a month or less we should get some very good news and we should be banyak, banyak baik (very, very good!) that everyone, including Miamoto himself, would be very happy. He said he could not reveal the nature of the good news.'

Fortunately there was not much time for rumour to run riot. Within a matter of days we were off by easy stages to the wide open spaces of Sime Road.

CHANGI, FAREWELL!

My last look at Changi was out of character. In fact it was the most beautiful of any I can remember. It was early morning.

The packing of our belongings in the cell was finished and everything was ready for the move. I walked up to the top of the 'Inside Garden', where David Molesworth was taking a last look at his plot, the scene of two years careful work. When I reached him I turned, the long line of the gaol stretching away on the left. In the far distance the whole of the eastern sky was a vivid blue, a back-cloth for every colour in the spectrum. It was staggering. Utterly beautiful.

'IF I KNEW THAT I WERE TO DIE'

March 15th, 1944. I wrote this 'reflection' two months before leaving Changi. When Buchan wrote *Sick Heart River*, his last book published after his death, he sends Leithen, a sick man, off into the wilds of Northern Canada to die. He knows he has not long to live and the book is really little more than an excuse for giving Leithen's thoughts on the approach of death. It is a remarkable book and so clear is the picture of the mind of such a man at such a time that one is forced to the conclusion that the writing is autobiographical. I wonder, did Buchan himself know that his own days were numbered? And did he leave this as the record of his own mind at that time? If so, then the book takes on an entirely new complexion — a new significance. But this is really beside the point — at any rate as far as my original opening is concerned, except in so far as it throws some light on what I might imagine my own thoughts to be under similar circumstances.

If I knew that I were to die. There must be many who are faced with that knowledge and the response to it one would expect to be as varied as personality itself. If *I* knew that I were to die, how, I wonder, would I react? Intellectually, if one can imagine emotionless thought in such a case, the certainty which I have of survival — personalised in the full Christian sense — would be a sheet anchor. Christian faith either meets that test or it is so much dust. Weak, uncertain and faltering as my own personal faith may often be, I thank God, and this in all humility, that He has given me a sense of His guiding and protecting hand in and through whatever this life — and its end — can offer. Ultimately His will is done and His children are brought home. But it is no denial of faith to say that emotion might give a slightly different form to the picture. However certain one may be of the joys which may lie ahead, there is always justifiable regret in the leaving of those which one has known.

In my Father's house *are* many mansions — that I know, but there are many mansions here, friends and moments which are very precious. Surely it is no lack of faith to take one backward glance at them when faced with death, even remembering Lot's wife! Regrets there would be in plenty — unhappiness caused, happiness missed, weakness of witness, of service and of love. 'Prepare to meet thy God'! Even so how can one prepare, when all one's preparation means a stripping away of everything until the soul comes naked and empty-handed into the presence of God? But still that empty-handedness is as He would have us come to Him. Christ went to the Father beaten, bruised, and broken, with one thing only left — the certainty of the Father's love. 'If I knew I were to die' — Of what use then the petty conceits of my own false values and pride? Oh, God, help me to make my life a daily death, living only for you. Yours I am — apart from you I have, I am nothing. Take everything from me — but not your love.

Figure 14: Elizabeth Choy, with her husband Koon Heng, was a brilliant light in the black story of the Double Tenth. Seen here in 1946, she was being received in audience by Queen Elizabeth at Buckingham Palace. She later received an O.B.E.

Section Four

Sime Road Camp

May, 1944 to September, 1945

Some parts of this section were written long after the diary entries. Where these occur a ¶ has been placed in the left-hand margin at the beginning of the item, at the head of each successive page and at the end.

Sime Road Camp

The wide horizons of Sime Road after the imprisoning, metaphorical as well as actual, walls of Changi, were a huge relief and a lift to morale. At the same time there were problems. The move itself was a major logistical exercise. In retrospect it is remarkable that we were given transport and were not forced to march the seven or eight miles from the Gaol on the east coast to Sime Road, adjoining the Bukit Timah Golf Course, in the centre of the Island. We were told we were leaving Changi surprisingly soon after the visit of General Saito and his promise of things to come, which we should find 'very, very good'. The move took several days and on the morning of May 2nd we in 'B' block were on our way.

Our first introduction to Sime Road left so much to be desired that any appreciation of our surroundings plummeted. The Camp had originally been R.A.F. Headquarters. Spread out in a former rubber estate covering about 70 acres — the P.O.W.s before us had used most of the trees for firewood — it consisted of a large number of long wooden huts with atap, or palm leaf, roofs, linked in the main by a system of concrete paths.

The accommodation allotted to us was, we were told, only temporary. It had better be! We were crowded into a space per man of less than one and a half feet — and the roof leaked! The next evening Tommy, Norman Alexander and I, with some others, moved ourselves unofficially into an empty hut, too late in the day for anyone to tell us not to. If anything, the roof had more leaks than the first, but we had more room to dodge the drips.

Four days after us, on May 6th, the Women's Camp moved from Changi. Their arrival had something of a party atmosphere about it. Some of the men had been detailed to act as

175

¶ baggage carriers for them and wherever we went there were glad and cheerful greetings. There were meetings too, for some of us for the first time.

In the middle of 1943 I had had a post card from a friend of my brother's, asking me to look out for Mary Scott, a Malayan Government Nursing Sister. We met, and this was the start of a massive correspondence between us about everything imaginable. It was also the beginning of a friendship which has lasted for more than forty years.

A SMOOTH TRANSFER

Amongst the P.O.W.s who moved out of Sime Road and into the Gaol at Changi, as we made the same journey in reverse, was Ronald Searle, the artist. The Women's Camp benefitted from his thoughtfulness. They found some delightful caricatures of his on the walls of the hut which they made into the Dispensary. Into his life-sized murals he had cunningly inserted messages such as 'Cheer up, girls. Won't be long now'.

On May 8th, six days after our move to Sime Road, Tommy, Norman and I were established in Hut 131 with more than a hundred others. It was to be our home for the rest of internment. Ideally placed, with open ground in front of us across a shallow valley to the south, a path led up a gentle slope to a distant clump of trees round the Pig Farm. Let it be said, those buildings were named after their potential rather than their actual population of livestock, which never amounted to more than a very few pigs at any one time. Ours was a good hut, still with not much space, but it had a good view and a sound roof — and the company was good.

Life began to take shape remarkably quickly. Health and medical services and kitchens were organised efficiently and smoothly in the four areas into which the Camp was divided. Other departments continued on a centralised basis as in Changi. The Men's Representative, with his office staff, was still in daily and sometimes uncomfortable contact with the Japanese administration and he was the means of communication back to the rest of us. The hospital and quartermaster's department both worked efficiently, though with woefully inadequate supplies. In the main, medical require-

¶ ments were just ignored by the Japanese. Other departments were well organised and worked well — tin smiths, plumbers, gardeners, carpenters, police, electricians, woodcutters, librarians and motor mechanics, to name only a few.

There was no break in the holding of regular Church services. Both Anglicans and Roman Catholics were fortunate to have the use of a chapel each, largely open-air, built and left intact for us by the P.O.W.s. The Free Churches soon brought into use a concrete site on the edge of our area, known as the Church-in-the-Glen. The Methodist Ministers, Hobart Amstutz and Tyler Thompson, turned it into a beautiful garden.

THE BISHOP RETURNS FROM THE KEMPEI-TAI

Just over three weeks after our move, on Thursday, May 26th, 1944, I was in the hut in the middle of the morning. A young internee came running down the path from the line of huts at the top of the far hill. He brought me a note from Palmer in the Front Office. 'I thought you would like to know that the Bishop has just come back.' I tore up the path to where, on the edge of the main road through the centre of the Camp, a small crowd were calling out their greetings to him as he went by. He had lost a lot of weight — about four stone — but he was fit enough to walk the half mile to the hospital.

TERROR AT THE Y.M.C.A.

For months he and others with him had spent time either in terrifying interrogations or in stolen conversations in the cell through carefully guarded whispers. For most of those who came back into the world again there was a very natural need to talk. This was certainly true of the Bishop. Fortunately there was a single side-ward where he could talk to his heart's content. In spite of his physical condition he was absolutely steady mentally and emotionally.

I had long hours with him. He spoke of those in the Y.M.C.A. who had helped him. First, Walter Stevenson, who, he said, through his care of him after torture had saved his life. Then there were people like Alan Ker, who, as they sat cross-legged in the cell, had taught him more than two

177

¶ thousand lines of Keats. I know how many there were. In the Bishop's anxiety not to forget them, I had to hear him! In exchange the Bishop taught Alan Ker several psalms.

Next to the Bible, Bradshaw's Railway Timetable was the Bishop's favourite reading. With help from A. Chettle, Thomas Cook's representative in Singapore, who was for a time his neighbour on the floor of the Y.M.C.A. cell, they planned elaborate tours and itineraries together, with the best ideas for hotels and restaurants. When they had done all they could in the British Isles they crossed the Channel to France!

A number of those who came back from the Kempei-tai spoke highly of those who had helped them. Several mentioned the Bishop. He did much for many people by his cheerfulness and by his efforts on their behalf. Literally the only way to get medical attention if someone was ill was to shout and to go on shouting whatever happened, until someone in authority came to see what the noise was about. This method the Bishop adopted. Walter Curtis, with his fluent knowledge of Japanese, followed the same courageous course at Smith Street, with similar good results for other people. They could be painful for himself.

No doubt there must have been times when it surprised and infuriated the Japanese, who were unable to subdue these extraordinary British. How, for example, explain the action of the Bishop, whose turn it was to lead the daily P.T. drill? For the Japanese numbers, on one occasion while conducting the familiar arms bending and stretching, he substituted the Sursum Corda — 'Lift-up-your-hearts!'.

BEARERS OF BURDENS IN THE Y.M.C.A.

Their concern for one another went even deeper. The Bishop spoke of the way the prisoners 'bore one another's burdens'. 'We formed' he said later 'a wider fellowship than any I had known before, a fellowship of suffering humanity. Prisoners knew that when they were taken out of the cell for questioning or torture there were others of us behind praying for them . . .'

Amongst doubtless other examples of 'lay evangelism', though they would not have called it that, were the actions of Robert Burns and Sam Travis, both of Changi. At different

¶ times they were in the same cell as a young Chinese, Lam Mau Fatt, to whom they talked a lot about Christianity. Burns advised him if possible to contact the Bishop. He was later transferred to the Bishop's cell, where, after further whispered teaching, he was secretly baptised, on Maundy Thursday, 1944, in the only supply of water available – the lavatory.

The Bishop told me of incidents which showed that he had made an impression on some, though very few, of the Japanese guards. There was one young Japanese interpreter in particular, who, on several occasions, warned the Bishop of answers which might be considered dangerous during interrogations and it was with the same man that he had long and really deep discussions. There were times when he would indicate that the questioning was over for the day. The Bishop would be asked to sit down and more than once they talked for several hours on questions of really vital importance, both political and religious.

After the war his example had almost certainly had some effect on one of the Japanese prisoners, by then in Outram Gaol, sentenced to ten years imprisonment by the War Crimes Tribunal. He had been one of those responsible for the Bishop's interrogation and torture. In 1947 he had been a member of a large group who, after preparation in the gaol, was brought to the Cathedral for baptism and confirmation by the Bishop. Of him the Bishop said, 'I have seldom seen so great a change in a man. He looked gentle and peaceful, even though he was going back to complete a ten year sentence. Later he received communion at my hands in prison.'

¶ It was not until Monday, June 6th, that I began once again to keep a diary, which began with this entry.

A DIARY RE-OPENED

Monday, June 6th, 1944. We have been away from Changi in the glorious freshness of Sime Road for a month – *and the Bishop is back.* With him came all the papers which had been removed when he went to the Y.M.C.A., including my two diaries, taken with other papers from the Cathedral, the one an account of the two months of war, the other various scribblings during our thirteen months together outside. Re-reading these last I have found so much of profit, and learnt so much from what I wrote that I am going to try and keep some record of events here.

'It was, I think, the return of the earlier diaries and knowing that they had been in the hands of the Kempei-tai without any repercussions, which removed most of the anxiety there might otherwise have been about the keeping of a diary. It was still very necessary to write with some discretion, which needs to be remembered in reading what follows.'

LIFE AT SIME ROAD CAMP

First, myself. Weight last Wednesday 8.12, for the first time under 9 stone and nearly half a stone lost in the last seven months, since the Double Tenth. I feel fit enough now we are here and can usually manage to get through a hard morning's work without too much loss of energy. The weight loss is general throughout the camp, but there is no doubt that this change to an open-air life, while meaning a vastly increased amount of work, has benefited most people's general condition.

Today's menu was better than most. Breakfast, 1 pint of kunji [rice porridge] and tea. Lunch, 1 pint of thin vegetable soup, 1 pint of rice. Supper, kunji, fish loaf, savoury spread, tea. Issue to kitchen — 122 lbs. rice, 100 lbs. maize flour, 800 lbs. vegetables. This area comprises about 800 people.

Only a few letters from Mother in over two years.

The Bishop is wonderfully well, very much thinner, bearded, with ghastly scars on his feet — perpetual witnesses to agonising days of horror — but nothing of himself has been lost or changed, unless it be some of his impatience. Certainly none of his love or wisdom. We have talked for hours.

Wednesday, June 8th. The reconstituted clergy discussion group met last night — Tyler Thompson and Hobart Amstutz, American Methodists; Presbyterian, Robert Richards; Jack Bennitt and myself, Anglicans. We were discussing the nature of sacraments.

First morning in the garden below this hut this morning as a regular gardener — carrying and watering, digging over and carrying compost. Glad to have got onto a regular fatigue at last, three hours a day, seven days a week, two morning to one afternoon shift.

Thursday, June 9th. To St. David's for communion this morning — Corpus Christi.

Long talk with 'John' last night. At last he is beginning to find firm ground under his feet — very different from seven or eight months ago when, in his own words, he was 'like a man trying to swim, but all the time groping for the bottom with his feet and often not finding it there'. Now he feels that he has a vocation to the priesthood in rural work at home, but sees the absolute necessity for testing things really thoroughly. The Bishop, now that he is back, does not intend to take any leading part in things clerical and I told him that the more he could leave himself free for personal work the better. John is relying on him for help and there are many others who need it.

Something in me has come to life again with the Bishop's return. After seven and a half months of a feeling of strain and anxiety, I feel as if I am living and breathing again. It has affected me strangely, too. Quite apart from the gladness, I

Figure 15: 'St. David's Church, Sime Road' from P.O.W. Camp Churches by the Revd. J. N. Lewis Bryan, C.F.

feel a much greater confidence than I did. It is partly I know the result of much of the reading I have done while he has been away; partly, too, the sense of liberation which being here means; but much of it centres round him and the relief of tension.

Friday, June 10th. Good morning in the garden, preparing a bed below the bank, digging in lallang [a thick tough grass] and compost for tomatoes. Some doubt as to how they will do here. Apparently, they don't like too much rain, but cherry tomatoes should do something, if only we can keep the blight off them. We look like having plenty of work ahead with new ground the other side of the valley to be broken up, probably for tapioca and root vegetables. The valleys, where the soil is better, will be used entirely for leaf.

Malaria is easing up a bit, although there have been somewhere around two hundred cases in the six weeks we have been here. But the health and hospital authorities have done extremely good work, getting to the root of the problem, with lallang grass clearing and cleaning up of doubtful spots both inside and outside the camp, as well as preventing the re-infection of mosquitoes by 'netting' patients, where possible putting them under mosquito nets at night. Our small area hospital has proved useful. In other areas, any but serious cases have had to remain in their huts. Fortunately, it is the benign tertiary malaria, but one or two people have had a bad spin.

The other snag is a type of Japanese 'river fever' — one of the tropical typhuses. There have been about ten cases so far. It is caused by a small mite deposited in the lallang by rats through their urine. This strain has not proved particularly virulent, but it seems an unpleasant thing to have. [Subsequently it led to six deaths.] Japanese medical authorities were up here today — taking tests, complete with guinea pigs — amongst them (Japanese — not g.p.s!) the senior bacteriologist from the College of Medicine. Whether from interest in our welfare or from interests of science remains to be seen.

Bought a 1 lb jar of Golden Shred for the Bishop yester-

day for $40! Also a bottle of barley water for $10. Small
Red Cross butter tins going for $25! Appalling!

Monday, June 12th. Another reminder of the love and
kindness of the *Annus Mirabilis* of 1942–43 at St. Hilda's,
Katong. First the mosquito net from Violet Scharenquivel,
then some tea, and yesterday $20 each for me and for the
Bishop. [How these things were smuggled in I have no idea.]

It looks as though we are going to be working elsewhere
for some time to come.

Wednesday, June 14th. Two hundred and twenty of us went
out with a hundred chungkols and about twenty axes, in
addition to the woodcutters, with saws and axes. We followed
the new road past Bukit Timah Golf Club, right round the
back of the camp, along the old bridle path by the side of
Watten Estate. We were working alongside the road about a
hundred yards from the junction with Dunearn Road, digging
the ground and felling timber. I was surprised to find how I
was able to stand up to a really energetic morning. The
Japanese in charge went off and bought us enough cheroots
for a general distribution of ten per man. Useful, since we —
Tommy, the Professor (Norman Alexander) and I — are all
nearly out of them.

Out again this morning — wood carrying today. It's difficult to see how this work can be for us, and even odder
coming immediately after the General's remarks that, with
the danger of grave food shortage we must grow food if we
want to eat it — 'Sindiri bikin — sindiri makan'! If that is so,
every available man should be working on our own gardens.
As it is, a total of four hundred men per day are being taken
from the camp and have to walk nearly two miles to get to
the job.

Japanese supplies for the next twenty-five day period
arrived today. Vastly improved Java rice — only 30% milled
and the difference between actual and nominal weight less
than 1%. That 70% of inner husk will give us invaluable
vitamin B and also a good deal more protein. Today I started
on extra 'fatigue rice' — ⅓ pint a day for those who are less
than 85% of expected weight. A good day to start — for the

first time we had savoury rice, fried in palm oil. Very good and filling. We were also due for 'seconds'. What a gorge!

Thursday, June 15th. The Bishop much better this morning. On Tuesday his tummy turned bad on him again, with violent vomiting during the night and feeling very washed out all yesterday. Considerable surprise, therefore, to find him at St. David's when I got there to celebrate this morning. He said he had had the best night since he's been back. But he's quite impossible. He 'skipped like a young unicorn' on his way back to the hospital for breakfast! I do wish he could get right. He lost half a stone last week.

Returned *Oliver Twist* and *Magnolia Street* to the Library.

Friday, June 16th. North Area Servers for Communion. At present there are four. We want one or two more. Try and arrange a meeting for Wednesday evening.

Tuesday, June 20th. How long I wonder? Perhaps not so very long. Black-out practice with sirens last night and, from now on, indefinitely. Our life here goes on unchanged and untroubled. Wireless messages were handed in on Sunday. Mine to Mother read — 'Peacefully fit June 1944 in better camp. Your latest letters July 1943. Overjoyed you have heard. Longing see you.'

At long last we are being better fed. Still very little of real value in the food but plenty of it. We are not likely to grow fat, but one has much more energy. Yesterday I was able to get through a hard morning's chungkoling down on Dunearn Road and today a really hard morning's lallang grass cutting behind the hospital without feeling unduly tired.

Not reading seriously as much as I should like, but nearly every evening I spend at the hospital with the Bishop, who continues to improve, and in the afternoon I feel pleasantly lazy.

Schweizer's lorry, our Red Cross representative, in yesterday with cheroots and cigarettes for free issue — first time for months. We each got fifteen and six respectively. Other supplies have been very intermittent, although 'Aldgate', the home of the Jews and of our black market, and others have

had plenty supplied privately for resale, prices ranging from
40^C to $1.50 for one cheroot! The actual cost of large
cheroots in town is no more than 20^C at the outside. Aldgate
also got 400 lbs of gula malacca, a fudge-like substance, on
Sunday, which they were selling at $10—12 a lb! It's an
appalling price but, oh, how good it is to get something
sweet. 5½ ounces of sugar every ten days does not go far.

Friday, June 23rd. This fatigue business becomes more and
more of a farce. The General comes and says 'Sindiri bikin,
sindiri makan' and immediately we are sent out at the rate
of four hundred, now two hundred, a day to Dunearn Road
to break up ground which cannot be for our produce, and for
the last two days a hundred and eighty men a day have been
on a special fatigue in the Japanese office compound. I was
up there this morning. Fifty of us were on lallang cutting
while the rest dug four funk holes and tidied up three old
slit trenches. They were quite obviously 'finding' jobs for us.
I suppose I worked for half an hour out of two and a half!
    An amusing afternoon yesterday down at Dunearn Road.
At about three it began to pour with rain and all but three
of us came home. We stayed down there climbing mangustine
trees for Osaki and another Japanese. The job done, I asked
Osaki if he could get us some cheroots. Money had been
collected in hope from the fatigue in case I could get any.
He very decently went off to get them while we waited but,
thinking they were for us three and not for the whole fatigue,
would only take $60 of the $130 I had with me. We looted
another mangustine tree while he was away, so altogether
not a bad afternoon — about twenty mangustines each and
two hundred and fifty cheroots for the seventy of us on the
fatigue.

Wednesday, June 27th. We have all been hard at it — from the
loftiest merchant prince down to the lowliest boy — for days
past giving the camp a bit of spit and polish for Lieut.-
General Dohiwara's visit on Friday. I've had two days in the
garden in the last nine. 'Sindiri bikin, sindiri makan'! And
how! The hillside opposite the hut, as a result, is only being
very slowly robbed of its lallang and, until we can get a good

area cleared, fresh planting is, of course, all held up. But what we have done is showing results. We took the first fruits of our planting today − a good full leaf and the rest is doing well. A few more downpours will see it leaping ahead.

A RARE FEAST

Bridge with Eddy, Sorby and the Bishop last night with delicious food afterwards. The Bishop had had a tin of bacon opened and cooked in the Hospital kitchens. That and a tin of butter beans and my rice loaf from tea were unbelievably good. After months of food completely tasteless of anything but pepper, or a very little sugar, the taste of that bacon was something long to be remembered. How long or how soon, I wonder, before our palates can begin to operate again?

I had hoped that here I might learn something about the life of 'birds', but I have seen none except the commoner varieties and not many of them. [In other words − no air activity by Allies!]

Thursday, June 28th, St. Peter's Day. Celebration this morning with many thoughts of Radley, being 'St. Peter's'. John Richards, O.R., and I kept it together for the second year.

THE BISHOP OUT OF HOSPITAL

Sunday, July 1st. Grand day yesterday − the Bishop out of hospital and back in the hut. Norman Alexander and I spent the afternoon rigging up the box for him, with his mattress on top of it as a really comfortable seat, so that it was all ready for him. To have him back with us again is the final step. Now he can put all the beastliness behind him and it's a great joy to be able to know that the whole thing is done with. He and I sat out together last night and prayed with a great thankfulness. This morning early we walked in the moonlight up the valley to St. David's where he celebrated. Praise and thanks to God.

Friday, July 13th. Weight yesterday up 5½ lbs. since last Wednesday to 9.3, very largely due to the fact that Norman has been off his oats since he had a surfeit of mangustines at Dunearn Road about five days ago! Result − considerable extra food for the Bishop and myself. Tommy usually has far more than he can manage anyway.

Siren last night at 9.45 with an alert at 11.30. Flares were dropped. Probably a surprise exercise.

Bobby Burns, Jilani, Travis, Hebditch, Blakstad, Goodall and Day back from Miyako today or direct from the Kempei-tai. Travis and Blakstad to hospital, the others to their huts, apparently fairly fit. Another chapter closed.

The Bishop steadily improving. He's been wearing a pair of my white shorts, but they have had to be returned to *my* store for fear of bursting buttons! His appetite is amazing — entirely changed from his pre-Double Tenth ways. Rice and kunji he can manage now in almost unlimited quantities and greens too — perhaps that's the most amazing of all!

Tuesday, July 17th. The Bishop has had an unfortunate set-back, but is better today after two days feeling very cheap, with aching limbs and fever — round about 101.5. He was tested for dysentery and it was positive, but he's been constipated since yesterday! Odd sort of dysentery. Temperature down today.

The Japanese have let us reopen the schools in both camps and we are to be allowed to preach again as from today — after ten months of neither.

New fatigue regulations. To earn our 50^C a day and 600 grammes of cereals daily, we have to work five hours a day — 9.30—12, 2.30—5.0, with half an hour's break in each period. The Dunearn Road fatigue counts as three hours net, which does not make it quite so bad, but it will be a sweat to have to work morning and afternoon. Those who only do three hours net drop to 30^C and 500 grammes. Most of us feel that, in spite of the expenditure of additional energy, the maximum food is important. I certainly do. I haven't felt so fit since we were outside; vastly improved from Changi where I felt and was completely flat, so much so that I had to have a fortnight off all fatigues at one time.

NORMAN COULSON — THE BRAVEST OF THEM ALL

Wednesday, July 18th. This morning came the news from the Kempei-tai of Norman Coulson's death. Leslie came over to tell us as soon as he heard. The poor old chap will feel it deeply. They were a greatly devoted pair of brothers. Norman would have been remembered for many things, if he had not had to work secretly. Very many people in Changi and Sime Road, without knowing it, owe him a very great deal.

¶ **A WORD ABOUT NORMAN**

Writing of the first days in Changi, the author of the Introduction to the report of the Double Tenth War Crimes Trial in Singapore, published in 1946, said:

> 'Almost the first interest of the internees was to obtain news of friends and relations, some of whom had been in the Forces . . . A records section was set up in the Camp at Changi and by devious means contact was established with other internment and prisoner-of-war camps.'

In 1942 much attention was concentrated in Changi on the fate of many of those who left Singapore in the last few days before the British surrender. More and more, those of us who were still free heard stories of the tragedies which had struck almost all of the small ships which sailed from the Island. Not only were we told of boats which had been bombed and sunk, but we heard also of many who had died, of others who had survived and got to Sumatra, and also of those members of the local community who had reached land and then made their way back to Singapore.

It was with these last that Norman Coulson had numerous contacts. He compiled lists containing a considerable number of names, many of them confirmed and cross referenced on more than one list. I saw them. They were remarkable for their detail and accuracy and for the amount of information they contained. Not content with those which he obtained in the first instance, he set people to work to add to them. With Norman's own personal contacts with the Gaol, they will have formed a valuable addition to the Changi lists.

When he died on July 17th, 1944 (not April 17th as recorded in Appendix II.D of the War Crimes Trial report), ¶ Norman's body was brought to Sime Road Camp for burial. I wrote in my diary:

'For us who were with him outside (in 1942—43) his going leaves a great gap. None of us who knew him then, his painstaking dogged persistence in anything which would help and comfort his friends in Changi, his unselfishness and his generosity and quiet efficiency, will ever forget him. Nothing was too much trouble and he seldom paused to let the risks he was running decide what he should or should not do. It was these qualities which cost him his life.'

Beside his tireless and often dangerous work, he was a wonderful companion. In 1942—43 he and his assistant, Bill Ross, were often with us at Bishopsbourne or Dyson Road. Often one or other or all three of us would call in on them at their workshop in River Valley Road.

It was inevitable that Norman would be arrested by the Kempei-tai. He had been very closely involved in illicit contacts with the Gaol during his official visits, particularly by smuggling money into Changi, of which the Military Police took such a terrifyingly serious view.

Mrs. Freddy Bloom was for many weeks in the same cell with Norman and a dozen others at the Smith Street Centre. In her book *Dear Philip* she said of him and of the extremes of torture he had to bear.

'It did not matter what they did to Norman, they never broke him and always on his return his main concern seemed to be for me. He told me much about his wife, who was a nursing sister, and about his daughter. I am certain that his remarkably kind attitude towards me was somehow evidence of his love for them.

During the months we were together, I spent many hours by his side. He was a deeply religious man and I would read to him from Walter Curtis's Douai version of the Bible. He knew the King James version and objected to some of the wording in this, to him, strange edition, but he would listen thoughtfully and be satisfied . . .

Once, when he came back more dead than alive, he opened his stiff, bloodstained hands and gave me a grubby aspirin. He had actually requested and received it, in the middle of all that was going on, because he

¶   knew I had toothache. As long as the world can produce
      even only occasional men like Norman Coulson, it is
      not a bad thing to be a human being. He was taken away
      from our cell two days before Christmas and I did not
¶   see him again.'

Thursday, July 19th. The Bishop was by no means fit this
morning but insisted on going across to St. David's for a
memorable service for Norman. There was a large crowd
there, including Freddy Bloom, Cicely Williams, Pat Williams,
Sandy Macnab, Mrs. de Mowbray and Mrs. Nairn, who were
allowed through from the Women's Camp with a Sikh guard.
As Vyvyan Frampton said, 'The Bish does know how to say
the right thing at the right moment'. There were so many
things which he might have said, and yet he chose just those
which were most true of Norman and of most help to those
who heard them. I went to Bidadari in the Bishop's place.
A large crowd was lining the road from St. David's all the way
to the Main Gate. 'Puss in Boots', the Japanese guard, was
very considerate, with a moment of respectful homage before
the grave was filled in.

    Confirmation at St. David's yesterday evening — a joyful
service as it always is, more especially in the case of adult
candidates, of whom there were thirteen — Hugh Bryson,
Wilfrid Ward, Charley Squire, Donald Cullen, Alec Morrison
and Harry Hesp (two "Asia Boys"), Dick Hill, Skipper
Thomas (who heard not long since in one of his letters he
had been given an O.B.E.), Bert Jennings, Jimmy Phipps,
Fred Gulland, 'Squibs' Elbury and Ted Hebditch. The Bishop
spoke of some of the stumbling blocks to Christian disciple-
ship, but the claims Christ makes admit of no compromises.
The Kingdom can only be brought in by our own courageous
action wherever we happen to be, in whatever vocation.

July 25th–27th. Hugh Fraser, Colonial Secretary and Alan
Ker back yesterday afternoon from Y.M.C.A. and the Kempei-
tai. Hugh Fraser died yesterday evening, of acute dysentery,
in the Camp hospital.

OF FOOD, AND WORK, AND BOOKS — AND, MAINLY, PEOPLE

August 1st. Another month and life goes on much the same. The letters which we know are here — our own Post Office have sorted them — are still denied us. There are now about 20,000, some of them from home as late as March, 1944.

Food continues plentiful in quantity, but no meat, and fresh fish only about once in six weeks. The kitchens are showing more enterprise — ⅝ of a lb. of fish pie made of dried fish — soggy in the middle, but good and crusty outside. It's good to get something to bite on for a change after slops, slops, slops. 'Sime Road bread', the usual evening addition to kunji, is an improvement on the old veg. and rice loaf. It's dryer and crisper.

We still go out to Dunearn Road, tearing the heart out of a small rubber plantation, felling the trees and carting the wood. Since we burn about eight tons a day in the kitchens we need all the wood we can get.

Rumours flying about that we are due for a move from here up country. Nothing to go on really, but some say Tanjong Rambutan Mental Hospital near Ipoh, others Port Dixon — wish father to the thought. Now we are settled here I hope to goodness we don't have another shift.

Very little reading these days. They are too full to be able to do much. Streeter's *Reality* is extraordinarily valuable — a book I shall always have by me after this. The chapter on 'The problem of evil' says, better than anything I have ever found, what my mind has been groping after for some time. A world free from risk or the possibility of moral failure is no world for men, no 'vale of soul making' in which men can hope to achieve any degree of moral stature. The natural response to suffering and pain is one of depression and submission to it. But the acceptance of it and right attitude towards it has redemptive quality both for the sufferer and for the witness of pain.

[There is a two month gap here in the writing of the diary.]

Sunday, October 15th. Mundane things still deserve to find a large place here. To read that the day was spent with Brock,

Norman Alexander and Tyler Thompson on the hill making
drills for sweet potatoes, will bring to mind far more than
the heat and sweat of straddle-legged chungkol work. There
will be Brock streaming with perspiration, lifting his sodden
topee to release the flood of sweat from his bald pate; Tye,
American Methodist Missionary, Apollo-like, 6'1", fair
crinkled hair glistening in the sun, showing in all he does and
says the competence and efficiency of the New World;
Norman, mahogany tanned, weaned from his former crazy
and feverish activity, wise and astonishingly astute, as quick
as any man I know to detect and pounce upon false reasoning
or sloppy thinking — and myself, like Norman, plodding on,
but without the feverish and foolish energy of three and four
months ago. It is a quartet as harmonious as it is international.
We come from Canada, California, New Zealand and England.
The talk flies between one and another or Tye and I burst
into song. Yes, the simple phrase 'bed-making on the hill'
carries with it many associations.

Perhaps the most surprising thing is that we are still here.
There is hardly a day when rumour does not raise its head,
but we grow wise and cautious. Perhaps when the end comes,
a great cry of 'Wolf, wolf' will go up from four thousand
sceptics, and tourists of the future will come to stare at us,
as we grow old here, refusing to believe that we are free,
however authoritative the source.

The Bishop seems very much better after a month in the
Camp Hospital. He had already had another month here in
the Area Hospital. Temperature still swings about a bit, but
he is far better than he was.

We've been allowed to send another postcard. Mine to
Mother read — 'well and bearded. Was Grandfather ginger?'

Food cycle slightly on the up-grade again after a long
decline. For about six weeks we have had little oil or polished
rice and not much fish. Now we have enough cargo rice to
last until the end of the month if issued on alternate days, a
good supply of oil and enough salt fish, ikan bilis, not unlike
whitebait, to give us fish paste daily for at least a week.

I find the daily food ration adequate, but no more than
that and only just that for the work we have to do. Today's
menu; breakfast, 1¼ pints of red bean kunji and coffee;

lunch, 1½ pints of fried rice, 1 pint of veg. soup and fish
paste; supper, plain kunji, a rice bun of about five ounces,
with a tablespoon of savoury spread and another of fried
spinach.

Work, 9–12, 2–5 with Wednesdays and Sundays as half
holidays. It sounds more than it really is, once the tea interval
in the middle of both spells spins itself out to something like
forty minutes. Half an hour is the official time plus one day
off a week. Norman, Tye and I are lucky. The garden where
we work is only a few yards from the hut and we can come
to read in comfort between whiles. The great snag of these
hours is that, with darkness at 8.15 there is all too little time
to oneself. For some weeks we shall be kept busy clearing
the hillside opposite for planting and preparing the beds.
Fortunately we are able to go at our own pace. Most of us
have found that we can't work as we once did – not on our
present diet!

Wednesday, October 18th. Yesterday a year ago the Bishop
was arrested. Since the Double Tenth Buchanan, Stephenson,
Bryning, Adrian Clark, Dr. Stanley, Norman Coulson, Hugh
Fraser, Pretty Perry and Alan Ker have died, the last three in
hospital here, Fraser and P.P. being brought back in a dying
condition and lasting only a few hours. Alan Ker's death
came sadly from heart failure after a slow two months of
battling, but apparently, we thought, successful. P.P.'s death
probably affected Alan deeply. Lionel Earle, Hugh Macintyre,
Hilary Rendle, Arthur Birse, Bobby Calderwood, Walter
Curtis, Bill Cherry, John Dunlop, Jack Bowyer, Wulfram
Penseler, Sam Middlebrook, Robert Scott and Mrs. Nixon
are still away. John Long has been back about three weeks
and is picking up well. His whole body was enormously
swollen with beri-beri when he arrived.

Reading has to be snatched in odd moments between and
after work, but I've recently finished Hensley Henson's
Christian Morality – and profited from it enormously.

Sunday, October 22nd. Middlebrook came back from Outram
Road gaol on Wednesday, terribly thin and weak, with
dysentery, but not apparently very serious. He was, naturally,

over-excited but, in spite of his physical condition, mentally alert and cheerful. The doctors had great hopes for him. He died quietly in his sleep the same night.

A GOOD READ!

Monday, October 23rd. Just finished Ann Bridge's *The Ginger Griffin* which, with *Peking Picnic, Four-part Setting* and *Illyrian Spring*, makes the fourth of hers I have read — and all of them enjoyed. Some of her descriptive writing is sheer joy — minute observation, and a clear sense of colour and form, together with the artist's exclusive eye for the significant, with a historical sense thrown in, all combine to give such passages as that in which she describes the general effect of Chinese architecture.

> 'Its supreme wonder lies in its use of space. It is not only in the curved pillared roofs, built to imitate the pole-propped tents of their ancestors, that the architects of the Forbidden City betray their nomadic origin. By a strange skill in proportions, by isolating great pavilions in immense stretches of flagged paving, they have succeeded in bringing into their palace courts the endless places of the Gobi desert. The eye travels over the lower walls surrounding each mighty enclosure to distant roof-trees, and beyond these to others more distant still, with a sense of beholding mountain ranges hull-down on vast horizons; the gold of the roofs suggests the wonder of dawn and sunset on far off snows.'

The great sweep of far horizoned landscapes, the massed heads of skilfully grafted chrysanthemums, the sights, sounds and smells of the bustling, hurrying streets, the restraint and delicacy of a beautiful room — and this from the Cotswolds.

> 'Down the valley the road passed through a marshy place, where the stream expanded on either side into reedy patches of water, masked and fringed with thickets of alder and sallow. In the soft February starlight she had stopped here, deliberately; she wanted to hear the silence, to smell the damp, leafy smell of the sedgy pools, to see the stars shine back from the dark water,

and watch the young moon low between the dim tracery
of slender twiggy branches.'

In all her writing there is the same certainty of touch, and
how she reaches us, so far as we are from the beauty of which
she writes.

KEMPEI-TAI VICTIMS

Wednesday, October 25th. Yesterday, Lionel Earle, Cherry,
Bowyer and Penseler came back from town. Lionel terribly
weak and emaciated, but after a good night there is much
more hope for him than yesterday evening. Someone who
had a few words with him this morning was surprised and
pleased to find him better than he had hoped, perfectly lucid
and cheerful without being too exuberant. Cherry too is on
the D.I. list, but the other two are better than any who have
come back since the Bishop and Yoxall. That leaves eleven
still away.

Theological reading – just read Dobson's *Worship* from the
S.C.M. Book Club. A short book, but excellent in its survey
of the current need for rethinking and revision of worship
forms.

Saturday, November 4th. About a week ago two more came
back from the Kempei-tai, Hugh Macintyre and Birse – but
we have had more losses. Rendle's body was returned to us
for burial. Bowyer and Penseler have both died. That they
should go, who were so much better than Cherry and Lionel
Earle, was a shock to us all, the more so since we had not
thought of them, until the last, as in grave danger. Meanwhile
Lionel and Bill Cherry seem to be going on well. But the
heart-breaking thing is to realise on what a very thin thread
their lives depend. So many things may go wrong and they
have so little resistance. Last night I was allowed to see Hugh
Macintyre for the first time, and Lionel. Both impressed me.
For about forty eight hours after he got back, Mac had been
delirious and I doubt whether anyone thought very much of
his chances. But apart from a certain difficulty in remembering names he was quite normal while I was with him. Always
allowing for unforeseen developments, his physical condition

does not seem too bad. He certainly has none of the beri-beri puffiness with which so many of the others have come back. Reports have been consistently good about Lionel, but even so it was still a delight to find him full of sparkle and mentally like a rock.

ALLIED AIR ATTACKS

Sunday, November 5th. Guy Fawkes Day and a morning of fireworks; real or not? Who knows? But small groups of large planes have been flying along the north of the Island from the west and swinging away over the Naval Base. Plenty of A.A. going up, but it's impossible to say whether they are firing on the planes. They may have been flying round and away to return again, in which case there were about twelve. But in all we have seen more than thirty, the largest a group of eight. One solitary siren went at about 9.45. Now at 11.15 there is still desultory firing.

(Later) No one knows for certain whether it was a raid or some large-scale exercise, but general opinion leapt immediately to the former.

The trouble is that, after two and a half years of waiting for something to happen, and having been fooled again and again by gossip and rumour, we are most reluctant to believe just those things we most hope for. The strange thing was the sounding of no more than one siren. But at the Green House Japanese H/Q there was consternation. The telephone went, the blue flag was hoisted; soon, after another telephone call, the red was run up. Figures rushed hither and thither in some alarm.

The total number of planes which passed over the Naval Base was forty-seven or forty-eight, including two which turned away to the south and flew east to west along the south coast. The story of four columns of black smoke from Tanjong Pagar just after these two had passed, I haven't confirmed. From our position here in the centre of the Island, it was impossible to tell whether or not bombs were dropped. All one can say is that, if it was only an exercise, it was extremely realistic!

Mid-day news from the Hospital says that Birse is seriously

ill. Another who has lost ground rapidly after getting back here.

The beard is a great success now that it's had its first trim. Twirling moustachios and a smart point on the chin. It's a good thick growth, without the barren patches of some. The colour is a rich Elizabethan 'orange-tawny'. I have been assured by Geoffrey ffoliott that if, although it seems doubtful, we are allowed to revive 'George and Margaret', I shall be allowed to play Dudley, like Pyramus, in 'your orange-tawny beard'.

General Saito has given permission for more entertainments, but Collinge is going to tell the Japanese that, unless we are allowed to rehearse in working hours, we can't do plays. 9–12, 2–5 in the blazing sun, even allowing for the forty minutes break in each period, does not leave one with much energy at the end of the day. Certainly not for the massive part of Karen Selby in Charles Morgan's *The Flashing Stream*, which was being mooted for me at the time of the Double Tenth!

John Woods is starting the Glee-Singers again which will mean the first good music for the camp in more than a year. Farrell has done some good work with his Wednesday concerts, but he hasn't been very enterprising with his music or his entertainers.

FRIENDS BY MOONLIGHT

Since May when we came here I have usually sat after lights out, early now at 9.30, with an interesting group. Tyler Thompson, 29, our American Methodist Missionary, very keen brain, with highly developed critical faculty. He has already appeared in this diary. I've got to know him really well working on our 'potato patch' recently. Leonard Morris, about 35, extremely well-read and well-informed, advanced Socialist, good talker. Norman Alexander, 39, the fourth member of our 'family' here in the hut. He took the Bishop's place in our B3 cell in Changi about a year ago when newcomers arrived in the Gaol and had to be accommodated in 'D' block. He is Professor of Physics at Raffles College, very clear thinker, hatred of anything smacking of loose argument or bad logic; generous, ready wit, with a great

natural and unassuming goodness. He was a very good cell-
mate in Changi and has got on splendidly with Tommy, the
Bishop and me. Brian Williams, 28, the youngest of us, a
Municipal Water Engineer. Good, quick, and analytical brain.
Macindoe, about 33, a complete enigma and the cynic of the
party. Sometimes irritatingly bitter and disillusioned. Jack
Bennitt, Diocesan Chinese Missioner, also well and widely
read. First in Maths at Cambridge and an original thinker.
'Doc' Tyson, 29, good at his job, and interesting when drawn.
Great Noel Coward fan. Pinnick, an economist by training
and in his speech. The Bishop and I complete a pretty motley,
but extremely interesting crew. We talk learnedly of many
things and always with interest, of food, books, the psy-
chology of sleep, engineering and of many kindred subjects.
We are never dull and God help anyone who is suspected of
false reasoning — usually me!

The Bishop has been out of hospital and back with us for
nearly three weeks. He seems to be completely recovered and
able to go off with Tommy every morning for one and a half
hours of leaf-cropping in the garden. He is far more at peace
than he ever was in Changi and, I think, happy.

Tuesday, November 7th. Today has been one of incident.
First came the rumours that Lionel Earle had been removed
again by the Kempei-tai — appalling if true, but the truth
was not as serious as it seemed. They did come, both for him
and Hugh Macintyre, but were convinced that Mac was too
ill to move. Lionel was carried off in a lorry, but Dr. Palester
was allowed to go with him — a clear enough indication that
it was only temporary. They were taken to Raffles College
and hung about outside for a time — long enough for Lionel
to have an attack of diarrhoea in the lorry! Perhaps it was
that which convinced the Japanese officer who approached
the lorry that Lionel was no very desirable companion.
Whether or not, they came straight back here and Lionel
none the worse, praise be!

Incident No. 2. Six nursing sisters are to be allowed (after
two and a half years!) to do day duty in the hospital, looking
after those who've been returned from Outram Road Gaol
and any others seriously ill. The last application was made

three months ago when Hugh Fraser came back, but met with the same blank refusal. Several doctors have said that careful nursing would have been of more value than anything else to some of those who were returned by the Kempei-tai, so weak were they. I imagine, too, that some at least of the six who died from typhus might have pulled through if this concession had been allowed earlier.

Incident No. 3. Mrs. Nixon and Dunlop came back this afternoon, both of them able to walk and generally much fitter than any of the others from Outram Road Gaol.

Thursday, November 9th. Kempei-tai in again this morning, but only to see Birse, now much fitter, to tell him that he had been tried in his absence and pardoned. Rumour has it that Mrs. Nixon and Dunlop will have been tried on the same charges and with the same result.

A solitary raider stirred up the whole hornet's nest this morning. Some heard a distant siren at about 11.30. At 11.45 we heard gunfire and saw a few bursts only over the town. One or two people saw a single plane making its stately progress westwards over the town. Jack Bennitt was at Bidadari Cemetery for a funeral and said that bombs were definitely dropped somewhere in the Kallang aerodrome direction. All traffic was stopped and people were running for shelter. Coming so soon after Sunday's effort, and after suspicious flashes and bumps in the night, it really begins to look as though we are at long last on the allied operational programme and that we may expect further and intensified visits. Fighters were taking the air in all directions, in addition to those which had been flying way up top since daylight.

Ours is an astonishing position here, placed as we are in the middle of the principal Japanese stronghold in the south western regions. It is now being attacked for the first time, and yet we might be on an island of the moon for all the apparent difference it makes. The whole thing seems completely unreal.

Saturday, November 11th. Armistice Day. Permission for a service in the Women's Camp this morning was refused, but we were allowed a mid-morning service at St. David's — quite a good crowd. Rumours fly around. Airy talk of 'no more work' and stand-by 'beginning in a few days' time'. What does it mean? Probably nothing. Weight yesterday − 9.8. That's better!

Monday, November 13th. Two local stories. (1) Internee to Kasimoto − 'I thought you said Singapore would never be bombed!' K. − 'A chicken always flaps its wings when its head is cut off.' I. − 'But there was Wednesday's raid as well as Sundays.' K. − 'They obviously aren't much good. They only come on half-holidays!' (2) Japanese to Internee − 'Soon there will be fighting here.' I. − 'Garn!' J. − 'Yes, there will − and you will have to stay in your huts!' Surely, a slight under-statement, since we are on the Island's main battle-field!

Stories of a possible move also persist. Not another, for pity's sake!

Thursday, November 16th. Weekly day off, always good. This morning as usual to St. David's. Tomorrow St. Hugh's Day. Thoughts of Lincoln, Hugh Blackburne and particularly Hugh Macintyre.

I haven't seen him again, but I hear he is going on well. The Bishop saw him yesterday and had some talk with him. I remember clearly, before the Double Tenth, a long talk with him one Sunday evening in 'B' yard. He had had a beastly internment with the gnawing uncertainty about his wife, who had left Singapore late, but through it all his mind had been searching for solid ground. For no apparent reason he had, on an impulse, decided to go to the service in 'D' yard that evening, not knowing that the Bishop was preaching. He found the answer to some of the questions which were perplexing him. That was only the beginning and I remember him saying that his own analytical and sceptical attitude made it difficult for him to accept before he had tried and tested his experience.

I gave him the analogy of a man climbing a tree, with the memory of past falls and disappointments, some of them heavy, testing every branch before giving it his whole weight. Having done that, faith in some degree is always necessary.

He cannot be certain that he will not be let down until he has put all his weight on the branch. As with others, Hebditch, Travis, Cherry, Long, Ker and, in some measure, Penseler, he has, through his experience found that the branch is firm and more than adequate to bear the weight of human pain, disappointment, sorrow and doubt. He has said he wants to be confirmed — 'And God saw that it was good'.

Evidence of a plane and gunfire over Seletar yesterday morning seems fairly sound. I didn't see it. One of our troubles is that there are no sirens within easy hearing of us here and their train whistles, like London buses, are very deceptive. That and almost continual rumblings of distant thunder make it hard for us to know if anything is going on unless it be really close as on the 5th. A good many say there were sirens at 4 and 7.15 this morning. Again, they may be right.

John Woods has revived the Glee Singers. It's good to be at it again, singing something worthwhile.

Norman is reading Wells' *Outline of History*. Pict, Scots, Danish and Norman invasions are dismissed in a single paragraph — and a short one at that. Wells may be overdoing it a bit, but at any rate it is a healthier attitude towards history than that which deals with battles, treaties and diplomatic niceties, while telling nothing of the people and things — the common stuff of life.

Saturday, November 18th. Ten thousand five hundred letters released yesterday. Three from Mother dated April 19 and 27 and May 4 this year. She had just got one of my wireless messages in which I told her not to worry. Her 'Insist on worrying!' pleased me. I liked its note of healthy common sense. Of course she is worrying. Would to God we were through the next few months. This time next year? How I wonder if I shall have been able to get home by then, but I think it more likely to be early 1946. Perish the thought!

Gardeners given extra rice today, some sort of Japanese harvest thanksgiving and four pigs killed. Yesterday it was announced that we were to have a whole holiday — today at lunch-time comes notice that that was a mistake. We are to work this afternoon and tomorrow, Sunday, afternoon to make up for this morning. Typical! But they haven't cancelled the pigs or the rice!

Sunday, November 19th. Siren at 10.15 this morning — the first time our own hand-moaner has been sounded, but nothing developed. I left for Bidadari and a funeral at 11, but town was quite normal, although there had been no all-clear. A fair number of people moving about, some of whom I knew. They seemed cheerful enough.

As a sign of change in the value of money, I watched a rickshaw coolie giving $7.50 to his client in exchange for a $10 note. $2.50 would have meant the hire of the rickshaw for about a week before the war! And the coolie who had change for $10 was then a strange phenomenon!

Monday, November 20th. Planes over this evening, only one of which was visible, flying over the town from the east, followed by A.A. fire. He swung away sharply to the south when somewhere over the harbour area, which looked as though bombs might have been dropped there. One or two fairly heavy crumps, but difficult to tell whether they were bombs or the sound of the guns. Some A.A. fire fairly close to the north, but the planes were invisible behind low cloud.

Thursday, November 23rd. The Bishop's birthday and a grand day. Large wad of 'medicine' and crackling, smuggled again out of the Japanese kitchen, large excellent cake from the Women's Camp, a beano with Ormiston, Peter Ellis, Dr. Harry Allen, and Dr. Gunstensen. Excellent menu of poached egg on rice toast, ⅓ tin of bully minced on bubble and squeak rissole, kitchen fish and veg. slice, hot and crisp, and coffee. Delicious. Then Vivyan Frampton in the evening with more rice and soup pirated from the Japanese kitchen.

Struggling most of the day with Sunday's sermon in the Glen. Brain completely addled these days, principally un-settlement caused by air alarms and excursions, or the possibility of them.

Friday, November 24th, More letters — three for me, one of them early 1943, a longer one — the other two, of twenty-five words, also from 1943. The Bishop had a letter from Mary in which she mentioned having had a wireless message and one from me — her 'nephew'. We were only allowed to send to 'relatives' in Australia on that occasion.

Smith and O'Neill back after two and a half years in Outram Gaol and both in very good shape. Three out of the six from the Cleansing Department died in the early stages. They were originally sentenced for views overheard in a coffee shop which were critical of the Japanese. Gow was the first to come back about two months ago. These two had more time to make up, having been longer in Miyako, where Smith especially had been desperately ill with beri-beri.

Thursday, November 30th. St. Andrew's Day. Winston's birthday, Thanksgiving Day and full moon, but none of these made any difference to allied strategy.

Figure 16: Bert Neyland's final New Year greeting.

ANOTHER GREAT CHRISTMAS
1945 — The first week in January.

I wouldn't like it to be generally known, *but*, we're still here! Rumours have been rife, but they don't get us out of here, nor do they bring the war to an end. Christmas was a great delight and added much to the store of memories of happiness we have, in spite of everything, known here and at Changi.

It began with a Carol Service in the Orchard on Christmas Eve, when the Women's Camp were allowed to attend. It was the first combined service we have had. It was very, very, lovely. Eight hundred men and about one hundred and fifty of the women in that beautiful setting. Hobart Amstutz, the American Methodist, and the Bishop taking the service, based largely on the traditional form of carols interspersed with lessons, Gordon Van Hien conducting about fifty of us in the Camp Choir. I wrote of it afterwards to Mary Scott, who was with Sandy Macnab in the front row.

There were three joyous moments. Diana Mary Macnab, now nearly two and a half, was looking adorable. She was thrilled to see the Bishop dressed, as she told me after our Christmas afternoon in the Orchard, 'in his blue'. She kept pointing her podgy finger at him, her lips framing a delighted 'B, B, B — Mummy, there's B'. And as one carol followed another, she began to dance. She's a lovely child.

The second impression, which almost brought me to tears, most moving with its pathos and such great courage, was the verse of Nowell which the women sang. It summed up so much of the way in which they have behaved these last three years. At all times life has been more difficult for them than for us. They have had none of the comforts to which they have always been accustomed and our hosts have done nothing to make things easier for them. From February, 1942, until the time of our arrival in Changi at the end of March, 1943, husbands and wives had been allowed to meet only once — on Christmas Day. They are, too, a complete menagerie of so many different types, and there have been times of real anxiety — the Double Tenth for instance, when they were cut off from all communication with us for several months and knew nothing of what was happening. Perhaps

" WE ARE NOT PRISONERS — WE ARE CIVILIAN INTERNEES "

Figure 17: 'We are not prisoners . . .' by Bert Neyland.

worst of all for them was the anxiety for Freddy Bloom, Cicely Williams and, later, Mrs. Nixon, all of them taken away by the Kempei-tai. But they have never wavered. Appalling as it is that they should have had to endure the privation and deprivation of these three years, their being here has made an enormous difference to us. Apart from the many acts of love and service which have come from them, contacts with people like Sandy, Mary Scott and Cicely Williams mean a very great deal and help to keep us more normal than we should otherwise be. Letters, under nominal Japanese censorship, pass freely between the two camps. Relatives — real or spurious! — are able to meet in the Orchard for an hour on Sundays, but beyond that all contact is barred. It is still damnable and unforgivable that they should be here.

The third and very deep impression at the Carol Service was the sight of Margaret Webb, standing alone under the trees with little Margaret in her arms, the child's head resting in the crook of her mother's neck. A great stillness and a great peace was over them both and a rare loveliness.

My mind went back to the great Carol Service in the Cathedral of which I wrote at Christmas, 1942, when people were standing in all the aisles, right up through the choir and chancel, into the Sanctuary itself. In the centre of the lowest step stood Alexander, the Bishop's Indian secretary, and his wife, holding their child, Mary, in her arms. That too was an unforgettable picture and said more to me of Christmas than all the carols. There was eternity in it. As long as people can look as they did then, and as the two Margarets did in the Orchard, all is not wholly lost with our tired world.

On Christmas morning the Bishop and I went across to the Women's Camp. Last year he was in the Y.M.C.A. and I, in Changi, held an illicit communion service in one of the cells on K 2. John Richards reminded me of it again after the Carol Service. Before the service the Bishop had a confirmation of four. It was lovely to be there in the open air on the Hospital Hill and afterwards everybody very cheery. Back down the hill, after a cup of coffee from Mary Hughes, with Diana Mary, a small blanket pinned round her and held by an enormous safety-pin. And there, at the bottom of the hill, Mary Bell in a kimono, swinging a skipping rope with Buster.

Home and happy to a large breakfast, followed by a visit to the Hospital and then on for coffee and a huge cheroot with John Richards, Tommy, Cecil Wilson and Christopher Dawson. A vast lunch and, from two till four, the meeting in the Orchard.

Each of the women was allowed to invite three guests and what a sight it was. Every available inch of shade crammed with people, the women looking grand, dressed in all their best, hair beautifully done, looking gay and fresh, and all of us in what few glad rags we have still got left. (As I write, January 11, Norman's wife, Mary Alexander's birthday, an alert is in progress at 11 a.m. with distant bumps and many fighters up high.) Sandy had sent invitations to the Bishop,

George Cessford and me. For the first hour I was with Mrs.
Williams and her daughter, Pat, and then with the two
Marys, Scott and Hughes. I'd never realised how deliciously
Irish Mrs. W. is. The broadest of brogues and used very freely.
There were only a few things which (another bump!) spoiled
the Garden Party atmosphere — one of them was the sight
of Mrs. W. beautifully gowned and groomed, presiding over
the coffee table — smoking a cheroot! (And it has developed
into a full scale raid.)

One of the astonishing things was the quantity and, still
more, the quality of food which they had produced. Mrs.
Williams had some delicious rice biscuits, spread with tomato
and chilli paste, while the Marys' cake had to be tasted to be
believed. Very light 'chocolaty' mixture with about half an
inch of gula malaka paste on top and a good sized wodge of
it. They had a biggish crowd there and I had only a few words
with Mary S. — very much the busy hostess — when I went
back for the last hour with Sandy and Diana. More eats —
ham roll sandwiches, delicious shortbread, conjured out of
nothing, rice 'hooch' and coffee. Sandy bubbling over with
good spirits, Diana very sweet — but all too soon came four
o'clock, and the end, after profitable use of Sandy's mock
mistletoe.

The Bishop and I wandered away, he very, I slightly,
nostalgic, he back to the hut to sleep, I to the top of 'Pig
Farm Hill' to hatch out a surprise for Denis Soul, who had
written a round as a Christmas card. David Coney, Gordon
van Hien, Tampsen and I rehearsing and then bursting into
song as he appeared over the hill. Back to the hut again, hot
and full, tired and content.

Good concert up on the road in the evening, but for sheer
enjoyment and atmosphere the children's concert on Boxing
Day in the Women's Camp was streets better. It flopped
badly, as I was afraid it would, when we repeated it here.
Charton, Harry Miller and Byrom conjuring, Bones Kirby
and Bob Storer, song and dance and 'the old sow', Al Greig
and his lightning sketches, and Grubbel with some good
conjuring, the last two admirably stooged by Sladek, formerly
a circus clown by profession. About the only calling not
represented amongst us would seem to be professional poet

or novelist. The orchestra played and I sang Jingle Bells, Old King Cole and 'The Good Little Boy and the Bad Little Boy'.

> I'll sing you a song of a good little boy,
> And a bad little boy also.
> There's really a moral to this little song,
> But what I don't quite know
> But list' to me and verily,
> I'll prove before I've done,
> That the good little boy gets all the praise,
> But the bad'un gets all the fun.

The second two verses were bright efforts of the Bishop's.

> The good little boy is kind to the child,
> And never tries to smack her.
> The bad little boy always beats the child,
> And he gets her gula malaka.
> The good little boy never walks in the road,
> And always says he's sorry.
> The bad little boy runs all over the road,
> But he gets his ride on the lorry.

> The good little boy is healthy and clean,
> And always rubs the Lux in.
> The bad little boy cuts open his shin,
> 'Cos he knows it's the day the duck's in.
> The good little boy climbs the ladder of life,
> He always is a trier.
> The bad little boy climbs trees with a knife,
> And he nips the biggest papaya.

We finished with ten minutes of community singing and then Auld Lang Syne. There was a concerted and spontaneous rush from the verandah of the hut, led by Mary Hughes, for a hand-joined circle and an enormous cheer as we finished. It was a real good end to a very lovely Christmas.

DEATH OF MRS. GRAHAM WHITE

Sunday, January 7. Mrs. Graham White, the Archdeacon's wife, known to her friends as Nobs, has died. She has had an amazing influence in the Women's Camp. Like the Arch-

deacon she has been unwell at intervals throughout internment, but no matter how she has felt, people going to her
with their troubles have found the help they wanted. In a
mixed community such as theirs, there have been many
personal problems and irritations. It has been due to her as
much as to anyone that they have achieved a community in
which friction has at least been reduced. I'm glad it was my
turn to go to the Women's Camp last Sunday when I was
able to give her communion. She could barely speak and was
terribly thin and very tired, but she had a firm hand clasp
and gave me a glorious smile. Last night she asked for the
Bishop and for me, but when we got there this morning
she had died. We feel sure she wanted to ask us to look after
Graham.

Monday, January 8th. Mother's birthday. The Bishop and I
celebrated with a tin of bully for lunch after I'd got back
from taking Jepson's funeral at Bidadari. Nothing to see in
town. In the evening, B had a scrambled egg for me. Delicious.
The first for eighteen months. Solitary raider over shortly
after lunch. We've seen no others for about a month. He flew
along the north of the Island. First we heard was two healthy
crumps followed by A.A. fire.

Wednesday, January 10th. Another plane, again just after
lunch, flying east to west over the town. Joint kongsi celebration in the evening for Mother's and Mary Alexander's
birthdays. The Japanese looked suspicious of such high spirits.
Large tin of tongue, with mustard!, and a tin of chicken soup
heated up and poured over it. Magnifique!

Weight in the morning up another two pounds to 10.1.
Hurray! Prewar 11.6; capitulation 10.10; lowest pre-Changi
10.3; Changi 10.10; May '44 in Sime Rd. 9.5; July 8.11;
November 9.7; December 9.9; January '45 9.11. Norman up
about a stone in two months. Tommy up 5 lbs. this month
and the Bishop over 11.6 gives us a pretty good record.
Practically everybody up this time.

Thursday, January 11th. Our second big raid — the first on
November 5. Sirens went at 10.30, followed twenty minutes
later by considerable noise from the north. Much A.A. fire

and heavier sounds as of bombs. Thin high cloud until about 11.20 when low cloud blew up. Our planes appeared singly through clóud breaks. Saw about twenty-five, flying over the Island from all directions. One straight overhead at considerable height we could identify as four-engined. Many fighters up and sounds of much machine-gun fire above the clouds. Saw several instances of fighters tailing the bombers, but none seemed to engage. Almost appeared at times as though they must be our fighters, but this most improbable. Saw two of our planes together far away to the north. A few seconds later a plane was streaking down in flames. Looked as though it must have been one of those two. Main target seemed to be Johore and the Naval Base, but thin cloud of smoke from Tanjong Pagar and the roar of two bombs falling, followed by the double crash of the explosions in the Kallang direction. Probably about fifty planes involved in all. Several bits of A.A. fragments fell in camp. Much discussion as to where these planes are coming from. Colombo possibly, but we have no means of knowing. One odd thing is that in a region where weather disturbances are always extremely local, they have not yet struck bad weather, whereas today, to have been half an hour later would have made accurate bombing impossible. Wherever the planes may be operating from, they seem to have accurate meterological information, which can only be obtained close at hand.

Friday, January 12th. The Bishop has plans for a camp-wide evangelistic campaign during Lent, each of the clergy to be responsible for about four huts, forming a small nucleus of three or four laymen in each, who would meet regularly with the clergy for prayer and discussion and to work quietly 'to arouse the careless and to open the eyes of the blind'. I have 121 — a good hut, the best of the four; 122, very tough. 135, an unknown quantity, and 129, the former Piccadilly, fair. The Bishop will deal with this hut, 131, and Jack Bennitt with the other four at the top of the hill.

Reading *The Golden Age*. I can't think why nobody has ever told me about Kenneth Grahame, and *Dream Days* too. They are sheer delight and really good writing. *A Tale of Two Cities* for the first time not long ago, which, except for

Pickwick Papers, I've enjoyed most of those very few Dickens I have read — *Nicholas Nickleby, Oliver Twist* and *David Copperfield. Dombey and Son* is having to be interrupted for the reading of Taylor Caldwell's *The Earth is the Lord's* which Brock has been urging me to read — the life of Genghis Khan. I'm only able to have it from the library for this week, but it is a magnificent study of the life of the Gobi and the gradual consolidation of the tribes.

Friday, February 2nd. And now *David Copperfield*, which Charles, Mother, Peter and I read long ago on one of Charles's leaves from Calcutta.

MANY MORE AIR RAIDS

Yesterday out at Watten Estate again, where we are clearing and ridging a large area for planting. 10.30 alert sounded in town, 10.45 wailer — long pause with no more than six fighters at considerable height. 11.5 four planes flew in from the S.W. and away over the Naval Base. For the next seventy minutes, with an interval of about five minutes, groups of planes were continually coming in on the same course, dropping their bombs and shearing away. First the group of four, followed by others of eleven, ten, seven and six, each of them greeted by considerable A.A. fire, but, in spite of a lot of machine-gun fire — three bullets came down in the camp — all above the clouds, no fighters engaged or came anywhere near our planes. As each of them flew over the Base we waited for the sound of the bombs, which, even at ten or eleven miles, was terrific. But more was still to come — much more.

At about this stage we saw low down over the trees what seemed like a pack of planes coming in, looking exactly like a skein of geese, nineteen of them, in irregular formation, but obviously drawn up on some plan. One suggestion was made that each of the planes had its particular target and flew in such a formation that, at a given moment, each of them would be over its objective. This of course would explain the single bomber which followed this big lot. He was after the loos! It was an astonishing sight and, if one didn't think too deeply, a very beautiful one, particularly at a moment when they were north of us, when the sun shone brilliantly on their flashing silver. One or two small groups followed on exactly the same course, the same absence of fighters, the same ineffectiveness of the A.A. fire, the same crump of the bombs, varying only in intensity, the same flash of silver as they sailed majestically on their apparently untroubled way. Then came a pause of five or ten minutes but, just as we were beginning to think all was over, more small groups, followed by a larger one of eighteen, came over just as before. In all about ninety planes appeared and not one of them was brought down. At 12.30 we could see a column of smoke from the Naval Base which, by 2.30, had extended over a wide area, but by 4 it had died right away.

Tuesday, February 6th. Reconnaissance planes over on three of the five days since the raid. The last one yesterday, at lunch time, flew very high, in a cloudless blue sky from west to east along the north of the island, back along the south, and eastwards again further south still, and then away to the north.

Ten more huts are to be put up immediately; two goats and two kids have been bought out of Camp Funds for $3000; by order of the High Command our rice ration is to be cut by 20% from the 10th. Albert Paley doing big black market business with 'Puss-in-Boots'. I've handed him my thick grey flannel bags with the possibility of getting something like $150!

'B' a bit weary and out of sorts these days. It's time he went home — and that goes for most of us! — but it doesn't affect him as it used to. He's much more patient with himself — and everyone else.

DANGEROUS FOOD SITUATION

Monday, February 12th. Notice from Men's Representative.

'The Nipponese have this morning informed the M.R. that the food situation is now such that it will be necessary to make a further cut in the rice ration during the current month, followed by further reductions during March. The position is one that is causing the Nipponese the greatest anxiety and they have warned the M.R. that it is possible that, within a few months, no rice whatever will be forthcoming, thus throwing the Camp entirely on its own resources. There is not a moment to be lost in taking every possible measure to bring about an increase in our own production of food within the shortest possible time, and for this purpose every single man engaged on less important work must be put to work in the Camp Gardens.' (Then follow various instructions re labour etc.) 'In conveying these Nipponese instructions to the Camp, the Men's Representative is confident that internees will realize their significance, and that they will stand and work together for the common good during these critical months. We must aim at the maximum effect in the matter of our future food production whilst other supplies (i.e. rice) are yet available, even if on a reduced scale, and whilst we still have a measure of physical stamina with which to cope with the task.'

Bulletin from Camp Quartermaster. The daily ration of rice for the Camp is reduced from 1750 to 1350 kilos and the additional rice for those on fatigues, and for the Camp Farm, increased from 50 to 90 kilos daily. Oil and fat reduced by 35%, sugar and salt by 25%.

Saturday, February 16th. About a fortnight ago returns had to be made to the Japanese of money in our possession on a given day. Easy for me — NIL. No one knew what it was for until on Tuesday an order came round that all sums previously declared over $100 had to be surrendered to be put into one of the Singapore Banks, and that withdrawal might be made against M.R.'s signature (!?) Big flap collecting it. Original returns by secret ballot, so no one knew who had declared what. Result, we were $400 short in this hut — one so-and-so failed to acknowledge his declaration of $500. Most others had spent a good deal of their cash — but 'General's orders', so had to be.

Considerably more air activity. Alerts — blue flag lasting several hours — reconnaissance planes over most days, coming and going at will. Yesterday at lunch time five were over ranging the Island across and across, incredibly leisurely, no

A.A. and no sign of fighters interfering, although there were many up. On several nights Japanese planes have been about lately. Many stories flying round of the evacuation of Penang — probably baseless.

Thursday, February 22nd. Nearly three weeks ago I cut my toe with a changkol in the garden, not a very bad one but it went septic under the nail, spread down the toe and has been extremely painful, with the result that I've had to lie up with it and it has been making no progress at all until yesterday, when Dr. Cammy Bain put on a sulphonamide dressing. Mary Scott had sent a little over, and the result that today it is really improved. These septic cuts and ulcers are the very devil. Once they go wrong, they take an age. No healing properties in the body and nothing the doctors can do except wet dressings.

Sky very overcast to the north two days ago at mid-day, when some of us remarked on an unusually heavy drone coming in from the west. Sure enough the sound of about a dozen bomb explosions from Sembawang aerodrome direction. A few people claim to have seen six planes through a cloud-break. Gloriously fine evening — sirens and blue flag up. Japanese fighters obviously expect something but nothing developed here.

THE SKIES OPEN

Saturday, February 24th. St. Matthias. A terrific morning. Sky absolutely clear, with some wispy cloud which thickened up a bit later. General direction of planes from west to east. Objectives oil installations.

9.30 Alert; 10.00 Emergency; 10.25 3, W—E; 10.30 7; 10.35 2. Bombs in NE. No planes seen. Thick smoke from SE. 10.40 10; 10.43 4; 10.45 10; 10.55 10; 11.00 9; Loud explosion; 11.05 8; 11.10 8; 11.14 10, SE—NW; 11.20 10, W—E; 11.35 10, W—E; 11.40 4, W—E; 11.45 4, S—N; 8, W—E; 12.00 8, S—N; 12.10 All clear.

Within ten minutes of the dropping of the first bombs we, even in our valley, with the Pig Farm Hill in between, could see the smoke billowing up. At about 11.30 I walked to the top of the hill. It was an astonishing sight. Through an angle of 25°–30° thick black smoke was bellying up from at least a dozen fire centres, all big ones.Very little A.A. fire and no fighters. The early planes an astonishing sight against the clear sky — like ghost moths and very difficult to pick up. Total of a hundred and three from W–E, twenty-two from S–N, checked with observers on Pig Farm Hill.

Thursday, March 1st. A new internee has brought the news that the fires from Saturday's raid were all on the Island in the docks and water front area. The big fire which lasted three or four days probably Texas Oil Co. plant in Cantonment Road. The others had all died away within thirty-six hours.

Sunday, Monday, Tuesday and today planes were on reconnaissance. Sunday and Monday's wandered about as they liked, one of them right over us, but ran into a lot of muck which was being thrown up from the Naval Base, possibly from ships there. A Johore fatigue, collecting wood for the new huts, have seen ships up in the Western anchorage.

The new arrival, one of the seven Dutchmen, who were taken off some time ago, was with a crowd of about nine hundred Dutch, mostly merchant seamen, working on some naval construction job out Jurong way. Their food and health bad.

Robert Scott back for treatment from Outram Road Gaol yesterday. Bad odoema of the feet, heart quite sound, some diarrhoea, and chronic, though mild, dysentery. Absolutely balanced and cheerful. My toe still bad — three and a half weeks now — but the hut have decided that all sick on a medical chit are to have normal rations, which helps a lot.

Latest performance of our hosts, that all children over ten are to work in the gardens.

Douglas M. has moved and not far from Karl's now. Groebells there already. [This last was written in code. A scrap of war news or rumour had reached us. I wrote that Douglas Montgomery (the Allies) had moved (advanced) and was not far from (near to overcoming) Karl (the Germans). Groebbels (the Russians) was there already (at the point of victory).]

Saturday, March 3rd. Another big raid yesterday — between fifty and sixty planes flying along the line of the Naval Base or the Straits of Johore from the west. Siren 10.35, wailer 11.20, first plane 11.30, last 12.20. Small groups this time, one of seven, three of five, three of four, two of three and the rest in ones and twos. Difficult to distinguish sound of bombs above noise of A.A. fire, which was the most intense we have seen. In less than thirty seconds between sixty and seventy bursts were seen round one plane. No sign of fires. Fighters much more in evidence — at least going through the motions, but never in concerted attacks of more than two at a time. The 'Prince of Wales Feathers' bursts, which have puzzled us, seem to be some sort of projectile put out by the bomber. Norman saw a flash from one of the bombers just before a burst. Whatever they are, the fighters have a high regard for them and sheer off immediately. A plane or planes came over in the afternoon, having a look. I saw it twice, very high through cloud-breaks. Heavy gunfire early this morning, I was told. I was oblivious.

Toe better, but still not working. Hungry in spite of full rations. Paley gave me $75 for flannel bags. No more petrol for lorries — we are to haul our own wood. Bored and want to go home. Declaration to be made of all gold and silver in our possession. Once bitten!

Friday, March 9th. No air activity since Saturday, a break which can't be accounted for entirely by the weather. Recce planes have chosen the clear spots in other spells of broken weather we have had.

Yesterday cards came from wives in Palembang written last September. Tragic news of the death of the wives of some husbands here in Sime Road.

A HUNDRED MEN IN A HUT

I wish I could catch the spirit of the scene in this hut. It's pouring with rain, so no fatigues, and nearly everyone asleep or resting on their beds — those who have them. Sitting here on Tommy's high stool at my trestle bed with wooden top — a permanent loan from Brock — I can look down the whole length of the hut. Behind me Sam Kemp and his endless cartons of cheroots; he is now our local purveyor of black market cheroots. Prices reasonable, small returns $4 profit on a carton of 100 at $75, $2 profit at $40—45 a hundred. (The pre-war exchange rate was about $8 Straits for £1 sterling.) On my left, in the middle of the hut between me and the door, Albert Paley, black market Palm Oil king — much larger profits, $8 for oil, which sells at $1 outside, but 'Puss-in-boots' — one of our hosts — has had his cut before it gets to Paley.

Beyond him, by the door, Turrell, sitting thoughtfully stroking his beard. Behind me, the other side of the door from Sam, Len Butler, an 'Asia Boy', flat on his face on his rope bed with my ground sheet on it and fast asleep. Bill Crook's empty bed in the corner — he's away in hospital. Next to him, at the end of the hut, Byrnes, grotesquely sleeping, a handkerchief over his eyes, and his feet up on a stool. Then Cundy, embracing his dutch wife, and in the corner Bert Will's feet — all that I can see of him. Tommy Hunter on his bed, Syd Chapman outside on the verandah — he's off work again with pellagra, a deficiency disease with unpleasant cracking of the skin, Turton, sitting leaning against Roeper's bed — on which R. is playing patience — with a towel round his shoulders fastened with a clothes peg under his chin. Roeper is astonishing — over seventy, thin and bent, with a voice which never rises above a husky whisper, but he keeps going apparently as healthy and enduring as the rest of us. Opposite him in the middle of the hut, 'Nick' Nicholson, beard still a bit patchy, sitting on his large table bed, leaning back in his characteristic position against his rolled up mattress, reading either Italian, German, French or Danish. Beyond him, also in the middle, Paul Forbes, lying on his enormous bed, looking like a catafalque, with its four posts at each corner for a mosquito net. Beyond Roeper, against the wall, German and Cruickshank sitting up reading, looking very old-maidenly. Then Jimmy Crowther, Doherty and Brock on the floor, and Coe, Managing Director of 'Sime Road Latex Production Incorporated'! He has produced all manner of uses for liquid latex — the juice of the rubber tree — medical bandages, children's rubber balls, patches for mattresses, and for shirts, shorts, pillow cases and what not;

beyond him Humphrey, for once not singing in his flat Yorkshire tones, Sturrock, Charlie Don, Drew Wallace, Sandy Simpson, Dicky Dickson, Robby, the hut Q.M. and Gordon Osborne, looking daily less Pickwickian in girth, but attempting to atone for it by a closer approximation to the supposed manner and conversation of the original. Away in the far distance Jimmy Edwards, one of Singapore's merchant princes, Davy Anderson and George Lewis. Closer at hand coming up this side of the hut, Benjie Human, our Hut Representative, Harry Foster, Collings and Lloyd Spragg, Brearly, Nicholl and Jacky Holland, Buster Findlay in the middle, and his blue pullover, one side blue, the other grey, Patchy Green, Graham and a large fleshy lump of thigh which is all I can see of 'Tiny' Lewis. There is still a lot of him — more than 13 stone! George Davis, a camp cop, has just gone off on 'point duty' — he's one of the better amongst our local humorists. Vic Parker in the middle, beyond the pile of our suitcases in my allotted space, Arthur Keen, for once silent, sitting on his bed reading and smoking, Tommy Yates, Skipper Thomas, Hall, Tommy sitting up in bed looking, as I am, quite determined not to go out working, although it is four o'clock and no longer raining, and the Bishop just awakened from deep sleep, looking slumbrous and bewildered. Benjy has just delivered a small parcel for him from Sandy Macnab in the Women's Camp — and he's off to sleep again.

And that is some of us — about eighty in all — each with three and a half feet by seven feet as our own private world. The whole length of the hut is festooned with ropes and wires for mosquito nets, which also support a maze of towels, shorts and other paraphernalia during the day. And there, over my left shoulder as I sit here, is the valley, cultivated on either side of the twisting path and rain-drain right up to the Hospital Orderlies hut on the top of the hill. Now after the rain it's a lovely contrast in greens, from the red-ribbed, wind-stripped jade leaves of the bananas, to the emerald of young bayam and the deeper green of the beans, on their tangle of stem and stick.

FOOD RATION SLASHED

Sunday, March 11th. Big cuts in our food. A month ago

workers were down from six hundred to five hundred grams of meal per day, with the threat of further cuts, which descended on us yesterday. Workers from five hundred to three hundred grams per day, part-time from three hundred and fifty to two hundred and fifty, non-workers from two hundred and fifty to two hundred and *all women* from three hundred and fifty to two hundred, regardless of whether they are working or not. Children from three hundred and fifty to one hundred and fifty grams per day.

Sergeant Major Tanaka further told Collinge that we might have to be cut still further and that, after August, there would be no rice at all. He said that he was giving consideration to the question of working hours — revised as from the beginning of February to four hours instead of six for heavy full-time workers, with changkollers and other extra heavies doing six hours with another one hundred and fifty grams per day. Now all workers other than the latter are to do as much as they feel they can — as indeed they do already! Extra-heavies working on Japanese jobs with extra rations are expected to *earn* the extra food, as they don't — and I don't blame them.

So far we have about fifty-four acres under cultivation in the camp, seven acres at Watten and another seven on the golf course. A large area outside the north gate has just had its first digging. All this development means a fairly large crop of sweet potatoes in about three months and tapioca at about the same time. We may need every bit of it before we've done.

Schweizer's lorry was in yesterday with two thousand pounds of barley and the same amount of maize, with four hundred pounds of red bean, which will help for a week or two, but no more than that. The women are hardest hit by the new ration scale. When we are at our present low level, it is ludicrous to say that women need less food than men.

The camp has bought three milking cows for $15,000 a piece. We have to pay for them with promise of a refund by the Japanese Red Cross at the end of the month. After three years, this is the first we have heard of Japanese Red Cross doing anything for us and still it's only a promise! [So far as I know, we were never repaid.]

Monday, March 12th. Another visit this morning, after a longish break — between twenty-five and thirty planes coming in from the west and flying over the dock area. One large fire — possibly oil installations at Normanton, or even Pulau Bukum, since we could hear no bombs. Sky overcast and we could only see through cloud gaps.

Today's menu. Breakfast, 1½ pints maize kunji and tea. Lunch, ¾ of a pint of vegetable soup, flavoured with fish and ½ a pint of rice. Supper, bean and rice loaf, about 6 oz. vegetable hash. Cheroots and pipes of tobacco continue to allay the pangs! Wet and cold spell still on after about a month.

Toe healing slowly, but still painful. St. David's last night for first time in five weeks. The Bishop was excellent on the Christ of the New Testament, describing Jewish teaching on the Messiah. St. Paul's preaching of Christ and St. John, in his first chapter, on Christ the Word of God, all of them attempts to describe the impact of Jesus and the impression He made. We need a restatement of His Divinity, that He was far more than the highest of men. His standards — the law of love — are those on which the universe is based. No one who can say 'Lord, Lord' and yet 'I do not the things that I say' regards Him as Divine.

Monday, March 19th. In Area Hospital. Last Monday — skimming bayam stalks — I split my left thumb-nail. Sepsis under the nail caused violent throbbing for several days. Fortunately for the thumb, the toe had a setback on Tuesday and was swollen, puffy and painful when I showed it to Dr. Bain in the morning. I asked him whether he could not send me into hospital as it had been so long and he agreed, so here I've been for the last week. Much better so. I can really rest it and it's enormously improved. Still a bit of muck to slough off, but part of it is healing well. Thumb still sore and I usually have to be up soaking it once in the night, besides steeping it in hot water most of the day. Otherwise I'm fighting fit and reading my head off. *Old Curiosity Shop* just finished and now, at the same time, Lin Yutang's *Importance of Living* and Forester's *Life of Dickens.*

No raids for the last week. Plane over on Wednesday.

Denis Soul has asked me to sing the Bass solos in the 'Crucifixion' on Good Friday. There is also a slight question of a birthday party — mine — with 'B', Sandy and Mary in the Orchard on Sunday. Get a decision from Dr. Bain on Wednesday.

Thursday, March 22nd. Toe much better — clean at last. Thumb still sore with muck under the nail.

Racing through Shirer's *Berlin Diary*. Intensely interesting day-to-day account from 1934 onwards. An absorbing book shedding light on many points. Reading his account of only newly occupied Belgium, I was reminded forcibly of many things in Singapore during the days immediately after the surrender. There was, for example, the crazed British soldier in the ambulance at the General Hospital on Sunday, 15th February, 1942, driving madly and dangerously round the roundabout at the entrance of the Hospital, or the strangeness of seeing the Japanese General in charge of Medical Services arriving at the General Hospital; the sight of a small group of British Tommies fraternising easily and naturally with a minute and very scruffy Japanese driver; the correct behaviour of the ordinary Japanese soldiers; derelict cars and army transports; the buying up of food and other stocks with useless 'banana' money; the Chinese shootings; the lost and unbelieving looks on people's faces; the arrogance of the Japanese officer who ran a dog through with his sword because it barked at him; the concealed smiles on the faces of the bystanders in Raffles Place as the Japanese officer caught his sword in the back wheel of his bicycle and ripped his spokes out; the helpfulness of Lt. Andrew Ogawa and one or two others. And now, are people hoping and praying, I wonder, for our bombers to come to Singapore, just as they did in the Channel ports, although it might mean death for some of them?

A MEMORABLE BIRTHDAY

March 25th, 1945. Palm Sunday. My 30th Birthday. What a day of days. I must try and get some record of it while it is in progress. First Syd Ross arrived last night, just as it was getting dark, with a bag from Mary Scott — the neck of a bottle sticking out of the top and other bottles clinking about inside. It was dutifully tucked away until the morning by the side of my bed, with a letter from Sandy Macnab clearly marked — 'NOT TO BE READ UNTIL SUNDAY'. A cheery letter from Mary had no such instruction. I awoke at about five and, while I gave the finger a soak, read Sandy's letter. Mac woke me at seven, but it was pouring with rain and I couldn't use the doctor's permission to go to the celebration. At the first glimmerings of dawn I groped down for my birthday sack and, like a child on Christmas morning, pulled out my treasures. A large bottle of rice 'hooch' and four cheroots tied onto it — being kept for our beano tonight. Two other jars — one of sago pudding from Mary Hughes with a chit 'Happier birthday next year, John. A bit of pudding you hated at school, but I am sure you will enjoy it here.' I am beginning to think they live on a very exalted plane over there! Mary Scott sent me over a similar mixture the other day and was horrified when I wrote back and thanked her for the jam! It's much too good to use as pudding, in great dollops. Nearest thing to marmalade I've tasted since I did taste marmalade. Sago flour, flavoured with gula malacca and lemon peel; delicious! The other jar, little round cakes from Mary Scott with a note:

'No flour
No butter } no Birthday cake.'
No eggs

'And what's more, Muriel would tell me thirty candles was extravagant!' Two of them went as soon as the jar was opened and another followed after breakfast. The Bishop had one when he came up after breakfast and I gave him one each for Norman and Tommy. At 4 p.m. they are no more!

The Bishop brought with him two packages — one from Mary and one from Sandy and Di. Mary's a small rubber purse-like thing edged in blue, with a press clip on the flap and inside a packet of tobacco, the whole wrapped in a bit of white cloth initialled in the corner, which now serves as my bed tablecloth. Sandy's a towelling flannel. Small things, all of them, but what thoughtful planning lies behind them. It's absurd that I should be so thrilled by sago, lemon peel and sugar — about half a dozen people have had samples here and all enthuse — its an indication of how starved is our sense of taste, the same old insipid stuff day after day. Sausages, brown and crisp and creamy mash, cold ham and poached egg, potato pie — WOW!! What couldn't I do to them!

NEW INTERNEES

During the course of the morning the new internees began to appear. The whole of the Jewish community, many of them, particularly the old men, of whom there seem to be a large number, a sad sight. All manner of stuff they had brought with them. One I saw carrying four fowls! Besides them most of the wives of Eurasians already interned here have been brought in, as well as the Eurasians interned and freed again in 1942. Amongst them was Roy Smith, looking extremely fit. Glad about him. He had a bad time from the Kempei-tai in the Y.M.C.A. when the Bishop was there. They were in the same cell together and a great help to one another.

Humphrey Potger is in the same bunch, but looking rotten. He's got kidney trouble and has been in bed with it for some time. Zehnder is also in, but I haven't seen him yet. All the Clunies-Ross family are here. Douglas, Gerry and Jimmy I've seen already. Gerry couldn't penetrate the beard and had to be informed who I was! Monty Armstrong greeted me by

Figure 18: 'Sime Road Woodcutters — Two of a Kind' by R. W. E. Harper.

wishing me many happy returns — heaven knows how he remembered. In spite of a long stretch in the Central Police Station and then in Outram Road Gaol — he was let out at the same time as Dunlop. He's looking wonderfully well and fatter than he was in 1943 when we were interned. I'm told the whole family are in, but I haven't seen them yet. Charlie Humphries, now about fifteen, with a broken voice, is here.

In addition, I have seen many I know but there are dozens more I haven't seen or heard of yet. There's going to be plenty of talk for the next few weeks. All these new arrivals have taken me right back to two years ago. They *were* good friends and it *is* good to see them. What a day! And there's a beano afoot for tonight — double celebration, my birthday and the possibility of another holiday with Sam.

[This is a reference to a strong rumour of the collapse of Germany. 'Sam' was my companion on a holiday in Germany in 1937, the Revd. Austin Williams, Vicar of St. Martin-in-the-Fields for many years.]

RED CROSS PARCELS

Monday, March 26th. The total of Red Cross parcels allocated to this camp from England, Canada, S. Africa and U.S.A. includes six and a half thousand parcels of foodstuffs for individuals, besides a bulk consignment of medicines, medical and surgical equipment, cotton clothing for men, English footwear, shoe repair materials, books and tobacco. Good! At last!! Everyone in camp on March 24th will get one parcel, new internees one parcel between five.

Later. But not so fast! We have just been told the parcels are to be held up 'till the General returns'. And when, pray, may that be?

Saturday, March 31st. Easter Eve. Many more than the estimated number of additional internees have arrived. There have been three batches, the first about two hundred Jews and a hundred Eurasians, all from Singapore; the second was about sixty Eurasians from Bahau, an agricultural settlement for Singapore Eurasians set up in part of Negri Sembilan; the third group were Eurasians from Penang. I don't know how many, but the total from all groups must be about four hundred and fifty to five hundred new men alone, with probably many more women. The numbers in the Women's Camp have about doubled and are well over the thousand mark.

The Bahau crowd have suffered terribly from malaria and lack of food, with many deaths. Between 30% and 40% of those who went up there. It has been known as one of Malaya's malaria plague spots for years. Devals, the Roman Catholic Bishop, died up there. His body was brought down to Singapore for burial. A festering mosquito bite led to gangrene. Amputation of the foot did not save him.

The people from Penang were arrested and kept for three days in Penang Gaol. They took four days over the journey cramped up in trucks. There was an air raid alarm in Malacca on the way down, besides heavy damage to the waterfront in two raids on Penang.

First night raid here on Thursday. There had been a blank two and a half hours of alert on the previous night. The wailer woke me, but it was a case of 'Wolf, wolf'. I rolled over, making the sleepy comment that a deep rumbling was thunder, but was moved to investigate when someone started saying something about a glow in the sky. Glorious starlit night with full moon and away to the south-west a big blaze. After a huge flare-up I could see light glinting on a plane flying east to west. Possibly ours, but no doubt about the two going west to east a moment or two later. A terrific deep orange glow showed them up quite unmistakably. There were several such outbursts, followed on each occasion by a deep dull rumbling sound of explosions. The biggest flare-up was from a point further east. Oil installations on Bukum and Sambu? Almost certainly, since there was still last night a bright glow to the south-east and a dull flicker in the south-west.

Still in hospital. Better. Stainer's Cruxifixion was in the Orchard in the evening, postponed from yesterday. Dr. Bain let me go and sing the bass part.

Wednesday, April 4th. I've just read J. M. Scott's *Life of Gino Watkins.* Watkins companion as a Polar explorer was Courtauld, who writes of the keeping of diaries:

'It is only when we dig up those faded records, which, once written, are stored away unread, that we remember with a shock the truth of those days, when weary in body we gave expression to the anxiety of our minds. We find in those close-pencilled pages the impressions of forgotten days which are happily erased from our memories.'

There's a great deal in that I expect to be proved true one of these days as I look back on this internment experience!

Voice in the early hours of the morning, from the Hon. Mr. Justice Aitken. 'Orderly . . . orderly, I thought you ought to know the emergency signal has been going for the last few minutes. Oughtn't something to be done about it.' He'd got it wrong. A pair of amorous cats had been disporting themselves with loud moans.

Sunday, April 8th. Out of hospital on the 6th, but today bandage off for the first time, with mercurochrome to dry up the last corner. Weak as a kitten all this last week — but no dysentery. The 'Parcel Crisis' in everybody's thoughts and on everybody's lips until most of us are sick and tired of the whole thing. But there's a cold fury abroad. We have few rights, and are allowed fewer than we really have, but there's no doubt that Red Cross parcels are ours individually and by right. On the 30th we were given details and told later in the day that no issue would be made 'until the General returned'.

After a day or two, Collinge — the Men's Representative — was called up to the Japanese Office and told that the parcels would be issued over a period of six months, and not to individuals but to the kitchens. Collinge refused to accept them on this basis and the following day a referendum over the whole camp showed unanimous support for this attitude. On the following day Collinge saw Sasuki, the Commandant, again and repeated what he had said on the previous day. Sasuki came out with a better offer, but still short of one a head and it was again rejected, but Collinge was allowed to write through Sasuki to the General on the matter. The General himself was in on Sunday and left the decision to Sasuki after some talk with Collinge.

Yesterday we were told that Collinge had had another interview with Sasuki, who had said that the parcels might be issued today, if not today then not at all. This was an order from a higher authority. 'All Nipponese orders must be promptly obeyed or there would be grave consequences for the camp.' All a bit obscure and it didn't seem to make much sense. The long and short of it is we have not got the parcels! At Christmas 1943 we had ¼ of a parcel. These latest ones have dates of issue June and July, 1942. Much of the stuff is already bad and tins blown!

Rice and maize being cut and cut, but our vegetable production good. Last month 8½ ozs. green leaf per head per day and a further 4 oz. potato, tapioca and papaya. My weight a week ago 9.9 − down 5 lbs. since February, but I've still got a big margin above my lowest of 8 stone 11.

May Day. Long gap since I last scribbled and much has happened. At long last we've had some of the parcels − enough for one a head and extremely welcome. I drew an English one in quite good condition. Best of the lot was an apple pud, our family dish! 'B' and I shared one with a tin of creamed rice on Saturday. There were howls of derision when the rice was produced from the parcels. Coals to Newcastle with a vengeance! But it was excellent. Really creamy, and with the use of a good deal of imagination, there was the illusion of Devonshire cream. The combination of the two was beyond all praise − except that there was not nearly enough of it.

A small 3 oz. tin of cheese I swapped with 'B' for a tin of syrup which he loathes; another good swap with Len Butler of a 10 oz. tin of galantine for 12 ozs. of vitaminised jam. A tin of bacon 'B' and I shared − very fatty, just like cold ham − in so far as I can remember what cold ham tastes like! Steak and veg., a tin of syrup, tomatoes, margarine, two small tins of sugar − one of which I sent to Mary. Condensed milk I've still got and shall give to Sandy for Di. The chocolate was slightly mouldy, but it would need to have been very bad indeed to have been condemned for this human's consumption. I managed to spin it out over three days. Even that was an effort. The biscuits were excellent — hard, crisp, dry and full of body. With marg. and golden syrup — very, very good.

'B' and I have pooled a certain amount of stuff and have decided to have a small binge every Wednesday and Sunday evening.

There are still enough parcels for an issue of ⅔ per man, but these have been held up. Further rumours too of the Japanese doctor who comes into the camp sometimes having said there were enough parcels in town for an issue of one per head per month for six months. He was also reported to have been rather drunk at the time! But it was he who gave us the first news we had of this lot.

A quantity of toilet requisites were also issued. One blade per man and in the draw what do I get but a razor! However, the beard remains and will remain. More fortunate on the following day when I drew a magnificent pair of khaki slacks — very good fit and excellent quality.

The parcels were eventually released on April 23rd, St. George's Day, which was a real gala day. The Japanese made a lot of fuss over it. Relatives meeting in the Orchard from 10—1, the General taking photographs of 'grateful internees receiving their parcels', of a service in the R.C. church, of children playing games and what-not else, and then, on top of it all we were given extra time for the meeting between two and four. 'B' sent a small boy back with a message at about half past two telling me to gate-crash. I pinched a blue ticket from Syd Chapman and dashed over there. Throngs of people — the first day the new arrivals had been allowed to meet and what a day for people like Doris and Charlie Maddox, meeting for the first time in three years.

Sandy and Mary had already got their parcels. Huge excitement opening them — 'What have you got?' — the first taste of chocolate and a Chesterfield cigarette! Mary and I had about an hour's talk — the first we have had of more than a few moments when I've been over for concerts or services, but by this time we've written reams of 'cabbages and kings' letters.

RED CROSS SUPPLIES

The Red Cross books have been released, sixteen religious books, eleven Bibles, thirty-eight N.T., twenty-five Prayer Books, eleven Soldiers' Song Books, five Children's books, four on Business, twenty-eight Science, twelve Accountancy, four Medical, nineteen Language, three Music, eighteen General Instruction, seven Biography, five Plays, eighty-four Fiction and six Miscellaneous. The Library say they are a good lot. The Medical supplies were released some time ago — some very useful stuff, particularly for dysentery. The doctors estimated the local cash value if sold in town as somewhere around $1,000,000!

The cash situation is simply chaotic at the moment. Up to the time of the arrival of the new internees at the end of March, the dollar, although its purchasing power was about 1% of pre-war, was still being lent at par here in camp, i.e. 8 to the £. Goods obtainable in the Black Market were

Figure 19: 'The Professor, Norman Alexander, shares out a Red Cross parcel — one amongst seven' as seen by Bert Neyland. The recipients were (left to right) the author, 'Tommy' Thomson, Henry Cowell, John Turton, George Davis, and Carlton Roeper.

cheroots at 45^c each, palm oil $8 a Pascall sweet jar, gula malacca $25 a kati [a kati = 1⅓ lbs.] — all stuff coming in through one of the Japanese to one or other of the Black Market kings in camp in exchange, sometimes for cash, but more often for watches, jewellery and new or nearly new clothes, which a few people have still got hoarded away. There were also a few tins of food about — large sardines and bully at about $80—$90.

Parcels like the one I got were being sold for Japanese $1250 each and I even heard of one offer of £125 by cheque being turned down in favour of a better offer! Klim, 16 oz. was going for $500 or $600, galantine $120, bully $250, Chesterfields $5 *each*. But many people were prepared to barter some of their food — say a tin, whose nominal cash value was $150, for a carton of cheroots. A week or two ago these could be got, in the Black Market, for $15 a 100, but now, on account of the shortage, you must pay $150 cash for 100. Actually the rate of exchange of banana money against Straits, repayable after the war, has dropped quite considerably, largely because those who have large amounts of cash are wanting to unload it. Straits notes are now worth 2½ Japanese notes. But even if you've got money, prices are astronomical and the more reasonably priced things like palm oil and gula malacca unobtainable. This is all a pretty good practical example of inflation.

¶ THE DEATH OF TREVOR HUGHES —
                                                    THE LAST OF THE DIABETICS

Particularly sad was the story of Trevor Hughes, a barrister in the Malayan Legal Service, whose wife, Mary, a nursing sister, was in the Women's Camp. One of a group of six diabetics, he came into Changi with a supply of insulin which would have been enough to see him through internment. At an early stage it was decided to pool supplies of insulin which had been brought in, each individual's needs being met as far as possible for as long as stocks lasted. In spite of repeated requests to the Japanese, no further supplies were made available.

On one occasion Mary Hughes had permission to speak to a Japanese doctor on Trevor's behalf. She received the

¶ reply — 'I don't know anything about it. We don't have diabetics in Japan.' Later, Doctor Worth, also interned, told Mary she would like to help Trevor by using one of the post cards allowed to internees from time to time. Nothing would come of sending a direct request for insulin. She therefore sent the following message. 'Tell Lawrence of Kings College Trevor Hughes in need.' After internment Mary heard that the message had been received. The insulin had been despatched. It never arrived. Trevor was the last of the six to die. His magnificent courage continued until the end.

Mary was also told that after the Japanese surrender ample supplies of insulin were found in the General Hospital in Singapore.

Although Trevor had been urged by his doctor, Hugh Wallace, to leave Singapore because of his diabetes, he decided to stay on, getting reassurances from a doctor at the General ¶ Hospital that there was 'plenty of insulin'.

Thursday, May 3rd. Archdeacon Graham White had an operation yesterday and has come through much better than they feared he would.

Wood supplies have been cut *to* 25% (not *by* 25%). Seven thousand letters arrived in camp yesterday, dates of writing to October and November last year.

'GAFFS OF MISS GRIFF'

Friday, May 4th. Miss Griffith-Jones produced a beauty the other day in the Women's Camp, even better than her Changi effort, which was a classic. 'The men are coming to tighten up the clothes lines. Hurry up girls. Take your clothes off'! On this latest occasion, giving her instructions to a group of women gardeners with regard to operations of pulling off the leaves of the sweet potatoes, 'You are to go to the bottom of the hill at the back of Hut 1, strip from the bottom upwards and the men will follow'! I was told that you could hear a gale of laughter from each hut as the story travelled round the Women's Camp.

Been back at work about three weeks now and feeling good. Food very inadequate but, even on this low diet, I don't get nearly as hungry as I used to. In spite of a spell of reasonably hard work in the garden, I still have a fair amount of energy, but it's only a very narrow margin.

Lionel Earle and Cherry, who were returned to us sick from Outram Road gaol, were taken by the Kempei-tai again on the 24th of last month after attempted and fruitless intervention by General Saito.

The Archdeacon is still very frail but slowly pulling round.

Two cows and a calf arrived in camp yesterday.

Mordecai, the internee Black Market King, but one who has been playing fair with us, is said to have ordered two hundred thousand cheroots to break the present cornering.

Rumours flying around — Australian Red Cross parcels have arrived in Singapore. Various Japanese alleged to have said that we shall get good news in seven, ten or twenty days according to the story.

Funeral at Bidadari Cemetery on Wednesday. Serangoon Road empty — no traffic. Rochore Canal Road street stalls of vegetables, rice and sago biscuit and cheroot shops open, but no others. Carton of cigarettes bought through Kamiya, the Japanese sentry — two hundred for $60.

Monday, May 7th. Rumours persist. This Japanese has said this, another has said that. Very difficult to sort out true from false, and even if one can, what to make of the residue? Possible that terms have been offered the Japanese. If they have and are accepted, it may be only a matter of weeks. If not, who knows? But it sounds as if the end of the year should see me out. If terms have been offered, how anxiously they'll be waiting for the reply at home. But we — we just don't know, so it's no good worrying.

Belgrave, our new Area Commandant, shows signs of enterprise. Reforms in area medical arrangements — four doctors on instead of two as recently. Signs of greater ingenuity in kitchens too.

Tuesday, May 8th. Weight 9.5. Down four lbs. — and I felt it this morning after a heavy morning digging out a rain-sodden bed, composting it and then two of us carrying up eighty-four lbs. of potatoes to the Fatigue Office!

DEATH OF ARCHDEACON GRAHAM WHITE

Wednesday, May 9th. Archdeacon Graham White died last night. He had recovered well from the operation and had managed to shake off a bit of bronchial trouble, but in twenty-four hours a sudden attack of diarrhoea took all his strength and he died at ten past eight yesterday evening. The Bishop was with him at five when he was still conscious and he knew the Bishop was there. I was up at the Hospital at 6.15 when the end was very near. 'B', Sorby and I took part in the service this morning. S. spoke excellently. The Archdeacon's years of service and his large number of friends. The contrast of his love and care for his books, for his birds and his garden — and his own carelessness of dress. His services to education and his great generosity. A war saw the beginning of his life with his wife 'Nobs'; another war saw his reunion with her after the briefest of intervals. A difficult task Sorby did excellently.

Thursday, May 10th. Ascension Day. Celebrated at seven at St. David's and back to assist 'B' at the Area Hospital where we went to administer communion after his service in the Glen.

One thousand four hundred of the letters out now. None between the four of us yet.

The General in yesterday. Commented on Burr Baughman's extreme thinness. The Men's Representative made the obvious rejoinder. Williams, Manager of Kelly and Walsh Bookshop, baptised this morning.

Gore died early today.

Saturday, May 12th. Cecil Loveridge died yesterday. He'd been ill for years, long before internment.

Allowed to put in wireless message to Australia today. Mine to Mary Wilson reads — 'Adams, King, Eales, Bennitt, Scott, Thompson, self, especially Len fit and cheerful. Loving thoughts. High hopes reunion. Georgina and Graham at peace.'

Rumours and public opinion running riot. Various Japanese reported to have spoken of 'Germany done'. 'Armistice in the East pending agreement — or not! We are all going on the

21st. All non-essential fatigues finishing in a day or two.' Can't believe any of it except the first. But I do believe another few months will see us through. And then —!

Thursday, May 17th. Rumours of peace on 21st persist, but as far as I can see there's nothing to go on. Two young Eurasians took a twenty-four hour holiday two days ago. They slipped away on Monday night, arranged for someone to report them in on fatigue, but their absence was spotted and they had to be reported to the Japanese as being away. They returned on Tuesday night at about eleven, getting through the sentries and wire without any trouble — both are a farce — loaded with food. They are now languishing in the guard room.

The quantity of food we are getting remains appalling. About ten days ago an exhibit was made up of one man's rations for a day. Less than half a 1¼ lb. Capstan tobacco tin of dry rice and the same of rice flour, ¼ of a tin of maize, 9 ozs. palm oil, (now up to 2 ozs.), a total of about 10 ozs. dry weight of veg. (about 6½ leaf, the rest root and papaya), 6/10 ozs. of sugar and at that time the average per day of dried fish was the equivalent of about 7 small whitebait, and that, with the addition of a pinch of salt, is all. Very occasionally we are able to buy eggs. I got one on Tuesday, the first for about a month, for $10! And also very occasionally palm oil at $16 a pint and gula malacca at $35 a kati! And yet we live and we are able to work. Why and how beats me.

AN AVERAGE DAY

The day's programme looks something like this:

7.00. Celebration at St. David's. I go once, sometimes twice a week, but it really is an effort.

7.30. Dawn and the bell.

8.00. Breakfast — pint and a bit of kunji (rice pudding), not even any maize to go with it now, but it's been good and thick lately, and a pint of tea.

9.00—10.30. Work in the garden.

10.30—11.00. Tea and break.

1100—12.00. Work — usually finish about 11.45.

12.45. Lunch. Pint of rice-and-veg stew, with a little dried ikan belis (whitebait) in it if any in camp. Sometimes I have to keep a bit of stew for tea.

4.00—5.00. Work in garden. If I did an extra hour from 2—3, I should get an extra 60—90 grams of rice and a little tapioca every day. But it's not worth it in the hottest part of the day and the only chance I get for reading and sermon preparation. I doubt if it's economically sound.

5.45. Tea — about ½ a pint of rice-cum-veg hash, or sometimes a rice and veg fritter with curry sauce, a pint of tea and a rice bun weighing not more than 6 oz. This I always keep until later. [A smear across the diary page was my blood, from a bed-bug I'd just squashed!].

Evenings actually free but, in point of fact, not usually for me. Mondays have been booked for Pat Sims, but now he's joining the Confirmation Class 'B' is starting. Wednesdays I meet Donald Cullen and one or two others for discussion of some religious topic. Fridays 'B', Norman and I have just started learning Malay with John Hodgkinson. Sundays always a service. Classical gramophone concerts on Monday, Thursday and Saturday, but I seldom get to them these days. The evenings are the time when I should get round seeing people and doing some pastoral and hospital visiting, but more often than not I'm only too glad to flop and read, or even just flop.

8.00. Evening bun, saved from tea, lately with a little marg. and marmalade from Red Cross parcel. 6 ozs. of jam, 5 ozs. of marg. and 6 ozs. of Golden Syrup all I've got left now. Cup of tea made in kitchen.

8.30. Dark.

9.30. Lights out. Usually sit out until about 10.30 — then bed and the comfortable thought of being one day nearer. I'm always hungry, sometimes weak and fagged, but usually cheerful. A plentiful supply of interests helps the first and last states.

Thursday, May 31st. The 21st disappointed us. No change in official attitude of our Japanese here, which remains civil, but entirely unhelpful. No signs of more food from the Japanese, although after a bad period the leaf garden figures improving again. No green vegetables whatsoever being brought in and no root, i.e. sweet potato and tapioca, other than for those getting extra fatigue rations. Hungry at most times and weary all the time. But tremendously cheered by two cards from Mother written in May and October, 1944. Someone had a card mentioning an Intercession Service in St. Paul's or the Abbey for internees and P.O.W.s in Malaya. Nice to know we aren't forgotten.

We began to think we were until yesterday when we had our first alert for over two months. The last raid was on the night of Good Friday, March 30th. The wailer was on for about an hour yesterday morning. Fighters up but nothing developed. Another alert this morning. No wailer, *but* a sharp burst of A.A. fire to the north with two heavy bomb crumps in the middle of it — quite unmistakable.

Schweizer, local Red Cross Representative, but never recognised by the Japanese as more than Neutral Agent, has been prevented from sending stuff in since the beginning of the year. Now we are told that Geneva will not advance any more funds and we are under the jurisdiction of the Japanese Red Cross which, we think, will make no difference whatever to the present situation!

Out to Bidadari a week ago for Roeper's funeral. He has, considering his age, put up a magnificent and courageous fight.

No sign of changes in town, except godowns near camouflage-painted St. Andrew's School. Practically no road traffic, few shops open and hardly any Japanese about.

Interesting group discussion on Wednesday evenings. Donald Cullen, George Human, Teddy Bolton and now 'Jan', discussing the Anglican Church — the basis of the sermon course of 'B's' and Colin King's, which begins next Sunday. Now I must go and make the tea and eat my bun — an insult to the stomach. One thing I know — that I nor anybody connected with me is ever going to be hungry if I can help it.

'OUR CHURCH IN ACTION' LECTURE COURSE

Thursday, June 5th. Celebration at Area Hospital this morning on the small plot by the Dispensary. Arranged with the M.O. for a monthly service, with fortnightly if numbers sufficient. This morning 'B' celebrated. There were eleven of us. He has begun the course which he is sharing with Colin King at St.

David's on Sunday nights — 'Our Church in action'. It was an excellent introduction to the whole course.

¶ This series, 'Our Church in Action', was given on Sunday evenings at St. David's. It had a regular and interested following, who each week joined in sessions for discussion. As its title suggests, the course dealt with Christian living both in worship and in daily life, relating to the two commandments of Jesus, love of God and love of neighbour.

It began with an introduction on the nature of the Anglican Church with a second talk on 'Personal discipline in the Church of England'. This looked at worship, private prayer and training of the mind by Bible and other studies.

The next two talks dealt with 'Problems of the Anglican Church', first through its forms of worship, both in the Prayer Book and elsewhere, and then through the organising of its life and of the links between clergy and laity, parish and diocese and so on.

Then came the influence of the Church as a body, and through its members individually, in politics and in economic and social problems.

In the sixth session Colin King, as a Priest-Schoolmaster and Head of a Government Boys' School in North Malaya, drew attention to the Church's role in education. The seventh in the series dealt with the Church and Christian Marriage, looking also at the problems of divorce and sexual laxity as it affects the 'Education of the young and the mischievousness of ignorance and of past bad teaching'. Above all in this context was stressed 'the paramount importance of parental responsibility and the problems caused by parental ignorance and neglect'.

The final talk concentrated on the Parish Priest as shepherd, as preacher and as teacher. At the end of the syllabus of the course appeared this: 'General Conclusion. The comprehensiveness and liberality of our Church and its Call to Clergy *and* Laity do not merely justify its existence, but encourage glorious hopes, if men and women will respond.'

The diaries of this time in Sime Road may give the impression that we were obsessed with thoughts of food and of our own situation to the exclusion of most else. This imaginative course does show that the Church was making it

¶ possible for those who wished to stretch out to the infinitely
wider world beyond the narrowest of limitations, which were
¶ imposed by a few strands of Japanese barbed wire.

Robert Soul claims to have seen a large 'bird' yesterday.
Present reading *Looking for Trouble, Land below the wind*
and now *Leaves from the Jungle* by Verrier Elwin, pages from
his diary of work with Muslim and Hindu helpers amongst
the Gonds of North India. Much entertainment.

Signs of burrowing into the north slope of Hospital Hill to
excavate tunnels. Light railway and timber shoring have been
brought in. We are told that they are preparing shelters for us
where we shall be parked with an armed guard in the event of
trouble!?!? To be ready in six weeks, we, of course, providing
the labour!

Talk with small group tonight on 'Why a Church?'.

ACUTE DANGER OF FOOD FAMINE

Monday, June 11th. Balance of parcels released yesterday.
Tommy and I share a Canadian one. Between five or six still
to come. No alerts, but increased air activity.

This is an interesting report by Medical Reference Committee on present food situation.

1. Only one major difference between the past week's diet
and one gravely deficient was green vegetables. We are depend-
ing on these for the avoidance of serious deficiency diseases,
and the minimum amount necessary per day to provide
minimum requirement of vitamin B2 is 10 ozs., or more if
much stalk is present. The Medical Reference Committee
reiterates its view that, unless the production of green vegetables is increased, the outlook is grave, and that such production should be regarded as the most important work in
the camp.

2. *Present position regarding production*:
   a. Crop for the past four days has fallen by nearly
      400 lbs. per day and now ration = 7 ozs. gross per
      head per day.
   b. Estimate for next week = 5¾ ozs. gross per head
      per day.
   c. A hundred able bodied men from the Gardens have

been transferred to heavy changkolling (temporarily). They are digging new ground outside the camp for tapioca and compensating for sixty men transferred to the tunnelling gang.

d. There is a likelihood of further calls on the garden labour by Nipponese and additional camp requirements.

e. The Executive Committee has decided that an emergency comb-out of Camp labour to assist the Gardens over the present difficulty is impracticable and would not provide a satisfactory solution!

It therefore is inevitable that garden production will fall, and this is the view of Messrs. Milsum and Jenkins, the two garden chiefs.

The M.R.C. considers that, unless immediate steps are taken to remedy the position, the result may be a catastrophe.

Drying guinea grass etc. When it was decided to improvise a plant for drying guinea grass and other green material there were two major objectives.

a. To grow and dry guinea grass tó supplement the present diet.

b. To make a machine capable of drying vegetable material which is unsuitable for cooking undried, or is too unpalatable for consumption, during a period of acute food shortage. Any addition to the diet under such circumstances will be important, and to be able to prepare material not usually considered as edible should be regarded as a form of insurance.

Monday, July 2nd. Long gap of nearly a month in writing of these notes is some indication of a complete absence of anything note-worthy. The war seems as far from us as ever. No planes over. Increased sounds of blasting by day and night and bombers have been going out northwards from Kallang for the last two days. Food still appalling. No cereals other than rice except for occasional issue of sago. Smokes are short. Japanese official sources bringing in only about 20 last month selling at 75^c–$1 each. Black market $3–4 a cheroot. They are small. Local cigarettes 30^c official, $2 Black Market.

I've been resting much more lately, lying off in afternoons. Not feeling so flabby. Work in garden has fortunately eased up a bit. Colin King's and 'B's' sermon course continues. We have discussion group here and at St. David's. Response to request for communion after evensong last night. Forty-five there. A lovely service.

Reading *For whom the bell tolls*, Mary Webb's, *Seven for a secret*, *Brazilian Adventure*, Barry's, *Relevance of the Church*, Antoine de St. Exupery's, *Wind, sand and stars*.

Cultivated area of tapioca and sweet potato outside the camp, forty-three and two acres respectively; inside the camp thirteen of each. Green vegetable not included in these figures. Still very hungry!!

Monday, August 13th. Long break of more than a month since above — little happened until last few days. I was badly pulled down and still losing weight. At all events I've been working outside for a fortnight now and, although I miss the free time from lunch to four and the reading I was able to do then, I'm feeling 100% better than I did. Black-outs and perpetual weariness a thing of the past — and also perpetual hunger. Small private garden I started some time ago bearing fruit. Onions plentiful, six Indian lettuce plants thriving and the dozen Ceylon spinach plants beginning to clamber up their scaffolding of bean sticks. Chilli bush yielding well too.

Rumours of the end rampant. Many say 11th was the day. Japanese busy on previous day.

RUMOURS OF PEACE CONFIRMED

Thursday, August 16th. P.O.W. over wire said 'Peace signed 11th. Military coming 21st.'

Saturday, August 18th. Work stopped on tunnels. No chang-kollers out. General addressing local Japanese. Tominaga in tears. Three hundred odd parcels released. Concert in Women's Camp. Battleship in Penang at midnight tonight. Little sleep.

Sunday, August 19th. 'B' sick. Five transport planes at Kallang. Rumoured staff officers in Singapore. Pouring rain in Orchard. Lionel, Walter, Calderwood and Cherry, Dr. Taylor,

Corner, Holttum, Birtwhistle, Hoffmann, etc. released by the Kempei-tai.

Monday, August 20th. Good sleep 11.30—5. St. David's early. Explosions and sudden blaze to the S.E. Died right away. Returning books a.m. Dhobying p.m. Terribly restless. 'B' to hospital. Broached bottle communion 'samsu'! Breakfast, four slices Kam; lunch ½ tin of meat and veg; supper, Tommy, Norman and I split a tin of bully. Bloated! Bad night. Up at 2.45 to find Tommy, Norman and Sam at top of steps. Tea from hospital. Appalling wind from tipple! Little more sleep.

Statement to Collinge by General Saito. Japanese still in control. Roll-calls to continue and instructions followed. 'You in this camp are well-educated men and you will understand the effect of the peace on ignorant soldiery, possibly inflamed by drink. Therefore, avoid occasion of incidents.' What an admission! No planes or any sign of our men. Hope for better things today.

Provisional arrangements from the moment of take-over. Raising the Union Jack — lighting — Orchard open for both camps 8—8. Women's Camp visits from Men's Camp 10—12, 6—8. Mail, essential work only. Still no news of when we shall be free. 'B' better after poor night.

THE BEGINNING OF THE END

Monday, August 27th. Official announcement has been made that early next month we shall be away. Individual issue of 7 ozs. Cold Storage butter, 1 lb. cheese. One parcel between six. 'B' back from hospital today. Japanese planes grounded since Saturday. Why delay? Air mail cards written and bagged ready for despatch. Camp quiet, the strain of last week lessened. Schweizer of Red Cross recognised. Instructions received by Japanese to provide best possible facilities in camps, especially for the sick and those in prison. Eggs $70 Japanese in camp. The 'banana' notes are worthless.

Tuesday, August 28th. Points arising from meeting between Men's and Women's Representatives and Schweizer. Japanese and British agreed on hand-over at Rangoon, but not here for another six to ten days. Japanese instructed to take good care

Figure 20: 'Bull, up a tree, where he could be out of sight of his fellow internees' by R. W. E. Harper.

of us. In Singapore, martial law by Japanese Military Police. In our interests that release be delayed until zero hour. British definite instructions we must stay in camp under good discipline. General Hospital and Alexander Hospital being vacated — soon ready for sick. Our Doctors to inspect on Tuesday. Raffles and Seaview Hotels and Grange Road flats vacated for use at zero hour. Everything that can will be done for us before zero hour. Free use of our own radio soon. Schweizer will receive our mail for earliest despatch at zero hour. British intend to drop tons of food from planes. Presumably delayed bad weather. Much food can't be got in Singapore. No eggs or meat. Adequate supplies at zero hour. At suggestion of Schweizer, Saito agreed release of Red Cross parcels in Singapore awaiting shipment to Borneo and Sumatra. Expected very shortly.

Saito and Japanese Military Authorities have been very helpful since the surrender. A visit of two officers from Changi is being considered. Absolute necessity of discipline. 'Nipponese troops in Singapore behaving in an exemplary manner. Their discipline is wonderful under extremely difficult conditions', says Saito. No information yet regarding P.O.W.s in Siam, Sumatra, Java and elsewhere. Being well

242

treated. Cabling to Tokyo list of essential requirements, especially medical supplies, clothes, mosquito nets and convalescent foods. They are trying to send supplies of writing paper. No envelopes available!

Japanese have furnished news dated August 26. Whole atmosphere easier, nervous tension and suppressed excitement greatly reduced. I was in the middle of reading out in the hut the first of the long *Domei* news bulletins we've had when my audience left me! A large plane flew low over the camp, and, on the second run, dropped leaflets. Great excitement, but rather an anti-climax at first. The plane had no marking recognisable to us and leaflets were in Japanese! While they were still falling, the valley was dotted with running figures to pick them up round the Pig Farm. A second lot fell all round the hut, one of the crew waving from the plane. Grand! The first real, though still remote, personal contact we've had with our world for three and a half years.

To the Orchard again after lunch sitting with the Hacketts eating home-made doughnut, biscuit and cheese, when another plane came over. More Japanese leaflets and two hundred Woodbines! The first English leaflets were dropped in the early evening on the edge of the camp round the Church in the Glen. Plane can't have been more than three hundred feet up. Liberator bomber, a glorious sight. Finished up in the Orchard with delicious tongue salad and cake at Fleur Ross's birthday party. All very cheery.

Got back to the hut to find boots being issued − about two thousand pairs of Japanese army issue have come in. Schweizer lorry in, bringing quantities of good cigarettes and numbers of individual parcels, amongst them for me and the Bishop a variety of wonderfully generous presents from the Schweizers, the Cathedral, the Hulermanns, Lee Peng Yam, Molly Lee, Savage and Houghton, Dong Chui Seng and Cecil Kaan.

Opening them I was taken right back into the atmosphere of 1942−43 when presents were continually being showered upon us. Camp issue of fifty Semangat cigarettes a head from Schweizer. Great stories of Catalinas flying up from Australia with food for us. It strikes me we're not doing so badly as we are!

Sorby to hospital again with dysentery. I can't see him being able to stay a single day here. He's not at all fit and ought to get home to Australia at once. I don't know yet what 'B' has decided. Weight two days ago up 2 lbs. in a month! Where the food has gone I just don't know. Obvious from dropped leaflet that our people are expecting to find us worse than we are. There's no doubt that our own food-growing, especially green leaf, has saved the situation.

Wednesday, August 29th. Breakfast of small plate of kunji and milk, sausage, bacon and fried bread, fried for us by Len Butler while 'B' and I were at St. David's, biscuits and butter. What a meal! And lunch too. A few spoonfuls of ration soup, ½ tin of bully, rice, salad and baked beans, biscuit, cheese and butter. Blimey!

No planes until now, 2 p.m. Our doctors, Winchester and Macgregor, to General Hospital yesterday. Japanese most anxious we should move our hospital there at once, but W and M refused. They brushed aside a carefully prepared inspection and found the place filthy, with no equipment. They and Military cabled Tokio Red Cross need for complete hospital and staff. Meanwhile we stay here until troops arrive.

Later. Wireless arrived and working by 8.30. Got over Pig Farm Hill just after 9.30 for a Will Hay quiz and the 10 o'clock news! To hear those six pips again! Hock and I sat in the tapioca half way up the hill and hugged ourselves with delight. The top and the bottom roads and the whole side of the hill were like a great amphitheatre, with one light shining from the roof of the electric sub-station where the wireless was pitched. Magnificent reception and a really stupendous moment. Cigarettes winking in the darkness, a ripple of laughter along the slope and a great content.

Thursday, August 30th. Outstanding event arrival of 'assistance party' by parachute at Changi, two officers, two doctors and two orderlies. Sudden mad rush by children from the Orchard up to the Green House during the afternoon meeting, shouting that airmen had arrived in camp. Even when Dr. Jock Winchester came through on his way to the

Hospital with the senior R.A.M.C. Colonel from Changi and a young officer in a red beret and battle dress, it seemed fantastic, in spite of the revolver at his hip. Terrific reception with everybody cheering and applauding. They couldn't understand the all-pervading smell which hung round us until we told them of the mysteries of red palm oil!

News again in the evening when we picked up a report being sent back to Colombo giving details of hospital accommodation available here on arrival of our troops. Good culmination to the day. More parcels. Delicious fruit from Richard Lim, and tobacco, including a tin of Balkan Sobranie!

Friday, August 31st. Parachute men in again. Mine-sweeping in Straits begins. Excellent feeding and camp food hardly touched. Feeling grand. If only they knew at home, this delay could be counted as of great value.

Saturday, September 1st. More and more parcels coming in, including many eggs. Issue of 2½ lbs. butter per man. Concert in Orchard in evening — enormous crowd but disappointing. Lacked pep.

Sunday, September 2nd. Thanksgiving service in part of Orchard partially ruined by noise in other parts. Many spent

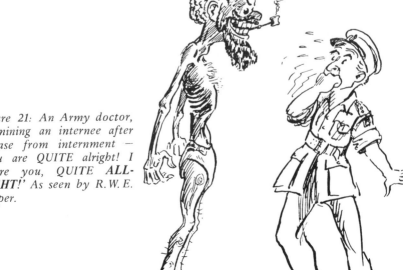

Figure 21: An Army doctor, examining an internee after release from internment — 'You are QUITE alright! I assure you, QUITE ALL-RIGHT!' As seen by R. W. E. Harper.

some time in town. Vengeance rioting going on. Great enthusiasm when any Europeans appeared. Two Swiss friends came
in and congratulated me on having survived my spell with
the Kempei-tai in the Y.M.C.A.! Apparently current rumour
outside. Also that Sorby had died recently after very bad
time there. This story all over town. It's said that troops are
expected hourly.

Monday, September 3rd. Glorious Eucharist in Orchard this
morning — the first opportunity men and women have had
of making their communion together since the beginning of
internment. Beautiful morning — really lovely and very
moving. K. T. Alexander came in in the evening to see 'B',
faithful as ever as his secretary. At noon the Union Jack was
hoisted by Lady Thomas. Big crowd there. Pricking at the
back of the eyes! As a symbol it's packed with meaning,
home, freedom, decency and order.

Good party in the Orchard during Victory Concert — Mary,
Mary Hughes, Nora Jones, Fisher, Shepp and myself. We
walked up the Women's Camp hill with them afterwards and
delivered them on their doorstep. Life gets more and more
normal! The move back from isolation and barbarism has
come very gradually, but there still remains the great link up
with the world outside this island.

Tuesday, September 4th. The *Sussex* and possibly other ships
have arrived!!!

Saturday, September 8th. Last few days before we left camp
this morning have been very hectic, with an incredibly
eventful forty-eight hours, leading up to this moment, when
I am sitting alone in my bedroom at Cathedral House — no
longer an internee, even under the British.

POSTCRIPT

The final word on Sime Road can best be left to a diminutive
Camp Policeman, a former member of the Harbour Board.
Arriving at the Main Gate on an informal visit, Lord Mountbatten, the Supremo and Commander-in-Chief, was greeted
with 'Where the hell have you been? You're late!'.

Section Five

———◆•◆———

Free — in Singapore!

September 8th to October 15th, 1945

This section was written long after the events

Free — in Singapore!

FREEDOM — UNDER THE BRITISH

The final entry in the diary in a hastily scribbled note was written at Cathedral House on our first day of freedom. The previous days had been packed with incident. Amongst the many friends from Singapore who invaded Sime Road and who came to see us with so many generous gifts, there was a very special welcome for the Revd. Leonard Griffiths, Chaplain of *H.M.S. Sussex.* Hardly was the ship alongside before he set off to find the Bishop, bringing with him a suitcase packed with chocolate, cigarettes, papers and magazines, amongst them several copies of the *Church Times.* One of these informed the Bishop that his brother, Leslie, also a priest, had been readmitted into the Church of England from the Church of Rome. The Bishop did not know that he had gone!

BROADCAST TO THE WORLD

Several within the Camp, headed by Mervyn Sheppard, had, with official approval, prepared a broadcast which was to be made available for the authorities if they wanted it. In it, besides a short service of thanksgiving, devised and conducted by the Bishop, there was to be a short message to the people of Singapore and Malaya, read by Lady Thomas on behalf of her husband, Sir Shenton Thomas, formerly Governor of Singapore. With other senior officers, he had been taken away from the Island early in internment.

There was also a message from Robert Scott, a member of the British Foreign Office, who had had frequent encounters with the Japanese in China and Japan in the ten years before the outbreak of war in the Far East. From the beginning of the Double Tenth enquiry it was clear that the Kempei-tai regarded him as the arch-conspirator of the espionage plot, which they believed, without any foundation, had its centre at Changi in October, 1943. He had served less than a year in Outram Road Gaol of the prison sentence passed on him by the Japanese. Although he made a full and complete recovery he was a sick man when he returned to Sime Road. He wrote his talk for the radio, but was unable to deliver it himself. I had the good fortune to be asked to deputise for him when the British Military Authority agreed to the broadcast being given on Friday, September 7th. The invitation led to a fascinating evening.

Cars were laid on from Sime Road to the B.B.C. studios in the Cathay building. On arrival we were faced with the astonishing sight of a hundred yards of jeeps nose to tail in Orchard Road. For anyone who had never seen a jeep, one on its own would have been remarkable. Three dozen of them 'on the hoof' was totally extraordinary!

Clearly overawed by the novelty of our surroundings and of the occasion, the broadcast lacked something in zest and sparkle. Whether it was that or the fault in the recording, given to us as the reason, we were asked to come back two hours later to do it again. As we had an invitation to a meal in the Ward Room of *H.M.S. Sussex* this postponement was filled with danger!

Naval hospitality came up to expectations. It was in every way an evening to remember. For the first time for years we had the unique experience of standing with a glass of beer in one hand, a cigarette in the other, a newly opened tin of fifty at our elbow, and there, no more than a yard away, row upon row of replacement cans of beer. Even more memorable was the company. Our hosts were concern and consideration itself. It would have been understandable if they had pumped us dry on our three and a half years behind the Japanese 'bamboo curtain'. Instead they were prepared to spend as long a time as we needed, answering all our questions about the world outside. Their generosity was total. For years afterwards I wore a comfortable tweed jacket given me by the ship's doctor — a Roman Catholic. One way and another it was a very good evening indeed.

We all felt that that showed in our performance when we got back to the Cathay for the repeat run of the broadcast! At all events it was put out on the radio waves of the world and relayed several times. Mary Wilson heard it in

Australia. She recognised my voice and immediately cabled home.

MOVE FROM SIME ROAD

On the next morning, Saturday, September 8th, the Bishop and I, with Muriel Clark from the Women's Camp, left Sime Road for Cathedral House in Cavenagh Road, the Archdeacon's house. It was unbelievably good to be there and to be welcomed by the Bishop's house boy, the faithful Ah Sing, who had been one of our first visitors in Sime Road and who now had everything ready for us.

As soon as the end of internment was in sight the Bishop realised that, by staying in Singapore for a time, there would be a great deal he could usefully do, both in the affairs of the Church and of the community as a whole. He was fit enough. I too was well and needed no persuasion to stay. It was one of the most fascinating and rewarding five weeks I ever remember.

CHANGI GAOL — P.O.W. CONFIRMATIONS

Without any pause the Bishop plunged into the huge amount of work waiting to be done, with me in sometimes panting

Figure 22: Confirmation of P.O.W.s by Bishop Wilson in Changi Gaol in September, 1945.

pursuit. It was not long before I went with him to Changi, a very moving return to the Gaol, for the confirmation of a large number of P.O.W.s

The over-crowding was indescribable. Every prison yard and open space was crammed with attap huts. The Warders' Quarters on the approach road to the Gaol were now used as billets for officers, very tightly packed. Amongst them was Edward Sawyer, whom I had known well for years. With him, as with other old friends one met, there was the huge relief that they had survived.

ST. ANDREW'S SCHOOL REOPENING

There was a great occasion, too, with the reopening of St. Andrew's Boys School, the pearl in the crown of the Anglican Church in Singapore. We knew that it had been left by the looters in 1942 with nothing but the bare bones of the building itself. It was picked clean. Even the grand piano was carried away on a bullock cart. And yet, there we were, so soon after the arrival of the allied troops, standing in the hall at St. Andrew's for the reopening of the school. Sorby Adams, the much loved and greatly respected Principal, was not there. He had been sent straight home from Sime Road to Australia. In his place with the Bishop, stood David Chelliah, the Senior Master, who had been an inspiring leader of the Anglican Church in Singapore for the whole time after the Bishop's internment in 1943. Numbers of former teachers were there too and the hall was filled with boys who had come to enrol.

For many, however, there were thoughts of a number of former members of the staff who had not survived. Some had died in the indiscriminate massacre by the Japanese of thousands of Chinese men in the first days of the occupation, amongst them Mr. Koh Eng Kwang and Mr. Chan Fung Wai.

Looking round in the packed hall it just did not matter that the place was totally bare and with no books or equipment. St. Andrew's was open again and here at its rebirth were the first of many generations, part of the life-blood of the new Singapore.

The Revd. Cecil Parr, School Chaplain, was one of those who also had died, as a P.O.W. in Thailand with the Singapore

Volunteers. It has been said of him 'that he had wonderful morale right up to the end of his life and he was of great spiritual help to his fellow P.O.W.s.'

His wife, Evelyn, left Singapore on one of the last small ships to get away during the final days of the war. Her ship was bombed. She died in internment in Sumatra.

JAPANESE SURRENDER TO LORD MOUNTBATTEN

An early highlight was the formal surrender to Lord Mountbatten by high ranking Japanese officers on September 12th. The steps of the Municipal Offices and a large area across the

Figure 23: Lord Mountbatten accepting the Japanese surrender on the steps of the Municipal Offices. Bishop Wilson looks on.

Figure 24: After the surrender a different kind of soldiering for the Japanese in the Cathedral compound.

road onto the padang, the open sports ground, were packed with a huge crowd as we saw the officers advance one by one up the steps and move into the building.

There was, too, another scene enacted only a few yards away at about this time. It spoke volumes. In the grounds of the Cathedral Japanese soldiers were put to work, as in many other places, to do a coolie job of tidying up. There were very few signs of 'triumphalism' on the part of ordinary bystanders. Amusement and great satisfaction, maybe, but very little more than that.

WAR CRIMES SENTENCES COMMUTED

In a different context, although in the middle of 1946 during the War Crime Trials in Singapore appalling crimes of cruelty against P.O.W.s and civilians were being revealed, motives of revenge were not always most prominent amongst those who had been in Changi and Sime Road.

254

Tominaga had been our Camp Commandant. His rule was unreasoning and capricious, callous and cruel. It was possible, though, as I remember, not absolutely certain, that one death could be attributed to him, even if only indirectly. He, Kawazai and Kobiyashi were sentenced to death. Suzuki was sentenced to life imprisonment and Myamoto to eight years. All these sentences were reviewed after protests led in the press by former internees. The three death sentences were commuted to ten years imprisonment and the others reduced accordingly.

DINNER AT GOVERNMENT HOUSE

Not long after our return to Cathedral House, when enough time had passed for us to begin to get into some sort of routine, however hectic, we could not understand why the Bishop had heard nothing from the Archbishop of Canterbury. However cursory a message, nothing came, not even 'Welcome back'! When he was on the point of cabling Lambeth himself, the Bishop was invited by Lord Mountbatten to an evening meal at Government House with me in tow. Early in the conversation the question of the lack of a message was raised by the Bishop. Immediately Mountbatten gave instructions which, by the next morning, produced a cable from Archbishop Fisher. For two days, it had been sitting unheeded in some errant Signals Office.

The conversation in the mess was fascinating. By one group of officers I was asked how much we had known of what was going on. After a brief history of our various phases of radio news gathering and of news blackout, I said that, with so much on which to catch up, it was all rather confusing. 'For instance', I asked one much decorated officer 'We hear a lot of a place called Arnhem. Can you tell me what it was all about?' 'I ought to be able to', was his reply. 'I was in command of the operation', and General Browning gave me a graphic description of the whole affair!

Dinner was the greatest delight. Four years earlier I had left my first curacy at Romsey Abbey for Singapore Cathedral. Sitting next to Lady Mountbatten she and I had Romsey talk all through the meal, with news of so many people.

SERVICE OF THANKSGIVING AT THE CATHEDRAL

St. Andrew's Cathedral will have known many supreme moments in its long history, notably during the Japanese occupation. For us there was the special magic of being back there again, knowing that on no Sundays all through those three and a half years, and on few week days, had services not been held.

Outstanding in my mind, fit to rank with Christmas, 1942, in the first year of the occupation, was the Service of Thanksgiving for Victory on Sunday, September 23rd. Representatives of the Armed Services, with their leaders, and members of the local communities, shared in a great outpouring of gratitude, of relief and of dedication. The Bishop asked me to read one of the lessons. The impression which that vast congregation made on me was unforgettable. In his address the Bishop was at the top of his bent. In his biography *John Leonard Wilson: Confessor of the Faith*, Canon Roy McKay quoted something of what he said.

> 'Our thanksgiving is first for the cessation of hostilities. There is a deliverance from battle, murder and from sudden death. Looked at from God's point of view this was a civil war between His children, though so few acknowledge Him.
>
> A second cause for thankfulness is that we were found worthy of victory . . . without priding ourselves too much on the height of our ideals, we have good reason to say that the war was between humanity and inhumanity, and we thank God humanity won.'

He then dealt with ideals of service and went on to stress the need for patience and sympathy.

> 'Our greatest need at the moment I think is to take upon ourselves the burden of the infirmities of the weak . . . patience is needed now, and something more than patience, an understanding sympathy. If we are going to help people we must for their sakes forgo something of our own strength and share the fear, the dimness, the anxiety, and the heart-sinking through which they have to work their way. We will have to forgo the privilege of strength in order to understand the weak and

backward, to be with them, to enter into their thoughts, to advance at their pace . . . If we are to serve aright God and our fellowmen we ought not to try and prove to ourselves and others that we are strong. Self-assertion, wilfulness or even standing aloof in critical reserve is not the Christian way of proving our greatness. The kings of the earth exercise dominion and power, but, said Jesus, "The greatest among you is he that serveth".'

This service, and particularly the Bishop's address, made a deep impression on many who were there. I had evidence of this on the following day when the Bishop sent me out to Tanglin with a note for the G.O.C., General Sir George Gifford, Army Commander of all S.E.A.C. – South East Asia Command – Land Forces. He spoke of the great value of the whole service, at the same time showing yet again the kindness and understanding of so many of those who led our forces in their return to Malaya. There was no reason why I, who was no more than a messenger, should not have been put into an anti-room to wait for his reply. For half an hour, rather, I was invited into his office while we exchanged questions, mine about the campaign, his about our captivity. That thoughtfulness was typical.

ENDAU – A HAZARDOUS JOURNEY

With the passing of time we became increasingly worried by the news we heard from a large group of people on the mainland. As communications improved information reached us from Endau, about a hundred and twenty miles up the east coast. With the arrival of new internees in Sime Road at the beginning of 1945 we heard of the enforced move of many from Singapore Island to Endau and further north to Bahau. Both of them had large populations, with grave food shortages, with appalling malaria and other diseases, and a frighteningly high death rate.

Immediately after our release we also heard of a situation at Endau made even more precarious by the complete domination of the whole community by the Communists. Throughout the Japanese occupation they had established themselves and operated from the Malayan jungle. They had now emerged and had taken control at Endau.

The Bishop was particularly concerned for the well-being, even the safety of some of those who were there. A number of Anglicans were amongst them, in particular the family of Dr. Chen and those who had gone north with him from Katong, as well as others from the Cathedral congregation. There was only one thing to do — to go and find out what was happening.

It was agreed with the British Military Authorities that we would drive up and back during the day in two cars, a civilian party, unarmed. This was important, as we knew we should have to go through a large area of South Johore in which Japanese soldiers had been concentrated. No one knew at that stage how they would react. In fact, although plenty of soldiers were about, we received no more than curious glances as we passed.

Arriving at Endau we found the whole atmosphere was very ugly. In a township of several thousand people the Communist element was clearly dominant. Dr. Chen and his family were acutely apprehensive and every word he had with the Bishop was monitored by one or other of a very sinister crew. The only true indication we were able to get of the state of affairs was a whispered message the doctor was able to give me to pass to the Bishop. Even without that message the anti-British atmosphere and hostility to us personally were clear.

As time passed the atmosphere grew more and more tense. The young Army Chaplain and a driver, both in plain clothes in the second car, who had come with us, joined me in urging the Bishop to leave before the light failed. There was also the importance of returning through the Japanese area in daylight. He was impervious to all our persuasion. He sensed that he was being of use by staying there and I don't think he accepted for a moment that he was putting himself or us in any danger, or, if he did realise it, it didn't matter.

It was almost dark when we left, the Bishop and I in the leading car. At one stage seven devils got into him — or at least his driving. The lights of the second car were left far behind until we finally lost sight of them. Both cars arrived back without incident, but I never want a drive like that again!

POSTSCRIPT ON ANDREW OGAWA

As the war in the Far East ended it became clear that the Church in Singapore had been, by Japanese standards, very reasonably treated. Apart from the Garrison Churches and the Mission to Seamen Chapel no church buildings on the island itself were closed, nor was there any interruption in the holding of services. The only restriction was a ban on preaching, which was eventually lifted.

None of this can have happened by chance, when, in other areas, so many churches were commandeered. St. John's in Ipoh, for example, became a sauce factory. In February, 1942, as was fully borne out later, we who were there in Singapore realised how much the Church owed to the Anglican Japanese Officer, Lt. Andrew Ogawa.

After the Japanese surrender two cables were sent to Sumatra from Japanese Headquarters in Singapore asking for the whereabouts of Ogawa, by now promoted Captain. The Japanese Army Commander and his Chief of Staff both advised him that, since he had been even for a short time the officer responsible for Changi Gaol for a few days after the fall of Singapore in 1942, it would be best to lie low. A reply was sent to Singapore that they could not locate the missing Ogawa anywhere in Sumatra.

A year later, on September 3rd, 1946, a third cable was sent from the Japanese Liaison Office in Singapore with instructions to search more carefully for Captain Ogawa. They had received a letter of appreciation from Lord Mountbatten, the British Commander, commending him for his efforts to keep churches open for regular services. It was pointed out that in Malacca and Ipoh, in many places elsewhere in Malaya and in Burma, churches had been destroyed or severely damaged by the Japanese army. In Singapore they were amazed to find they were in such good condition. Captain Ogawa later wrote to me that he was glad the authorities had not noticed the name of King George had been crossed out in the Cathedral prayer books — but he added that he had only used a pencil!

Two days later he boarded a British hospital ship in Medan, which sailed for Singapore. He was met at the docks by the Port Chaplain and by the Revd. Dr. David Chelliah, who knew

Ogawa well and who had played such a prominent and leading part both in the life of the Church and of the schools of Singapore for the whole of the Japanese occupation. Also with them at the docks were K. T. Alexander, the Diocesan Secretary, and several members of the Cathedral congregation, who presented Ogawa with one of those same Cathedral prayer books. It was an expression of their gratitude for all Andrew Ogawa had done for them while he had been in Singapore, often in the face of serious difficulties for himself from the Kempei-tai.

His journey home to Japan to his wife and family [he now has five daughters] continued on the hospital ship. He has made three return visits to Singapore, once to share with Bishop Wilson in the making of a film by the B.B.C., and twice with football teams from the Tokyo University, where he was a Professor and a member of the teaching staff until 1982, three years before his eightieth birthday. He still plays a leading part in the life of his Church nationally and in his local congregation in Tokyo.

JOURNEY HOME

The Bishop's achievement by staying was considerable, not only in what amounted to widespread first-aid for the Church throughout the whole diocese, but also in implementing emergency welfare and relief in Singapore. On the strength of all this he obtained air passages from the R.A.F. for himself and for Muriel Clark and me. Early in the morning of October 14th, 1945, a small group of us were at Seletar to see him off by flying boat to Australia, to join Mary and their children Susan, Tim and Martin, with James, born in 1942, whom he had never seen. For Muriel and for me it was a dress rehearsal for our leaving for home on the following morning.

MURIEL CLARK – 'A SPLENDID NURSE'

Muriel had arrived in Singapore as an S.P.G. Missionary Nurse at the end of 1940 to work at St. Andrew's Hospital. She went into internment. There were many who spoke of her quiet and gentle efficiency. Of her a fellow internee from the Women's Camp wrote 'She is very much liked and respected, and many of my friends who have been patients have told me how pleased they have been when it has been her turn for duty, because she is such a splendid nurse'. When the Japanese authorities eventually relented and agreed to a small number of nurses being allowed to work in the Men's Hospital, Muriel was one of those who were chosen and who proved her worth. She was also a housekeeper par excellence for us at Cathedral House, and was a delightful companion for me on the journey home.

At the appointed time early on the following morning, October 15th, we were again at Seletar. Muriel and I were the only passengers in the flying boat which, as it took off, matched our mood, as it seemed to throw out its tall twin plumes of spray particularly joyfully in the bright morning sunshine.

All through the day we plodded across the Indian Ocean for Ceylon. Our coming in to land down a blinding path of evening sunlight reflected from the water, produced a monumental bounce, more like a leap. Those who saw it chalked it up as one of the biggest ever seen!

The two nights in Colombo were bound to be very special, with Bishop Douglas Horsley as my host. He had been about five curates ahead of me at Romsey, and was always the very best of company. With Muriel comfortably billeted and lapped in luxury at Government House there was a marvellous welcome from the Bishop, with help from his Chaplain, John Timmins, my contemporary at Lancing.

Our departure from Colombo was almost as spectacular as our arrival in Ceylon. In a downpour of rain a plane taking off a few ahead of us had crashed and was ablaze on the other side of trees beyond the airfield boundary. However, we boarded the plane and taxied across the runway. The heavens opened and the rain came down in torrents. Take-off was impossible and was delayed for twenty-four hours.

At the second attempt we got away. All day our Dakota flew northwards, the interior of its fuselage stripped down for wartime duties. On sofa cushions we sprawled full length on the floor or sat propped against the side. The first guarantee that we really had left the tropics came late that evening with the delicious feeling on our skins of the cold night air, when we landed for a brief stop at a hutted aerodrome out-side Karachi.

Through the night the superb mountains below us shone in the moonlight as we flew westwards to Cairo, arriving with the dawn and first light to a distant view of the Pyramids. It was pure magic. As we stepped out of the plane at Cairo aerodrome there was that same feeling of cool dry air.

After a short break for breakfast we were off again to Malta. Sadly the flights during the day made little impression, so difficult was it to see out of the small windows, but Malta when we got there was fascinating. Muriel and I cadged a lift into town from the R.A.F. station and spent hours just wandering round the streets, savouring it all. We were aware of a certain amount of amused comment as we passed, dressed in an odd assortment of clothes, looking like a couple of tramps.

On the final leg of the journey there was heavy cloud until, crossing northern France, we were shown from the flight deck some of the horrifying war damage. Quick glimpses of the blessedly familiar Isle of Wight and the Solent were all we could see, but we were only a few minutes away from Lyneham R.A.F. Station.

From there, after what seemed only a quick dash up the Great West Road, the coach put me down in the forecourt of Reading Station. In minutes a phone call brought Mother and Michael, the dog, from Pangbourne. Both went mad and I knew I was home.

Section Six

———◆◆◆———

A letter from the Women's Camp

A letter from the Women's Camp

Thursday, April 12th, 1945. 'A Good Thing' has happened. Winnie the Pooh might well have said that. '1066 and All That' certainly would. A fortnight ago Mrs. Doris Maddox was amongst the large number of those who were newly interned, although Charlie, her husband, has been an internee since the beginning. Doris was one of the very best of the younger people at St. Hilda's in 1942 and 1943. Both then and since she has played a leading part in its life. The 'Good Thing' was the arrival of a long letter from her in the Women's Camp, full of news of many people, all of it entertaining and very encouraging. Here is the greater part of what she wrote yesterday, much of it giving a clear picture of the Church under Japanese occupation.

'St. Hilda's has spread, but not without a scrap or two. However, the Revd. John Handy has nine committees to cope with the work, the idea being to keep nine groups of people, old and young, interested and busy.

About finance — St. Hilda's is well off and all the other Churches, too, are able to manage. Mr. Handy is not drawing any salary from St. Hilda's or other Church funds, which is a help. Up-country they are poorer. The other committees are for the Sick and Needy, Choir, Servers, Sunday School, Mothers Union, Prayer Circle, Study Group and Musical Evenings.

The Revd. Dr. David Chelliah carries on as Dean and in charge of the Cathedral. He gave up his job as assistant to the Japanese Director of Education and Religious Affairs. He is now able to do parish visiting again and the Cathedralites give him $300 a month.

George Daniel continues as Manager of the S.P.C.K.

Bookshop and lives in the Chapter House at the Cathedral. He also runs the Church Library, which is very popular, as well as organising the Cathedral Choir. He also does a lot of missionary work.

The Sunday School did well, although many of the teachers had to leave because they were not free every Sunday. However, we found new teachers and the boys' class improved, because of football every Saturday. Then tapioca planting in the grounds prevented football-cum-netball-cum-rugger. Then the boys began to get work and so did the big girls.

Rosemary Scheideggar does all Mr. Handy's typing for him. His sermons! They run to pages and weeks ahead. During Lent we endured many an hour and a half morning service because of the sermon. Every 'plain' Sunday there is a lecture — very instructive, but difficult to live up to all the time.

The Choral Communion Sundays are now of two kinds, Mixed Choir and Men's Choir. The Lay Reader and the Choir Master find it difficult to get sopranos and altos, but the Men's Choir is very good. Now and then there is a special choir and those whose work necessitates missing regular choir practice turn up in force. Sometimes we borrow from the Methodists down the lane. There were practices in the Cathedral throughout Lent for the Easter music. Many Churches had representatives in the United Choir, although the Christian Federation has been banned. The ban tends to cement "the tribes".

The President of the Mothers Union at St. Hilda's is my Mother, Mrs. Mark Moss. The cosy meetings they have once a month! Owing to this and that, theirs is the only group who have high tea at every meeting. They meet on the Musical Evenings, an hour later. Mum is an offshoot of Mrs. Graham White's Mothers Union, so her work is still going strong and just as she liked it. They had the loveliest, liveliest and cakiest party of the season. Just because they invited the Papas? However, very few Papas did turn up and for punishment they made the tea. Some cupfuls were too sweet, with two doses of sugar, some had no sugar. As they served the tea they raided the cake table which was literally covered with cakes and sweets. But it was the jolliest meeting St. Hilda's ever had. The children, too, were visited by Santa Claus, who was attracted by the large and brilliant Christmas tree. Mr. Handy and I enlisted the aid of many a generous Father Christmas and the children had a very gay party.

St. Hilda's had a friend in the Revd. Matsumoto of the Tokio Diocese in Japan. He rounded up those who missed Church, stressed the importance of regularity and was pained to find that all four hundred members did not come every Sunday. He advised Mr. Handy when there were tricky knots to unravel. Just before I came in to Sime Road he left for Taiping and this is what he said — "You do not cooperate enough with the Government. You are concerned only with helping people. You must make some gesture towards the Government." So we arranged to give Good Friday's collection to the Japanese Red Cross. He also noticed that we never played or sang Japanese songs. The Study Group did not discuss "Oriental Culture".

The Japanese Director of Religion and Education requested a syllabus of Church doctrine and ceremonial. All the lawyers of the Church and all the priests (on the q.t.) drew up the code or syllabus, which was censored and revised by the Director, who is quite understanding and does not interfere much. Any hymn with reference to the King and any prayer for royalty is taboo. Sermons have been allowed since last Easter. Now and then visiting priests come to us and Mr. Handy goes to the Cathedral.

The Musicals are highbrow; lowbrow when the jollier members have a turn. The Study Group is learned. The poet Milton scared me away! "For and against large families" attracted a crowd. "History of the Church" is now on the programme. There is a group of young men under John Tan, who meet regularly and practise reading the Bible aloud. Ian Hope has the best voice, trained by Karl Lawson, the local actor. These men are called "Trainees" and occasionally they read the lesson during the evening service. Some sound grand and some so sincere. Mr. Handy can at last chant Merbecke, with a few notes thrown in — or out. He has also learnt to pronounce God correctly, because he found out he was calling Him "Almighty Gaawd"! John Tan coaches him. He learns quickly.

Quite a crowd of Chinese went up-country to the agricultural settlement at Endau. The Eurasians went to Bahau, which the Revd. Gnanamini visits from Seremban. To make up for these losses Mr. Handy has converted as many as went. There have been many baptisms and the new marriage register is filling up.

Now for un-marrying! Poor Mr. Handy has been very loud in denouncing Mr. This, who sent his wife away and consoles himself with Mrs. That. He made himself quite unpopular. Lucky no one rooted his Sunday School Superintendent out! His latest round was a challenge to a hand-to-hand fight. He was accused of being "not like Padre Hayter"! He was a little stiff, but within the letter of the law. But he refused to fight and kept absolutely silent, all the while he was called all the unsavoury names in the dictionary of an angry man. He is little the worse for many new and trying responsibilities.

St. Hilda's Sick and Needy Fund is very full. The Church gets an income of about $250 a month and we spend nearly all this. This Fund and our General Funds are quite separate. We have a bank account of $3000 as reserve. Recently Yap Pheng Gek gave us a windfall. In fact the wind causes many a fall. So the needy get $5 or $10 a month per head. In addition the sick are visited regularly. A kind soul donated free medicine for those in need and free medical attention.

All the religious and charitable institutions recently joined the Black Cross Society, whose members wear a small badge of a black cross in a circle. They look after the homeless after air raids, feed the hungry and bury the dead without charge.

The Moss family have had their problems, but have got over them. Dad met with an accident on the way to work. Three lorries were racing, tearing down the road, loaded with about seventy people and one banged into his lower ribs. On the way to the hospital he caught a chill and contracted pneumonia. M. & B. cured him in a month. Mummy got tapioca poisoning, but an injection or two put things right. She is very thin but full of fight. Betty works for a Chinese lawyer, Babs cooks and Coral does the marketing. Zoe is also a blessing — the pillar of the family. Bill works at Jurong and comes home once a week.

K. T. Alexander, the Diocesan Secretary, is working and comes across now and then to chuckle. He is always in a good humour, and Padre Baboo, the Indian priest, is doing well too; and so are the Chinese clergy, John Lee, Yip Cho Sang, Ng Ho Le and Gwok Kuo Moh.

All the people I know are still very fond of the famous three, the Bishop, John Hayter and the one and only Padre Adams!'

Section Seven

———— •◆• ————

Sermons to a 'Captive Audience'

Changi, Ascension Day, 1943
Changi, July, 1943
Sime Road, June, 1944
Sime Road, New Year's Eve, 1944
Sime Road, Holy Week, 1945
Sime Road, Ascension Day, 1945

Sermons to a 'Captive Audience'

Some of the things we did or which were done to us in Japanese internment nearly fifty years ago spring readily to mind. Not at all so simple is it to remember what some of us were thinking. A slight indication of our thoughts may possibly be seen in sermons preached at that time.

CHANGI, ASCENSION DAY, 1943

On Ascension Day in June, 1943, remembering our Lord's promise 'Lo, I am with you always', I said at a service in Changi,

> 'Many of us have experienced during the last eighteen months since internment began something we did not know before. If we can think back to the war period, to the events at the end of 1941 and the eight weeks which followed, there are many who would admit that we felt the presence of a strange "something" in ourselves, steadying and supporting us. That "something", that unexpected strength was, I believe, a sense of the nearness of God. We may not have realised that it was Him. But how else can we explain it? Need we explain it in any other way? . . .'

CHANGI, JULY, 1943

Even as early as that, with more than two years to run before the end of the war against Japan, we were already looking ahead to what would follow and to our share in rebuilding the world after 'this war and the world's slow death'. At a United Service on July 25th, 1943, I said:

> 'The Church is necessary if the world is to be saved and reclaimed for God, and God knows the world needs it. But the picture need not be one of unrelieved gloom.

This world can never be given over to complete pessimism. The feet of Christ have trodden it and there is still light in the path that He has walked.

In the book of Daniel are these words, "There was darkness over all the earth". As against that St. John, in the Book of Revelation, has written "There was a rainbow round about the throne". The world of men — darkness. The world of God — light and loveliness.

. . . The time is coming when many of us will have within our own hands the rebuilding of some part of the broken, shattered world. There can be only one true building which will last, the building according to God's planning. The value of our work will depend, not only on our own knowledge and intelligence, but on our willingness to be guided by God.'

SIME ROAD, JUNE, 1944

In another sermon, preached in Sime Road after the move from Changi, while referring to some of the new experiences of many of us, I did also point to what the move had cost us in terms of 'time to stand and stare'.

'Someone has said "The ultimate ability to do useful things constantly and well depends on a prior courage to enjoy useless things." So, what bearing have these things for us now and in the years on the other side of events which lie ahead?

Many have found in Changi and here a new satisfaction in things which previously meant nothing to them. Some have discovered real pleasure in music, others in painting; some a completely new interest in books and reading. These are all occupations which have no immediate practical value. In the eyes of many they are useless, but it is just these on the credit side which will live longest in our thoughts of internment.

It is significant that, since coming here to Sime Road from Changi, many of these activities have had to be crowded out, and we are back to a way of life more akin, in certain limited respects, to life outside. Time has become an enemy again rather than an ally and we are bound by the clock. Perhaps we may begin to see in this transition how easy it is to let opportunities for "useless" activities slip away. Martha becomes more and more "encumbered with serving" or, in our language, overloaded with fatigues.'

SIME ROAD, NEW YEAR'S EVE, 1944

Sometimes I wonder whether those of us who went through Changi and Sime Road are still, years later, able to keep an accurate balance between our memories of what was bad and evil in our conditions and treatment, and on the other hand the good we were able to make out of such huge adversity. I don't believe that I was overstating that good in a sermon preached in Sime Road on New Year's Eve at the end of 1944. Talking about St. Paul's 'Whole Armour of God' I said:

'One used to hear much talk in the earlier days of internment of what we had lost. Of course it's true — all of us have lost so very many things we value, and I do not mean only material things . . . There is a very great deal on the debit side, but I do not believe, true as it may be for some of us, that there is nothing on the credit side, that we are not in some way the richer . . . There have been many new experiences in two directions. Haven't there been times when we have known that we have been supported by the prayers of others all over the world? God's love and strength came to us through their prayers. How else can we possibly account for the sense of security and ultimate well-being which so many people felt during the weariness and the horror of the last days of Singapore before the fall? Say at least that that may have been the answer to the prayers of many who knew us and of hundreds of thousands all over the world who didn't . . .

Our second gain is this. There are few of us who have not learnt something of the art of human companionship — and it *is* an art, calling for great sympathy, subtlety and patience. Most of us do now find it easier to be tolerant of one another than we once did. And, too, many of us have found, with surprise even, enormous help from the most unexpected people. In the days which followed the Double Tenth there was in Changi a widespread spirit amongst us of sympathy. The same solidarity was most noticeable in England during the latter part of 1940 and, I believe, still may be now in 1944. I am not suggesting that our communal life has been by any means that of an ideal community. There has been in it a great deal of selfishness and there are few of us who are blameless. But many of us have found solid gains in a greater adaptability and a deeper understanding and we have seen them in other people.

We are just passing through the gate of another year and as we look forward we can see, but dimly in their details, great changes for the world and for ourselves. We hope for a return to a new life, not necessarily, as so many people in their heart of hearts would have it, to the old . . . Our time remaining here should be a time of preparation, looking to see, if we can, what exactly we have gained from this experience. We have withstood "in the evil day". Many of us have gained power for living by having been brought close to God. Pray now that in the years ahead we may not, through any forget-fulness, lose that sense of His hand in ours. Only by such a preparation shall we be able "to stand having done all".

SIME ROAD, HOLY WEEK, 1945

In 1945 preaching in Holy Week naturally meant thinking about the Cross and especially the forgiveness of God. At that particular time the question of the forgiveness of enemies was for obvious reasons, one with which we were closely concerned. What would happen 'after the war' was of real significance to us. While there were some who would cheerfully have said of our captors 'Shoot the lot!', it was impossible to pass through Holy Week standing in the shadow of the Cross of Christ, without facing such questions as justice, retribution, mercy and punishment, as well as the right attitude for a Christian towards forgiveness. We hated and could never forget so many of the evils committed by the Japanese, but hatred is a bad bed-fellow for any Christian.

In this sermon I started from the words of our Lord 'Father, forgive them'.

'Those words seem almost incredible, until we remember who it is that is speaking. That He should be able at such a moment to utter such a prayer is yet another indication of the greatness and uniqueness of Jesus.

The Cross of Jesus stands at the parting of the ways of history. From it He looks back over the years of the nation's long story and forward through the years that are to come; for both it is the same, "Father, forgive". Remember that this is no isolated incident in the life and teaching of Jesus, for forgiveness holds a large, even the chief place in both. The keystone of the gospel is the reconciliation of man to God and man to man . . .'

After thinking of the need for forgiveness in personal relations, seldom greater than in the close quarters of internment, I turned to the terrible wrongs brought on by war. Grave and grievous, still they need to be forgiven.

'I am convinced Christ's words were not meant for private wrongs alone. Wider issues of far greater urgency are involved and the fate of civilisation itself may depend on decisions made and actions taken in the next few years. "Ye have heard that it hath been said 'An eye for an eye, a tooth for a tooth' . . . Ye have heard that it hath been said 'Thou shalt love thy neighbour and hate thine enemy'. But I say unto you 'Love your enemies, bless them that curse you, do good to them that hate you and pray for them that despitefully use you and persecute you."

Bitterness blossoms in the rank growth of war. The winds of discussion and propaganda scatter the seeds still wider and no one knows where the process will end. Here I must speak both frankly and provocatively. I make no apology for doing so because I believe that there are some things which must be said and still more must be thought out clearly and honestly.

There are some things we find it practically impossible to forgive. On all sides there are millions homeless and starving. Many hundreds of thousands have died, leaving behind the pain of sadness and loss. We too here in Sime Road mourn the death of some of our number (at the hands of the Kempei-tai) and there are still some

277

under arrest about whom we are desperately anxious. Others, thank God, have returned to us, but bearing in their bodies the marks of their suffering. How can these things and so many more be forgiven?

One thing is clear from that lonely cross on a hill-top, the symbol of all that is best in our world. The gravity of the wrong done can never be a barrier to forgiveness. All the wrongs which men could they heaped on Christ — and yet He bore them and carried them and was still able to send that cry echoing out across the years — "Father, forgive". His love for mankind was deepened even further when He saw the great, the awful need in which they stood. Dare we aim any lower than Jesus Himself? Dare we, seeing the highest and knowing it to be the highest, turn away from it with a careless shrug?

. . . In forgiving men Jesus was not indifferent to the repetition of their wrong-doing. In the affairs of nations after the war it is certain that there will have to be controlled discipline. Anything less than that would be a shirking of the Christian duty of love. Punishment is not incompatible with an attitude of forgiveness. Lessons have to be taught and the learning may be painful for those who have to learn them. Further, the punishment if it is to be effective, must in some cases be severe.

Equally, however, punishment without any higher motive than that of imposing suffering for its own sake, is no better than the primeval urge for revenge — "an eye for an eye, a tooth for a tooth" — and its effectiveness in settling wrongs is about as effective as a Corsican vendetta!

Any policy which does not consider the welfare of our enemies — a fair paraphrase of Jesus's injunction that we should love them — will be unchristian and, in the long run, doomed to failure. Literal or economic annihilation is the talk of extravagance and thoughtlessness. Jesus did not rub His hands with glee at the thought of the coming destruction of Jerusalem. He stood outside the walls and *wept* for those who were His declared enemies, as He thought of the suffering which He knew was to be theirs.

I say again, I am not forgetting what has been done. Jesus had good reason to remember what had been done to Him. But still we hear His voice "Father, forgive them", as if to say "Bring them to a right mind, O Father. Help them to know what is involved in peaceful living. Grant that they may know thee and play their part in building a better world." You will remember how St. Peter asked Jesus whether seven times would be as far as he could reasonably be expected to forgive his brother. To him, as to us still, Jesus replied "I say not unto you until seven times, but until seventy times seven". In other words, Christian forgiveness is without limit.'

SIME ROAD, ASCENSION DAY, 1945

As we advanced further and further into 1945 we became increasingly aware that the end was in sight. More and more our minds moved towards freedom and a return into the world. On May 6th word rushed round the camp that Tominaga, one of our senior Japanese custodians, had let it be known that Germany had capitulated. It was not surprising that a sermon I preached on May 13th, 1945, had a strong forward look to it. It was the Sunday after the Ascension. I talked about the awful distress and total sense of failure and of loss felt by the disciples with the death of Jesus on Good Friday. Then I spoke of the new life for them on Easter Day when they knew that He had risen and was alive. This grew in certainty during the days leading up to the Ascension. And then came Pentecost, or Whitsun, with the pouring out on them of the strength and power of the Holy Spirit.

'These men had lost none of the freshness of their earlier daily companionship with Jesus . . . That had not changed. Nothing had been lost. However altered the conditions of their lives, whatever new situations they were called on to meet, they applied what they had learnt of God to each problem as it arose. They had a spiritual poise and balance which, in a world of flux and continual change, meant that they were able at any time to draw on the whole of their spiritual resources. They were never caught unawares. The picture of these men has a very great deal to say to us . . .

As we look at the future we cannot fill in the details of what it will hold for us. It goes without saying that the immediate changes between this life here and that new life will be enormous . . . That will be the time when we shall need to take a fresh grasp of the fruits of our own experience of the love of God and of the demands which love makes.

Either we shall remain in the confused, despairing bewilderment of the disciples on Good Friday and Easter Eve or we shall go forward to share something of the stability and the certainty which the disciples held after Easter and Pentecost. Which is it to be?

On Easter Eve it seemed to the disciples that Jesus was to play no part in their future. Their life with Him, they thought, was finished, a thing of the past. Somehow, it seemed, they had to remake their lives without Him. Family life and friendships without Him to share in them; new work without His interest to keep theirs alive and fresh, stimulating them and drawing them out; the many new problems of conduct and behaviour without His hand on their shoulder to comfort and reassure — it is little wonder they were broken as they faced the future.

What of ourselves? When we are in the centre of that future to which we now look shall we remember what He has been to us and what He can be again — closer and greater by far than we have even known Him already? As we look forward we shall be wise if we recognise that none of our relationships will be the same as they were — all of us have changed during these three years. Not that change means loss. It doesn't. But to reach the highest we and those we love will need to walk together in God's presence.

We look forward, too, to whatever work the future may hold. It will not be the same as it used to be. For some it may be along completely new paths, but, whatever it is, our need of God will be the same as it has always been. Perhaps we have not recognised enough in the past that there was much place for God in the office, on the rubber estate or the tin mine, in the servant's quarters, the Club or the hospital ward — or in our own homes. Life would sometimes be more comfortable if He were not there. But it is to those who have known Him there, who have tried to give Him entrance there, that I would say, He will be waiting to come as He did before, however changed the scene and the nature of your life may be . . .

It is not going to be easy to readjust ourselves to the life of the future — infinitely more difficult if the house of life is built on the sand rather than on the solid unchanging rock. But the house built on the rock of the Christian faith does not fall.

"What is precious is . . .
Never to allow gradually the traffic to smother
With noise and fog the flowering of the Spirit."

So writes Stephen Spender. Eleven men did allow the traffic of lack of faith and of despair to smother them temporarily in the midst of change. God grant that change may not smother the flowering of the Spirit in us, or, through our carelessness, find us unprepared.'

Section Eight

———◆·◆———

Where did they go?
Where are they now?

Where did they go?
Where are they now?

The two principal characters in this story, Bishop Wilson and Sorby Adams, both returned to Singapore after the war. In 1948, however, Leonard Wilson was back in England, first for five years as Dean of Manchester and then, until 1969, as a most notable Bishop of Birmingham. His retirement to his beloved Yorkshire was brief. In 1970 he attended in St. Paul's Cathedral the annual service of the Order of St. Michael and St. George, of which he was an impressive Prelate. On the same day, travelling home by train with his daughter, the Revd. Dr. Susan Cole-King (in 1987 she was ordained Priest in the United States) he suffered a stroke. He died at his home in the Yorkshire Dales on the 18th August, 1970.

For ten years after the war Canon Sorby Adams carried through the building up again of St. Andrew's Boys School. In 1956 he went home to Adelaide, where, successively, he was in charge of two parishes. However, 'the lure of the east' was still strong and in 1966 he returned, this time to Brunei until 1970, when he was back in Adelaide. He never retired. For the remaining six years of his life — he died suddenly from a heart attack in 1976 — he had a general licence for pastoral work in the diocese. The Archbishop of Adelaide said of Sorby 'He was one of those men who became a legend in his own time. He is remembered with great affection in Adelaide, but his great life work was during nearly thirty years in Singapore'. Thousands at St. Andrew's, whether as boys or parents or staff, would agree. His wife Eunice, his unfailing support, survived him by ten years.

The Revd. Eric Scott has been working for many years far 'up river' in Borneo. He died in Kuching at the age of 80.

Colonel Herbert Lord of the Salvation Army, may well have thought, as he left Sime Road, that that was enough experience of captivity for one lifetime. He was wrong! In 1950 he was arrested in the British Embassy in Seoul and taken as a P.O.W. to North Korea. He had a very hard time. He was released in 1953.

From the senior member of the Salvation Army in Changi to someone who was then one of the more junior. He is now Commissioner Stan Cottrill. His career has been eventful and varied, with service in Singapore, Southern Rhodesia, Korea, Britain and Japan. His final appointment before retirement in 1982 was of the greatest distinction. He was Chief-of-the Staff or Second-in-Command of the Salvation Army world wide.

The Revd. Tyler Thompson, an American Methodist Minister, has spent the greater part of the time since 1945 in teaching, particularly, for twenty-seven years, as a Professor of the Philosophy of Religion in Evanston, Illinois. In the spring of 1987 he survived a seven hour operation on a growth in his neck. As part of his recovery he had to do 'one hundred and sixty exercises six times a day, besides a daily walk of at least three miles'. With that regimen it was hardly surprising to hear him say 'I expect to be back on the tennis court in three months, but it's not yet clear how well I'll be able to hit the ball when I get there!'.

The lectures in Changi by Norman Alexander attracted a large following. They showed clearly why he achieved such distinction as Professor of Physics, first, from 1936 until 1949 at Raffles College, and then, until 1953, still in Singapore, at the University of Malaya. From there he moved to Nigeria to the Chair in Physics in Ibadan until 1959, when he spent a year in Turkey at the Middle East Technical University in Ankara. Returning to Nigeria until 1966, it was as Vice-Chancellor of a new university that he received his knighthood.

Four years followed on various university planning operations in Fiji, the West Indies, Mauritius, Ghana and Southern Africa. Before final retirement in 1973 he had what he describes as 'a few painful years' as a Civil Servant with the Ministry of Overseas Development. At the age of 82 his industry is still prolific. Describing himself as 'amiably disposed towards the Church' he mentions seemingly endless jobs preserving 'the fabric of our little church, mending great cracks in the walls by setting large lumps of flint in mortar'. He speaks, too, of 'making a whole set of bench ends and I am now commissioned to making a new notice board'. He doesn't change much!

Tommy Thomson, whose cell the Bishop and I invaded on B3, became our close friend there and in Sime Road. He learnt in internment the tragic news that his wife was one of those killed getting away from Singapore. He returned home to Scotland and spent the rest of his days with his sister at Milltimber in Aberdeenshire.

Yahya Cohen, frequently a young companion as he and I bicycled home together after days in Katong in 1942-43, was later interned. After the war he qualified as a doctor and became Senior Surgeon and Professor of Surgery at the University of Singapore. He became a Fellow of the Royal College of Surgeons of England.

Just before Christmas, 1941, with the Japanese not far behind them, Kerr and Jennie Bovell came south to Kuala Lumpur. We met at the northern end of the Padang, outside St. Mary's. Would I marry them? Regretfully I had to pass them on to the Registrar, who was able to help. Jennie returned home. At the end of internment Kerr had various appointments in Malaya. He became Chief of Police in Pahang in 1954. From 1956 for six years he was Inspector-General of Police in Nigeria. He was knighted in 1961 and retired in 1962, when he became Bursar of Worksop. In 1968 he moved to Radley, again as Bursar. He died there in 1973.

In 1946 Dr. David Molesworth returned to Malaya as Medical Officer-in-Charge of Sungei Buloh Leper Colony in Selangor. Some years later he moved to Ghana as Director of Leprosy services. In 1966 he took charge of the Pilot Leprosy Control Project in Malawi until retirement in 1978. This was his greatest work. After his death in 1987 it was said of him, 'It was due to David's charm and way with people that such extensive groundwork was carried out, enabling the scheme to grow . . . to a nationwide control scheme. By the time he left 24,000 cases were under treatment. He died at his home in Devon after several years of illness.

With few instruments and only a primitive pedal-driven

drill Peter Ellis worked wonders of dental make-do-and-mend in Changi and Sime Road. Because of his improvising many teeth were saved which might have been lost. After the war he was for many years in private practice in Oxford, where he lives in semi-retirement with his wife, Lyn.

On release from internment Mervyn ff. Sheppard, now Tan Sri Datoh Mubin Sheppard, set himself the task of rounding up some of the leaders of the Japanese Kempei-tai, who had been responsible for the torture and death of many civilians in Singapore. He learnt that the men he was hunting had left Singapore hurriedly in small boats and were hiding on one of the Riau Islands.

Two sections of a Punjabi Regiment were laid on to go with him. He also obtained the cooperation of a Chinese, who owned two motor boats. By making them available he hoped to avoid punishment for his own close collaboration with the Japanese. With an interpreter and a large white flag they set off for the island of Kundur on September 23rd, 1945. A number of prominent Kempei-tai were known to be hiding there.

The Japanese garrison on the islands had not as yet surrendered, but after hearing an order from the interpreter they duly did so and were rounded up with the Kempei-tai and taken on board. Sheppard also had the satisfaction of discovering ten crates of British Regimental Silver which the Japanese hoped to dispose of in Indonesia.

Three more similar expeditions followed in which many leading Kempei-tai were captured and handed over for trial on War Crimes. For all of this Sheppard was awarded the Military M.B.E.

Returning to Malaya after three months leave Sheppard was given the task of setting up a new Department of Information to cover the whole of Malaya. After being made District Officer Klang he became British Adviser Kelantan. Later, for more than four years, he served as British Adviser Negri Sembilan. There followed a successful Food Denial Organisation to prevent the Communist terrorists from obtaining food, in particular, rice.

When Independence came Sheppard applied for Malayan citizenship and became a Muslim. The list of his activities is formidable! He was made the first Director of Archives and also set up a new National Museum. In 1963 he chose to retire in Kuala Lumpur. He then reorganised the Ex-Service Association, besides building their nine-storey headquarters. He was the first Secretary-General of the Muslim Welfare Organisation and took over the posts of Honorary Secretary and Honorary Editor of the Malaysian Branch of the Royal Asiatic Society. Besides all this he wrote more than a dozen books, including a two-volume pictorial biography of Tunku Abdul Rahman. Most recently he helped to form the Heritage of Malaysia Trust to preserve old and historic buildings all over West Malaysia.

For his many works for Malaysia, Mervyn (now Mubin) Sheppard has received four Malaysian awards carrying with them the titles 'Tan Sri' and 'Datoh' as well as an Honorary D.Litt. Besides all this he has received a C.M.G. from Britain.

Those who have known him over the years will not be surprised that his industry does not wane and that, even at 84, he still has the energy to support it!

Mrs. Elizabeth Choy, O.B.E., and her husband, Koon Heng, paid dearly for their concern and self-sacrificing work for internees. His health was always bad after torture and imprisonment in the Double Tenth enquiry of more than forty years before. He died in 1985. Elizabeth served as a member of the Legislative Council during the early 1950s. She then returned to teaching at St. Andrew's School. In 1986 'Not Afraid to Remember', a play based on her experiences during the Japanese occupation, was performed publicly in Singapore. It attracted a lot of attention and showed the great respect and affection in which she is still held.

In 1942 Sandy Macnab was taken from Changi to the Kandang Kerbau Hospital for the birth of her child, Diana, whose health was poor from the start. She was, however, a beautiful child and she delighted all who knew her and who saw her growing up in Changi and Sime Road. After the war she suffered further acute health problems. Even so, she qualified as a nurse and married very happily. She died while still in her mid-30s. Sandy died at the end of December, 1990.

After the war Muriel Clark returned to Singapore as a missionary nurse. With the departure of Bishop Wilson and his family Muriel accompanied them, first to Manchester and then to Birmingham. Her tasks were manifold, but can best be described, affectionately, as 'Comptroller of the Household'. With the move of the Wilsons to Yorkshire on the Bishop's retirement Muriel lived nearby in a small house of her own and later moved again when, after the Bishop's death, Mrs. Wilson lived at Ledbury in Herefordshire. She died in 1984, but Muriel is still there in the house she bought for herself.

Two years after the war Mary Scott was married to Alec Mosley of the Shell Company, a former P.O.W. with the Volunteers. He died in 1967. Mary still lives at West Moors, between Ringwood and Wimborne, in the home she and Alec made for their four sons and their daughter.

Dr. Cicely Williams became a world authority in paediatrics. She was the first to identify kwashiorkor, a deficiency disease in African children. She lives in Oxford, within a short distance of her former college, Somerville, by whom she was paid high honour at her 90th birthday celebrations in 1983.

Mrs. Freddy Bloom was one of those who, like Cicely Williams, spent many months with the Kempei-tai after the Double Tenth enquiry. At the end of internment she and her husband, Philip, returned to England. Very soon their elder child, Virginia, was born. She was 'profoundly deaf'. As a result Freddy's experience led her to found and become Chairman of the National Deaf Children's Society. She has written several books, mainly on the care and development of the handicapped.

And the author? In 1946 there began three good years at Ipoh in North Malaya, where my wife, Rosemary, and I met. Our marriage in England in 1949 was followed by parish work in the Midlands and at Winchester, and by six very rewarding months as Chaplain of the Royal Free Hospital in London.

In 1955 I began twenty-seven happy years as Vicar of Boldre on the southern edge of the New Forest.

We retired to nearby Lymington in 1982. Sadly in 1986 my wife was diagnosed as having Parkinson's disease, at the same time undergoing an operation for a mammoth brain tumour. This very heavy double blow has caused her many problems, with all of which she copes with the greatest courage.

Before her illness I was part-time Chaplain of a prep-school and of the Fortune Centre, a unique research and training centre for the education of learning-disabled people through horses.

I have also, incidentally, written a book — this one!

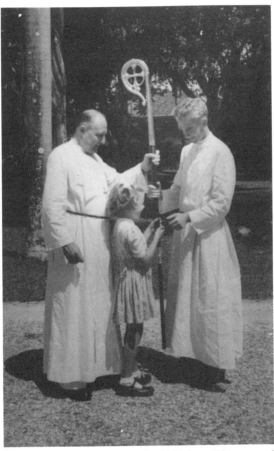

Figure 25: 'Under Instruction!' Bishop, Vicar — and Parishioner, Jane Taylor, in Ipoh in 1947.

Section Nine

———•••———

Forty years on

Figure 26: Bishop Wilson and his family in Birmingham in May 1967. Left to right, top: Susan Cole-King with Stephen and Adam; Paul Cole-King; Muriel Clark; Mary Wilson; Mary, wife of James Wilson; Mary Wilson, the Bishop's wife; James Wilson; the Bishop; Mickey Wilson; Tim Wilson. Bottom: Michael Cole-King; Nicola Moll, Mary's daughter; Helen Cole-King; Isobel Wilson, the Bishop's stepmother; Mark Wilson,

Forty years on

Diaries make it possible to judge years later the long-term effects, both for good and for ill, of events as they first happened. So, after nearly fifty years, looking back on the whole span of December, 1941 to October, 1945, do I really mean it when I say 'I wouldn't choose to go through that experience again, but I don't regret it'? Yes, I do mean it!

Twice in the diaries I wrote 'I would not want to be anywhere else'. The first was in a letter I wrote to my mother on the last day of January, 1942. A friend carried it out of Singapore. Nothing that happened changed that.

The second occasion was at St. Hilda's, Katong, later in 1942, during the first year of the Japanese occupation. In the midst of daily fears, uncertainties and personal problems and pressures a small but soundly based Christian community was beginning to take shape, though it would be truer to say it was being shaped by God. It was a thrilling time.

They were a real community, strengthened by the worship and prayers they shared together and growing in their understanding of the Christian faith. They were learning more about God and about themselves and what it meant to be part of God's Church.

I wrote at the time that I would not want to be anywhere else but with them at St. Hilda's.

When I left England a year before the cry was being heard 'Let the Church be the Church'. The 'Parish and People Movement' were its chief exponents. They were as responsible as anyone for the popularity now, in our time, of the Parish Communion. Spontaneously and without any direct planning I saw Church life in Katong developing along very similar lines.

For me since then, wherever I have been, the Church has been nearest to its true self, and most true to its Lord, when those hall-marks of worship and prayer, of learning, of fellow-ship, and of love and care for one another have really been present. They certainly were at St. Hilda's. Again and again I have looked back on our time together then as a very special example of the closeness of relationship there can be between a priest and God's people. I thank God for it.

THE GOOD COMPANIONS

Many times since 1942 I have had reason to marvel at my good fortune as a young priest to have been chosen to spend more than a year in the close company of two such men as Bishop Leonard Wilson and Sorby Adams, who was out-standing as a school headmaster and as a priest. They were both of them nearly twice my age, but we were a wonderfully harmonious trio. It is not for nothing that I have dedicated this book to them as 'Two Very Good Companions'.

It is to those two that I owe many things, amongst them the first beginnings of a greater facility in framing my own beliefs and being able to talk about them.

One thing we had in common was the same kind of sense of humour, frequently ribald and Rabelaisian. This quick-silver appreciation of the comic which we shared did have dangers. There was, for example, the memorable occasion when we were saying evensong together at the Bishop's house. A regrettable misreading of some word from one of the prophets reduced all three of us to devastating, overpowering hysterical laughter!

A catchphrase Bishop Wilson and I shared emerged again years later in a very different context. Any mistake he made, or anything he forgot, was greeted with 'Silly Old Bishop'. This, of course, we abbreviated to S.O.B. When he became Bishop of Birmingham his diocese thought that the car num-ber plate he had chosen, SOB 1, referred to the 'See of Birm-ingham'. Only he and I knew another use of those letters and, too, that there are many words besides Bishop which begin with the letter B!

APOSTLE OF UNITY

There are numerous fresh insights I owe to Leonard Wilson from this time. One of them was an awareness of the scandal of a divided Church and of the urgent need to put it right. Christian Reunion was a passion of his. My own background had been typical of the period. I had not thought it strange, certainly not wrong, that, in the English country town of about 5000 people from which I had come, there should have been ten whole-time, salaried ministers of religion — three Anglican, two Salvation Army and one each from the Roman Catholic, Methodist, Baptist, Congregationalist and Elim Four Square Gospel Churches, not to mention the seven places of worship, clergy houses and organisational set-up which all had to be maintained at huge cost. Nor was there up to 1940 even the most formal cooperation, least of all shared worship, between those seven separated Churches.

The Bishop faced up to that kind of situation in Japanese occupied Singapore. For me the Federation of the Churches which he initiated was a great awakening, even though it was only designed as a first step of cooperation between the Churches in a shared scheme of welfare at a time of acute and urgent need, of which even the Japanese approved.

Nor shall I ever forget one other aspect of the Federation — the combined services in the overflowing cathedral, especially at Christmas, 1942. They were an inspiration which has always lived with me.

On arrival in Changi Gaol in March, 1943, we found the whole Church climate was shot through with the closest cooperation and the friendliest of relationships between the clergy and all the members of the Churches.

BISHOP WILSON THE TEACHER

It was there that Bishop Wilson's great gifts as a teacher really came into their own. His natural sympathy with his audience came from someone who, in his youth, had himself worked through very considerable doubts of faith.

When he left Singapore in 1949 he became Dean of Manchester. Barbara Saxon, who came to know him well, said of him, 'He really had a superlatively good voice and knew how to use it in a knock-out sense of timing, which gave incredible force to his wisdom, humility, forgiveness and awareness of weakness'.

Colonel Herbert Lord, of the Salvation Army, a friend of

the Bishop's in internment, said that the strength of Leonard Wilson's powers as an evangelist could be described as 'salvation through seduction'!

More than forty years later Commissioner Stan Cottrill, in 1942 a young Salvation Army Captain in Changi, said 'The Bishop made the Gospel he preached so attractive by his own dedicated personality. Times without number since then I have acknowledged my indebtedness to him for opening for me something of the great grandeur of God. Never do I read John 17 or speak from it without recalling the evening when he and I led the service together in Changi. The passage came alive for me just by his reading.'

THE CLERGY LIVING AT CLOSE QUARTERS

On a broader front in Changi we began to experience what was to be for us, for two and a half years, a complete form of community living. Life in the Gaol was lived totally without precedence or privilege, with everyone on exactly the same basis. It was, incidentally, a type of existence from which every Christian minister could profit if, early in his ministry, he could experience it for long enough!

In our own times in England local congregations most often decide that a priest, a minister, is a person apart. He is often isolated from them. They may not knowingly intend it, but that is how they think of him and what he frequently becomes. The minister who encourages and even develops this separateness from his people is turning his back on one of the essentials of the Incarnation, of Christ's coming amongst men. He identified Himself with His people. He came amongst them as one of them, and fortunate is the Christian minister who can be in that sort of relationship with those around him.

With all its problems and very many disadvantages, living at such close quarters did help us to understand people. It taught us all, too, the need for forbearance and tolerance, and that without them there could be chaos. On the whole people were remarkably tolerant.

For that element in Changi and Sime Road I have always been grateful. It gave me a standard against which, over and over again I have been able to judge the way my life has gone.

For the clergy the overcrowded living conditions meant that we knew more people and were better known. We were far more approachable and available for those who wanted help, whether to sort out their beliefs or their personal problems or attitudes or whatever. I remember that we were so used.

ATTITUDES – TO THE JAPANESE

Most people have found it infinitely harder to be tolerant in their attitude towards the Japanese. This was scarcely surprising for those whose only experience of them was limited to the day to day petty tyranny of our camp guards and, even worse, who knew at second hand the appalling cruelties of the Kempei-tai.

My own attitude towards the Japanese was and always has been conditioned by the qualities of Professor Andrew Ogawa. His outstanding service to the Church in Singapore in 1942, saving its buildings from desecration, and his many acts of kindness to the Bishop, to Sorby and to me will always be in my mind. He and I are still regular correspondents.

ATTITUDES – TOWARD GOD

Whether or not the average Christian became more aware of the presence of God than he had been before internment varied as much as it does in the world at large. Many were at Church services and some returned to their communion. Without reservation I could say, however, that those who had any faith in the care and the love and the trustworthiness of the Father had a huge advantage under conditions which were so totally adverse. Most especially was this true of the way so many people faced their sometimes appalling anxieties for the members of their own families.

At no time was there any marked movement either towards or away from the Church and its worship and Christian belief. There are, however, many who, during and for a time after the Double Tenth enquiry, felt acute anxiety, dread and plain fear. Amongst them were, I know, those who felt some kind of stability from the knowledge that, somehow, God was there.

That kind of awareness of God under those circumstances has acted as a beacon of light for many people for the rest of their lives. They can say — I can say it — 'I know God will be good to me now, because I knew His goodness to me then.'

Our experience in Changi Gaol and Sime Road Camp was as nothing compared with those who were on the Thai-Burma Railway or the Death March in North Borneo. However, if asked I still say 'I would not have chosen to be anywhere else'.

Section Ten

Afterthoughts

Afterthoughts

Soon after *Priest in Prison* was first published in October, 1989, several incidents came to light which are now included in this second edition.

PERILOUS DEPARTURE

Dr. Austin Adams, youngest of the four sons of Sorby Adams, wrote:

> 'My mother left Singapore on the last plane to make the exit successfully. She was able to get a seat on that plane because she was pregnant with me. The driver, Lakim bin Osman, drove through an air-raid to get her to the airport on time. Kallang was intact when she arrived, but while waiting for departure there was another raid, in which the airport buildings were extensively damaged. During all of this she hid under an office desk. Sitting on one side of her at the airport was a Persian lady bemoaning the fact that her money was in carpets, while on the other side was someone who clutched a bag, obviously with the family gold and diamonds in it.'

AN ARCHBISHOP'S VIEW OF SORBY ADAMS

After Sorby's death in 1976 the Archbishop of Adelaide said of him:

> 'Sorby Adams was one of those men who became a legend in his own time. He was a brilliant scholar, a fine teacher and a great priest and pastor. He was the kind of man whom it is hard to label. His interests were varied and his influence was immense. He is remembered with great affection in Adelaide. However, his great life work was in Singapore, where he served for nearly thirty years.'

Sorby's second son, Graeme, has written:

'I have wondered why he did not take the job offered here in Adelaide as Headmaster of his old school, St. Peter's, the most prestigious school in South Australia. Reading *Priest in Prison* has shown me how deeply he was attached to the people of Singapore, and how loyal he was to the Bishop, to whom he had promised to return.'

TED HEBDITCH REMEMBERS

In a letter written after reading the first edition of *Priest in Prison*, Ted Hebditch, Chief Electrician in the Gaol, wrote of . . .

Lt. Andrew Ogawa at Changi

'A Japanese Lieutenant, an Anglican, English-speaking and very pleasant, was very briefly in charge of Changi from the first day we moved there. He lived in the Prison Superintendent's house, where he had a G.E.C. short-wave radio. He used to get me in very often to tune it to London for news from the B.B.C.'

What would the Kempei-tai have said about *that*?

Norman Coulson's Smuggling

'I once sent a sewage pump out to Norman Coulson for repair. When it arrived back at the Gaol two weeks later I found it was full of ten dollar notes. After a great trouble getting the Japanese sentry out of the way I hurriedly got rid of the money to the Camp Treasurer.'

Holy Communion in a Strange Place

'Sam Travis, Blakstad and I were sent by the Kempei-tai to the Miyako Hospital for three or four weeks. Travis, a layman, set up a table. On it he put bread, a substitute for wine and a flower in a cup. He did the full service and we all three had communion — the first time I had ever had it.'

It was not, however, the last. Ted was confirmed by the Bishop when they were both returned by the Kempei-tai to Sime Road.

'THEY HAVE NO WINE!'

By coincidence *Freedom in Internment*, a fascinating book, was published in Singapore at the same time as *Priest in Prison*. By even greater coincidence it was written by the Revd. Tyler Thompson, who features in this book.

Writing of the custom in internment of using only a few drops of wine added to water at Holy Communion, he speaks of the occasion when Sorby Adams had gone to the Women's Camp in Changi with Eric Scott, 'a priest of the deepest Anglo-Catholic convictions'. 'The slender supply of wine had given out. Eric had not been told. When, during the service, he discovered this, he looked round with such deep distress written on his face that Sorby was able to grasp the situation immediately. He was fearful that Eric would falter and not even go on. With his puckish sense of humour and, wanting to be as helpful as possible, he said (in a stage whisper audible throughout the room): "Go ahead, Eric. Jesus turned the water into wine." And Eric did!'

THE BISHOP AND ALAN KER WITH THE KEMPEI-TAI

After the war, on July 21st, 1946, Bishop Wilson visited Mrs. Alan Ker at her home in England, when he told her of his time with Alan in the Y.M.C.A. She wrote a brief account of his visit for her family.

'The Bishop seems most thoroughly to have enjoyed Alan's character, for so much he told me was typical. For instance, Alan taught him thousands of lines of Keats. (Alan had suddenly realised in Changi that he had the power to learn by heart. From a copy he acquired by chance in the Y.M.C.A. he learnt practically the whole book of Keats.) If the Bishop asked him "What does all this mean?", Alan replied "Learn it first and don't ask questions". Repeating the poetry and dwelling on this or that line seems to have taken them right out of themselves.'

Mrs. Ker continued 'I asked the Bishop what he taught Alan? "Psalms mostly", he said, "but Alan was angry with me because I could never go right through anything!" . . . The Bishop said that he and Alan argued endlessly on every subject, including religion. Alan said that no one had ever really explained it to him before . . . The Bishop said they may not have seen eye to eye on everything, but they richly appreciated one another. "I loved the man. He was so real and alive and honest, eager to live and make the world better, burning for business integrity and honest dealing".'

The Bishop finally told Mrs. Ker that he had counted on Alan's support in the rehabilitation of Singapore after the war. While in hospital in Sime Road Camp after his return from the Y.M.C.A., Alan had asked the Bishop to celebrate Holy Communion for him on the birthday of his son, William. He died suddenly just six days later.

THE CHANGI QUILTS

After the fall of Singapore in February 1942, P.O.W.s had no way of finding out what had happened to their sisters, wives or fiancees, or, in some cases, their mothers. They did not even know if they were alive. Those in Changi Gaol's Women's Camp hit on a way of getting round this. They embroidered four patchwork quilts of sixty-six squares each. The squares on three of the quilts bore the name or initials of those who had worked them.

With the permission of the authorities, three of them (the fourth being a 'sweetener' to the Japanese themselves) were sent to the Military Hospital in the P.O.W. Camp, providing lists of the women who were at least alive. These names were rapidly circulated amongst the P.O.W.s.

One of these quilts now hangs in the Museum of the British Red Cross at Barnett Hill, Wonersh, near Guildford in Surrey. Two others are in Australia, at the War Memorial Museum in Canberra and with the Red Cross. The whereabouts of the fourth is unknown.

Figure 27 (opposite): This photograph, by courtesy of the British Red Cross Archives, is of the Changi Quilt which hangs in their Museum at Wonersh.

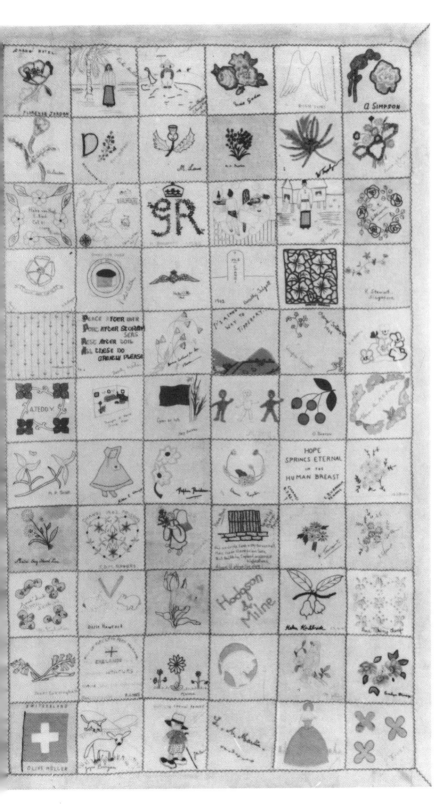

THE REVD. CECIL PARR —
P.O.W. PADRE EXCEPTIONAL

On page 253 reference is made to the death as a P.O.W. in Thailand, of Cecil Parr, Chaplain of St. Andrew's School.

Sir Edward 'Weary' Dunlop, the Australian surgeon, was and is one of the most respected of all P.O.W.s from the Burma-Siam Railway. In his diary, published by Penguin Books in Australia, in an entry for 21st February, 1943, Sir Edward wrote of Cecil:

'Unexpectedly Padre Parr (C. of E.) and Padre Bourke (R.C.) turned up . . . Padre Parr ran a very good conventional service . . . his robes and communion kit battered, travel stained and with water stains. Above this a gaunt, bearded, spiritual face (at times I caught a distinct resemblance to a bedraggled, ill Jesus of Nazareth), below were a gaunt, thin pair of legs and army boots.'

And again, on 24th April, 1943, writing of the arrival of Cecil Parr in camp:

'Easter services were arranged for 20.30 hours, just after evening roll call, the C. of E. in the concert area between the tents. Rain had just fallen so the ground of course was sodden. It was in some ways as lovely an evening as you could wish to see . . . the sky, positively aflame with crimson banners and mass cloud formation, broke the fading light into all colours of the spectrum.

Some hundreds of men attended the C. of E. service . . . As the light faded the padre's candles and a few fires lit the scene fitfully. The theme of the address was suffering, the cross and the empty tomb. The suffering of which we had experienced something, only a little of that endured by millions of others, was not in vain; if all suffering ended only in muddled stupidity the sacrifice of the cross would not have been made. This service was followed by the Last Post and Reveille, beautifully played by Page, and God Save the King.

Then came Holy Communion with more than sixty communicants. It was a strange sight, the robed and bearded figure fantastically lit by candlelight, the communicants moving forward out of almost complete darkness from the little surrounding islands of men around the fire.'

In a footnote Sir Edward recorded that Cecil Parr died soon after these events. The figure in Salisbury Cathedral at the south-east corner of the crossing at the entrance to the choir, is his memorial.

A STATEMENT OF SINGAPORE'S PAST

On the wall of St. Andrew's Cathedral there is a tablet bearing the names of forty men of the Malayan Civil Service who died during the Japanese occupation. Most of those remembered there were Prisoners of War or Civilian Internees.

At the service of dedication in 1989 Sir Percy McNeice, the oldest survivor of the then Malayan Civil Service, referred to the memorial in the words used by Mr. Lee Kuan Yew, Singapore's Prime Minister. He called it 'a small statement of Singapore's past'. 'But', said Sir Percy, 'what these men gave . . . was all they had to give.'

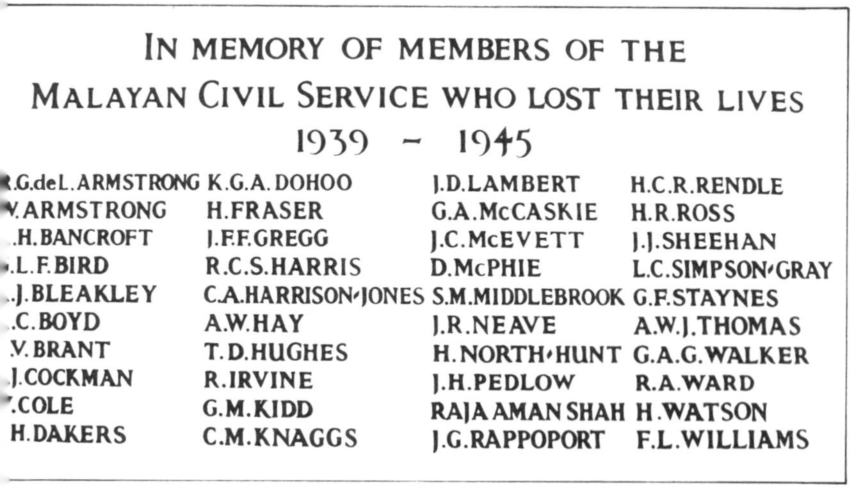

IN MEMORY OF MEMBERS OF THE
MALAYAN CIVIL SERVICE WHO LOST THEIR LIVES
1939 – 1945

R.G.deL.ARMSTRONG	K.G.A.DOHOO	J.D.LAMBERT	H.C.R.RENDLE
V.ARMSTRONG	H.FRASER	G.A.McCASKIE	H.R.ROSS
H.BANCROFT	J.F.F.GREGG	J.C.McEVETT	J.J.SHEEHAN
L.F.BIRD	R.C.S.HARRIS	D.McPHIE	L.C.SIMPSON-GRAY
J.BLEAKLEY	C.A.HARRISON-JONES	S.M.MIDDLEBROOK	G.F.STAYNES
C.BOYD	A.W.HAY	J.R.NEAVE	A.W.J.THOMAS
V.BRANT	T.D.HUGHES	H.NORTH-HUNT	G.A.G.WALKER
J.COCKMAN	R.IRVINE	J.H.PEDLOW	R.A.WARD
COLE	G.M.KIDD	RAJA AMAN SHAH	H.WATSON
H.DAKERS	C.M.KNAGGS	J.G.RAPPOPORT	F.L.WILLIAMS

Figure 28: The Malayan Civil Service plaque in St. Andrew's Cathedral.

MR. SCHWEIZER AND 'THE BLUE ANGEL'

It has taken forty-five years for the unveiling of a remarkable story. Without knowing it many people who were prisoners of the Japanese in Singapore owe their lives to the persistent and heroic efforts on their behalf of Mr. Hans Schweizer. A leading Swiss business man in Singapore, for three and a half years he fought a continuing battle with the Japanese for recognition as a Red Cross Representative. He was never given it. Even so he persisted in his attempts to bring essential food to P.O.W.s and also to Civilian Internees, first in Changi Gaol and later in Sime Road Camp. In a time of increasing crisis and a dangerous drop in food supplies he and his helpers, amongst them especially Mr. Yeo Joo Song, a member of the staff of Diethelms, Mr. Schweizer's firm, never had official sanction for what they were doing.

Often in acute personal danger he was repeatedly interrogated by the Kempei-tai, who, because of his contacts with those who were interned, suspected him of spying. They maintained that those who gave help to those who needed it were helping the enemies of the Japanese.

The details of Mr. Schweizer's story came to light after the first publication of *Priest in Prison*. Purely by chance I heard that now, aged ninety, he is living with his wife, Hildi, in Western Australia. Remembering something of his part in the story I sent him a copy of the book. His reply when it came was astonishing.

Thirty years ago, in 1960, he had written a German version of *The Experiences of a Delegate (unrecognised) of the International Committee of the Red Cross in Singapore between 1941–1945*. After reading *Priest in Prison* he had within weeks, for my benefit, translated that German account into English and typed it onto twenty-three single-spaced pages.

It is an incredible document, describing what lay behind those visits, particularly to Sime Road, with his heavily laden elderly lorry, which, with very great affection and with good cause, we nicknamed 'The Blue Angel'.

While acknowledging the very real help over a long period from a Japanese Army Sergeant named Fujibayashi, 'without whom' he said, 'I would have been lost', he has given in some detail, not only an account of the extreme difficulties and

Figure 29: Hans Schweizer, head of the Swiss firm of Diethelm and Co., was never recognised by the Japanese as Red Cross Representative in Singapore. He suspects that, on National Swiss Day in Singapore in 1942, 'Captain Tanaka dropped in, probably to see that we did nothing anti-Japanese!'

frustrations with which he and others were faced in dealings with the Japanese, but also the very real and frequently repeated dangers in which he stood from the close attention of the Kempei-tai. The interrogation he had to go through on a number of occasions was intense, frequently lasting as long as ten hours, though always without torture or detention overnight.

It was only later he discovered that on several occasions he had been near to execution. His opposite number in Borneo was less fortunate. He and his wife were executed for no more than sending food parcels to friends in internment.

Mr. Schweizer describes one occasion of his own great good fortune. He writes, 'A Kempei-tai officer had proposed my execution, but he was transferred to Bangkok and took all his papers with him. So the matter could not be followed up!' That was not all. 'Some of the other things he took along were his office and flat furniture, including the light bulbs and' (wait for it!) 'water taps!'.

Besides much else Mr. Schweizer has shed light on another mystery. In a personal letter he sent with the typescript he wrote, 'My connection with Bishop Wilson is still vividly in my mind. We used to go to the same second-hand bookshop in Bras Basah Road, where I used to deposit in a book the money I advanced to him as a loan to the Anglican Church. He usually entered immediately after I left and got hold of the sums of money placed there for him. We thereby avoided visible contact, as we both were mostly supervised.' So, the previously unnamed neutral from whom the Bishop borrowed money on behalf of the Central Committee in Changi Gaol was Mr. Schweizer. The risk was very great that he might have become involved in the Double Tenth enquiry.

These are only a few of the long list of courageous and perilous enterprises for which countless people have owed Mr. Schweizer their admiration and gratitude. It must be to the real regret of a great many that there has not been until now any recognition or acknowledgement of the actions of such outstanding courage nearly half a century ago.

Section Eleven

———◆•◆———

Postscript

CHANGI PRISON CHAPEL – 1989

Photograph by courtesy of Adam Corres

Figure 30: The new Chapel which has been built outside the walls of Changi Gaol.

Postscript

CHANGI PRISON CHAPEL

That's not quite the end of the story. Outside the walls of the Gaol at Changi a Chapel has been built. While not a copy, its simple structure is similar to the more elaborate Church of St. David's built by P.O.W.s. at Sime Road Camp and later used most gratefully by internees.

The Chapel is a reminder of the 85,000 soldiers and civilians imprisoned at Changi between 1942 and 1945. Many people are paying visits to it and to the Museum nearby. Both, under the initiative of the Singapore Tourist Promotion Board, serve to bring to mind our experience whose story is told here in *Priest in Prison* and in even more acute form in the history of those who suffered as P.O.W.s.

As a continuation of this book and on behalf of those others of us who came through those years I ask you to join in gratitude to God for our survival; thanking Him, too, for those who stood beside us as our companions, but who died in captivity, or, later, as a result of their privations.

Ask, if you will, for comfort for families bereaved, as well as for those who still, after half a century, carry with them the marks of their captivity in body or in mind. Nor can we forget the needs of all prisoners, hostages and captives everywhere, praying above all that wars may be no more.

Index

'The Descent from the Cross', as used in St. David's, Sime Road, was drawn from the original sketch still in the possession of the artist, Stanley Warren. The figures were drawn from life using other P.O.W.s as models. The figure holding the body of Christ is a self-study.